The
Coastal
Headlands
of
Mainland
Britain

A practical guide and much more

GRIFF J FELLOWS

Grosvenor House
Publishing Limited

This book is published by
Grosvenor House Publishing Ltd
28-30 High Street, Guildford, Surrey, GU1 3EL.
www.grosvenorhousepublishing.co.uk

A CIP record for this book
is available from the British Library

ISBN 978-1-78148-905-5

First published in eBook format in 2014 by eBook Partnership

By the same author: The Waterfalls of England
ISBN 1-85058-767-1

Whilst every care has been taken in the preparation of this book, no warranty
is given by the Author or Publisher as to the accuracy or completeness of the
information contained within it. Neither the Author nor the Publisher shall be
liable for any loss or damage arising by virtue of such information or any
instructions or advice contained within this book.

Front cover picture: The Foreland and Old Harry Rocks: Griff J Fellows
Back cover picture: Hartland Point: Griff J Fellows

Contents

Preface

As I have visited these headlands I have been surprised by two things, first the richness and diversity of interest that they hold ranging through their natural beauty, flora, fauna, geology, history (military, civil and ecclesiastical), lighthouses and shipwrecks, industry (mining, quarrying, power generation, fishing), art and a variety of recreational activities. There is something for everyone. Secondly almost all headlands have free public access and many are supplied with car parks and clear direction signs.

What is a headland? This is not an easy question to answer. I suppose the best answer is that you know one when you see one. Scale comes into it. A headland should be walkable within a day and often in a matter of minutes, otherwise it is a peninsula. Height is irrelevant. It may tower above the sea or be a shingle spit almost covered at high tide. If it is cut off at high tide is it a headland or an island? With a few minor exceptions I have defined them as headlands. There are many more headlands than are described in this book. I have chosen those that have particular features of interest and are accessible to the public. They are sequenced in geographical order running clockwise round the coast starting at the Thames estuary.

Each headland is introduced with its name, the county or unitary authority, a nearby town, its grid reference, and the relevant Ordnance Survey maps. Those that are accessible by wheelchair carry a wheelchair symbol on the title strip.

Headlands are dangerous. Keep away from cliff edges. Watch the tides and the weather. Keep children and dogs under control. Stay well away from nesting birds, particularly those that nest on shingle or in grass. Obey the country code.

v

Be safe, plan ahead and follow any signs.
Leave gates and property as you find them.
Protect plants and animals and take your litter home.
Keep dogs under close control.
Consider other people.

Headlands are a rich heritage. May we enjoy them to the full and do all we can to preserve them for future generations.

Acknowledgments

My thanks to all I have met as I visited each of these headlands who have told me things I would never have discovered on my own.

Thank you Andy Graham for piloting us in a light aircraft round the coast of Wales, the Southwest Peninsula and the Channel coast to take aerial pictures. You patiently circled round yet again skimming the waves or high above the land to get the best view.

I thankfully acknowledge the sources of other aerial photographs as follows: St Bee's Head, Skyscan.co.uk © B Evans. Isle of Whithorn, Royal Commision on the Ancient and Historical Monuments of Scotland (RCHMS). Mull of Galloway, Skyscan.co.uk / B Evans. Rudh' Arduaine, Skyscan.co.uk / K Whitcombe. Dunstaffnage Castle, RCHMS. Ardnamurchan Skyscan.co.uk / B Evans. Cape Wrath, RCHMS. Fort George, (RCHMS), Kinnaird Head, RCHMS. Girdle Ness, Skyscan.co.uk © K Whitcombe. Fife Ness, RCHMS. Headlands at Elie, RCHMS. St Abb's Head, Skyscan.co.uk K Whitcombe. Tynemouth, Skyscan.co.uk © Skyscan. Scarborough Castle, Skyscan.co.uk © J Webb. Flamborough Head, Skyscan.co.uk © I Bracegirdle. Spurn Head, Skyscan.co.uk © Richmond and Rigg.

I am grateful to Dave Souza through Wikipedia for the close-up photograph of the unconformity at Siccar Point. I am indebted to Pembrokeshire County Council for providing the picture of a portion of the Last Invasion Tapestry (see Carregwastad Point).

A special thank you to Scilla, my wife, for your company while visiting these headlands in all weathers. You first introduced me to the delights of the Cornish coast. Without your helpful suggestions, energy and unfailing enthusiasm for this project this book would never have been completed.

Introduction — The delights of headlands

Imagine the scene. You walk along a crowded beach through an aroma of sun-lotion, negotiate your way round sprawling bodies, ducking the occasional flying frisbee and you reach the zone of rock-pools. Here children are scrambling around discovering an ancient pre-human world of seaweed and shellfish. Climb up the steep steps past clumps of sea campion to an area of worn grass criss-crossed with paths, the haunt of dog walkers and ice cream sellers. Continue along the cliff-top rising ever higher above the crashing waves. The paths thin out and the turf gets springier. Thyme, thrift and kidney vetch abound. The path cuts across three banks and ditches which are all that remain of the defences of an Iron Age cliff-castle. There are round circles, difficult to discern, marking where Bronze Age people built their huts. Pass the concrete remnants of Second World War defences, ugly to some, but with stories of human courage to tell. Stone remains can be made out in the long grass and heather, remnants of fortifications of previous wars. A curious small stone structure appears. It is clearly ecclesiastical. Could St Bedroc, the obscure ancient saint who gave her name to this headland, have lived in this building? It is widely accepted that she is buried nearby beneath the turf. The cliffs are changing. The rocks are more jagged. A fine natural arch comes into view and off-shore stacks provide safety for sea-birds. You are now virtually alone with nature, sharing the path with an occasional back-packer. You reach the end of the headland where a lighthouse built two centuries ago still acts as a warning and a reference point to ships. The views have opened up to left and right revealing a wild and windswept shore as far as the eye can see.

Is St Bedroc's Head a typical headland? Each headland is unique and a typical one does not exist. This imaginary headland with its imaginary saint contains features that are frequently seen. Even in Britain some headlands are so remote and wild that evidence of human influence can hardly be made out, while others are dominated by buildings as varied as holiday hotels, military forts and nuclear power stations. Many are stunningly beautiful and attract those who appreciate our varied coastal scenery. The flora and fauna on land and in the sea are rich and diverse. Cliffs around many headlands are a lure to geologists and rock-climbers. Headlands have played a significant role in the history of Britain. They provided the front line of observation posts to warn of the approach of enemy ships and offered ideal locations for defensive fortifications. In peacetime day-marks and lights warn ships of danger and act as navigation aids. Many headlands are named after saints, often dating back to the days of the early Celtic church. Headlands hold interest for everyone.

The Formation of Headlands

All land is subject to the opposing processes of deposition and erosion. Wind, water and ice are responsible for both.

If material is deposited at one site on the coastline faster than it is eroded then a headland is formed. Longshore drift refers to the movement along the coast of sand and shingle by the action of waves and currents. If waves hit a beach obliquely carrying sand and shingle with them they then retreat at right angles to the beach. In this way material is moved along the coast. This can build up headlands of shingle such as Spurn Head and Dungeness. Some shingle headlands are unstable affairs and change their shape with winter storms. The severe storms of the winter of 2013/2014 did major damage at Spurn Head and Blakeney Point in particular and led to cliff falls at Beachy Head and other sites. Some shingle spits are remarkably stable. Hurst Point for example carries a 16th century castle which appears to be as secure now as the day it was built. Deposition of material in vast quantities can be the result of volcanic eruptions. Lava flows and intrusions of igneous rocks have produced headlands along the northwest coast of Britain, most famously the Ardnamurchan Peninsula.

Many headlands are composed of hard rock. The rocks on either side being softer have been eroded away by the sea. Examples include the Dolerite rock that supports Dunstanborough Castle, the Schist of Start Point and Granite of Land's End. Sometimes a headland is made of the same rock as the coastline on either side and the hardness of the rock cannot be the explanation. At many sites around the southwest peninsula headlands are the ridges between ancient river valleys. Subsequent rising of the sea level has flooded the valleys forming long sea inlets called 'rias' that make safe natural harbours. A range of hills running into the sea, even if made of rock no harder than surrounding rocks, will form a headland simply because it takes longer for the sea to erode it away. Examples are Foreland Point in north Devon, Beachy Head in Sussex and St Bee's Head in Cumbria.

In general the oldest rocks in Britain are in the northwest and the youngest in the southeast although there are many exceptions. Also the younger rocks are usually the softer and are subject to faster erosion by the sea. The Holderness coast of Yorkshire is being eroded faster than anywhere else in Europe.

Around the British coast are headlands with rocks from every geological period. These are described in the texts of the relevant headlands.

PERIOD	MILLION YRS AGO APPROX	SOME ROCK TYPES FOUND ON HEADLANDS	SOME LOCATIONS
Neogene (includes Quaternary)	23 — Present day	Sand and Shingle	Spurn & Dungeness
Paleogene (includes Tertiary)	66 — 23	London Clay Basaltic Lava	Suffolk Morvern Peninsula
Cretaceous	144 — 66	Chalk	Dorset to Kent & Yorkshire
Jurassic	206 — 144	Sandstone and Limestone	Yorkshire, Dorset

PERIOD	MILLION YRS AGO APPROX	SOME ROCK TYPES FOUND ON HEADLANDS	SOME LOCATIONS
Triassic	251 — 206	New Red Sandstone,	St Bee's Head Cumbria
Permian	290 — 251	Granite	Cornwall, Lands End
Carboniferous	354 — 290	Limestone, Sandstone, Dolerite	Gower Peninsula. Northumberland
Devonian	417 — 354	Old Red Sandstone, Mica Schist	Caithness, Moray Firth, Devon
Silurian	443 — 417	Greywacke and Shale	E and W coasts of Southern Scotland
Ordovician	490 — 443	Dolerite, Basalt	Pembrokeshire
Cambrian	543— 490	Sandstone Dalradian Schist	Lleyn Peninsula Mull of Kintyre
Precambrian	4600 — 543	Lewisian Gneiss, Moine and Dalradian Schist, Monian Sandstone Schist Tuff & Lava	W & NW Scotland & Lleyn Peninsula,

Headlands show many other important geological features. At Siccar Point James Hutton first demonstrated the principle of 'unconformity' where nearly horizontal beds of Old Red Sandstone overlie almost vertical beds of Silurian Graywackes. The Highland Boundary Fault cuts through headlands on the east and west coasts of Scotland. Other headlands are a rich source of fossils, notably those along the Jurassic coasts of southern England and Yorkshire.

Flora and Fauna

At Dungeness, of all places, can be found 600 species of plants, one third of all native species found in Britain. Many headlands are nature reserves or Sites of Special Scientific Interest (SSSI) because of the unusual or rare plants which they support. The actual species will depend on the underlying rock and climatic features. Porous rock like limestone will produce dry conditions, but boggy ground overlies impervious rock. Shingle banks and spits are the driest of all. The rock also determines the acidity of the soil which in turn influences the species of plants which flourish there. Igneous rocks like granite and lavas are acidic whereas limestone and chalk are alkaline. Climate is another factor. Headlands, being exposed to strong winds, tend to have few or stunted trees. Gullies and cracks in rocks provide a sheltered microclimate enabling unusual and delicate plants to thrive.

Many species of familiar seaside flowers are widespread throughout the country and are not fussy where they grow. These include sea campion *(Silene maritima)*, thrift or sea-pink *(Armeria maritima),* kidney vetch *(Anthyllis vulneraria)* and spring squill *(Scilla verna)*. Others are confined to specific areas. The Scottish primrose *(Primula Scottica)* can only be seen on the mainland along the north coast of Scotland. At the other end of Britain the fringed rupturewort *(Herniaria ciliolata)* is virtually limited to the Lizard peninsula. Other treatments for hernia are recommended nowadays! Bluebells *(Hyacinthoides non-scriptus)*, which are often considered to be woodland plants, also grow on exposed headlands in the southwest. Rumps Point is a carpet of blue in the Spring.

Plants growing on shingle deserve a special mention. The harshest conditions are nearest the sea where drainage is rapid and salt spray is a problem. As one moves inland, often just a few metres, plants increase in number and diversity until the shingle is hidden and a covering of soil is formed. One of the common and most dramatic plants on shingle is the horned poppy *(Glaucium flavum)* with its large yellow flowers and thin curved seedpods up to 30cms long. Other striking flowering plants that can tolerate shingle and sand dunes include sea holly *(Eryngium maritimum)* and viper's-bugloss *(Echium vulgare)*. Marram grass *(Ammophila arenaria)* is the principal species to stabilise sand dunes. As shingle and sand become progressively vegetated woody plants can gain a foothold, such as sea-buckthorn *(Hippophae rhamnoides)* with its needle-sharp thorns and bright orange berries.

The sea is home to plants in the form of seaweed, a type of alga. Rocky shores, in particular, are rich in seaweeds. Different species live at different depths or zones. Seaweeds are classified according to colour: the red, green and brown. Brown seaweeds are far the commonest. Kelp is a general term referring to large brown seaweeds forming forests mainly below low-tide level. Seaweeds provide shelter for many marine species of molluscs, crustaceans and fish. Several species are edible, for instance Purple Laver for making laver bread. They are used today as a source of alginates which have a wide application in paints, foods and pharmaceuticals. Seaweed used to be harvested in huge quantities for fertiliser. It was also, at one time, burnt and the ash produced soda and potash used in glassmaking and the manufacture of soap. In the splash-zone between high water and the domain of flowering land plants the rocks are often covered with colourful lichens.

Shellfish found on rocks also tend to be confined to different tidal zones according to their ability to withstand desiccation. Barnacles and limpets are found nearest to high water mark and can easily withstand several hours exposed to hot sunshine. Periwinkles and whelks are intermediate, whereas bivalves such as mussels need to be submerged for a greater proportion of the time. Mussels are often so densely packed together as to completely cover the underlying rock. Worm's Head on the Gower Peninsula is reached at low tide by walking across extensive mussel beds.

It takes sharp eyes to see fish beneath the surface, though gannets appear to experience no difficulty. The exception is the huge, but harmless, basking shark seen round our southwest coasts each summer. Fish there are though, and headlands afford popular sites for anglers after bass, conger eels, wrasse, pollack, ling, dogfish, mackerel, ray, turbot and other species.

Sea mammals are always spectacular. Otters are increasing in numbers, but need patience and local knowledge to find. Seals, both common and grey, are a frequent sight and can often be seen observing the humans as intently as they observe the seals. Resident populations that can be seen every day of the year, at Blakeney Point for instance, are popular tourist attractions. Totally aquatic mammals that never come ashore are known as Cetaceans. Dolphins, porpoises and whales make regular appearances. Chanonry Point on the Moray Firth is the national capital of dolphin watching. Here pods of dolphins and porpoises pass along the firth through the narrow gap between Chanonry Point and Fort George.

Headlands attract bird enthusiasts throughout the year for the variety and quantity of bird life to be seen. On open headlands larks, stonechats, meadow pipits and wheatears are widespread. The chough, an attractive crow-like bird with a curved red bill, is the emblem for Cornwall. It no longer breeds in that county, but does in west Wales and can be seen regularly on Pembrokeshire headlands. Peregrine falcons nest on remote cliffs. They frequently prey on birds caught in flight. They are the fastest of all living creatures on Earth as they stoop with folded wings onto their prey. Cliffs provide nesting ledges for many seabirds such as fulmars, kittiwakes, gulls, guillemots, razorbills and gannets. Vast nesting colonies of sea birds are one of the great natural sights of Britain's coast. Sadly their numbers have recently diminished to an alarming degree due to the reduction in the number of sand eels which form an important link in the food chain. Many Scottish and Welsh headlands are home to large sea bird colonies. In England St Bees Head on the Cumbrian coast and Becton Cliffs on Flamborough Head in Yorkshire are outstanding. Sand martins nest in burrows in the soft cliffs such as at Hengistbury Head. High headlands command an expanse of sea for observing ducks, geese and other seabirds on the surface of the water.

Shingle headlands such as Spurn Head provide nesting opportunities for terns and ringed plovers. Thousands of gulls nest at the south end of Walney Island, which is not entirely separated from the mainland, so is included in this book.

A headland is often the first landfall for migratory birds from Scandinavia, Iceland or the Continent where they may be observed on their Spring and Autumn migrations. Occasionally rare visitors get blown to these shores by storms.

Navigation

Ever since man took to the sea in boats headlands have reaped a dreadful harvest of wrecks. The scale of loss of life and goods at sea is difficult to comprehend. Just over 100 years ago in 1909 alone no fewer than 733 vessels were wrecked around Britain's coast with the loss of 4738 lives. There are known to be over 30,000 wrecks round these islands' coasts. Sailors, and society at large, used to take a fatalistic attitude to the loss of ships and men at sea. It was widely believed that if a sailor were rescued from drowning then the sea would simply claim another victim in his stead. The view was that the sea should not be cheated of what it regarded as its own. In the 18th century the losses were enormous. Nearly one third of seamen died in the course of their work, many through shipwreck. Many gained from all this loss. Presumably ship builders did well. Also wrecks were highly prized by land dwellers who would strip a wreck of everything of value before the excise men arrived. Wreckers were those who lured ships onto the rocks, but it is doubtful that this happened as often as some have thought. No-one was ever convicted of this offence. Looting of cargo from wrecks is not just a thing of the past (See Beer Head). At first ship owners resisted the building of lighthouses as they were obliged to pay a fee each time they sailed past a lighthouse. Eventually, and not least because of the value of cargoes that went to the bottom, opinions changed.

The world's first known light was on the promontory of Sigaeum guiding ships from Troy. The most famous lighthouse of ancient time was the Pharos of Alexandria built about 300BC. This was one of the seven wonders of the ancient world and was destroyed by an earthquake in the 13th century having stood for

1500 years. Romans built a 'pharos' at Dover on the orders of the emperor Caligula in AD 90. The remains are within Dover Castle. Romans also built towers along the Yorkshire coast and it is probable that fires were lit on these towers to guide ships. The base of one such tower is in the process of being eroded away by the sea at Filey. The oldest surviving light tower in Britain is a chalk tower on Flamborough Head built in 1674 and designed to carry a coal and brushwood fire as a signal to shipping. The heyday of British lighthouse building was the 18th and 19th centuries. In Scotland lighthouse building was dominated by four generations of the Stevenson family. (See the appendix) They were brilliant structural engineers who built the first permanent stone lighthouses on wave-washed rocks as well as numerous lights on headlands. Thomas Smith (1752-1815) was employed by the Northern Lighthouse Board and founded a firm of lighthouse engineers. He took on and trained Robert Stevenson (1772-1850), the son of his wife by her previous marriage. Robert married Thomas Smith's daughter and had three sons who all joined the firm: Alan (1807-1865), David (1815-1886) and Thomas (1818-1887). Thomas's son Robert Louis (1850-1894) trained as an engineer, but found his real forte was as a writer. David, however, had two sons who were both lighthouse engineers: David A. (1854-1938) and Charles A. (1855-1950). Finally Charles's son D. Alan (1891-1971) was the last of the Stevenson dynasty of lighthouse engineers. Not only did they build offshore and onshore lighthouses, they also made many technical innovations in the light mechanisms and optics.

Lighthouses round England and Wales were built at the same time; the most famous English lighthouse engineer was the Yorkshireman, John Smeaton (1724-1792) known as England's first civil engineer. In the next century James Douglass (1826-1898) was pre-eminent. One of the last classic stone lighthouses to be built can be seen at the foot of Beachy Head. Since then steel or concrete lighthouses have been constructed on land (Dungeness) or offshore using a caisson technique developed by Swedish engineers. A British company, Chance Brothers of Smethwick , glass makers and engineers made great contributions to the design of the optics of lighthouses. They surrounded the light with Fresnel lenses and made the whole mechanism to rotate thus causing the light to flash intermittently.

Originally lights were powered by candles or burning wood or coal, later by oil lamps, then acetylene and finally by electricity. Twenty-four tallow candles provided light at Smeaton's Eddystone lighthouse. The first experiment with electric power for a light-house was by Faraday at South Foreland, Kent in 1859. Souter lighthouse at Lizard Point near South Shields was the first in the world to be powered permanently by electricity. As the means of generating light evolved, so the optical systems for projecting that light improved. The light was made to rotate, first by clockwork, but later by electric motors. Each light had a different 'character', a term used to define the number, colour, length and frequency of the flashes. A ship would then never confuse one light with anoth-er. By taking bearings of lights along the coast the exact position of the vessel could be charted.

Lighthouses were originally all manned. The work was exacting and often dangerous. The lights had to be checked every 2 or 3 hours throughout the night. Often the keepers in offshore lighthouses were marooned for weeks or months by storms. Now there are no manned lighthouses round the British coasts, all are automated. The absence of resident keepers has led to problems, not least the fouling of windows by seabirds with nobody on site to clean up.

The Northern Lighthouse Board controls all Scottish lights while Trinity House operate those round England and Wales. The original title of the Corporation of Trinity House, which was given a charter by Henry 8th in 1514, was 'The Master, Wardens and Assistants of the Guild, Fraternity or Brotherhood of the Most Glorious and Undividable Trinity and of St Clement in the Parish of Deptford Strond in the County of Kent'.

Do lighthouses have a future? Certainly in this age of global positioning systems and satellite navigation they are not needed to the same extent as previously. However technology can fail and small craft may not be fully equipped and then the lighthouse can be a lifesaver as before.

Round our coasts are lookout stations on HM Coastguard Service. In Scotland many are still manned giving direct visual surveillance of inshore waters. Round England and Wales they are no longer manned, but this function has been partially taken over by the voluntary National Coastwatch Institution providing a valuable service along Britain's busiest stretches of coast.

Defence

Headlands with steep cliffs make ideal defensive positions. Iron Age people exploited this property energetically before the Romans invaded our shores. These so-called 'cliff castles' can be seen particularly round the coast of Cornwall, but also elsewhere. A suitable headland was chosen and defensive ditches and ramparts surmounted with wooden palisades thrown up across the neck of the headland. Occasionally a large headland was chosen where the ramparts enclosed an area of several hectares such as Flamborough Head, Hengistbury Head and Dodman Point. Here whole communities could live. Most cliff castles are small where a community could retreat when attacked. The defensive ramparts are particularly well preserved at Trevelgue Head near Newquay, Cornwall and Nash Point, Glamorgan. Scotland is home to Duns and Brochs. The former are found mainly in the southwest and the taller brochs in the north. Both are dry stone structures built for defence.

Headlands were chosen for the same reasons during the period of the building of great stone castles. These were built not only for defence, but also to house troops who could go on the offensive when required. Bamburgh Castle and Dunstanburgh Castle on the Northumberland coast and Criccieth Castle in Wales are fine examples. Castles in Scotland, often the seat of the chief of a clan, served a similar purpose, for instance Sinclair Castle near Wick and Dunnottar Castle just south of Aberdeen.

Shakespeare might describe this Scepter'd Isle as "This precious stone set in the silver sea, Which serves it in the office of a wall, Or as a moat defensive to a house." True, but the sea is also the route by which invaders attack. For centuries Britain felt vulnerable to invasion from the continent of Europe. Headlands have provided vantage points for lookouts scanning the horizon for French, Dutch, Spanish or German fleets. With the advent of gunpowder, forts were built on headlands looking out to sea to protect our shores from foreign attack. Henry VIII built a chain of magnificent forts around the southern and eastern coasts of England. He incorporated some of the best military planning of his day by keeping walls low to provide a small target for enemy fire and building a tiered wedding-cake structure to accommodate as many large guns as possible. They did, however have serious design faults. The walls had no earth embankments to absorb or deflect canon balls. The upper gun platforms were roofed with wood making them vulnerable to fire from mortars. These forts might not have withstood a sustained attack and it is fortunate that they were never put to the test. Many are in a good state of preservation and are open to the public. Pendennis Castle and St Mawes Castle guard the entrance to Carrick Roads and Plymouth, while Hurst Castle protects the western approach to the Solent.

Arguably the most impressive of all Britain's headland forts is Fort George on the south coast of the Moray Firth. It was built by George II to prevent any further Scottish rebellions following the defeat of the Jacobites at the Battle of Culloden in 1746. Though open to the public it remains a military establishment to this day. It has never been attacked and is a prime example of military deterrence.

The early 19th century experienced another threat to our shores, this time from Napoleon Bonaparte. In 1803 Captain William Ford proposed the building of a chain of towers round the coast and the following year William Pitt ordered them to be built. Known as Martello Towers a total of 103 were eventually constructed. They were designed to be 600 yards apart so that the whole coastline was in range of 24 pounder cannon mounted on top of the towers. Not one was ever fired in anger.

By the middle of the century Palmerston again perceived a threat of a French invasion and ordered the building of a series of forts, some defending against a sea invasion and others protecting naval installations from attack by land. They were often called

Palmerston Follies because of their high cost and the fact that increased firepower rapidly led to their obsolescence. At this time Hurst Castle was extended with long casemated wings on either side of the 16th century Henrician castle to make it one of the largest of all Britain's coastal defences.

Coastal forts continued to play a significant role in the defence of our shores until and during World War 2. When Hitler threatened our shores in 1940 General Sir Edmund Ironside was put in charge of defence against invasion. Within four months no fewer than 18,000 pillboxes had been constructed. Gun emplacements were positioned on headlands guarding important ports. These would be low and camouflaged behind earthworks. Magazines would be underground and the whole surrounded with tank traps, barbed wire and pillboxes. By this time, however, it was air supremacy that was the crucial factor and the planned invasion never happened.

Headlands are a happy hunting ground for the military historian with ample remains to be studied from the Iron Age to the present day.

Saints and Monasteries

Many headlands are named after ancient saints, some are well-documented historical figures and others lost in the mists of legend. Why should headlands be associated with these early Christians? There are two rather conflicting reasons. First there were those who sought remote locations to remove themselves from the world and devote their time to prayer and there were others who came as missionaries and wanted to be close to centres of power and influence. It must be remembered that in those days there were no large towns, travel overland was hazardous and coastal sites were ideal for the spread of ideas and information by boat. Lindisfarne is an example of the latter and the chapel at St Govan's Head of the former.

The Romans were the first to bring the Christian religion to these islands. Constantine, the first Christian Roman emperor was declared emperor in Eboracum (later called York) in 306 AD on the death of his father, Constantius in that town.

It is reasonably certain that towards the end of the 4th century AD, well before the departure of the Romans, the Christian community in Carlisle sent St Ninian as bishop to the people of what is now Dumfries and Galloway. According to tradition St Ninian arrived in 397 AD and founded a church at the Isle of Whithorn which is a headland on the Scottish coast of the Solway Firth. St David is shrouded in legend. It is certain, however, that he was a bishop in Pembrokeshire in the 6th century, probably in or near the town and headland that bear his name. The Irish influence on the southwest coast of Scotland was profound. St Columba (521 – 597) came from Ireland and founded the Christian community on the island of Iona. Irish stone-carvers introduced the art of carving stone crosses and grave slabs to Scotland (See Rubha na Cille). It was from Iona that St Aidan travelled to Lindisfarne as its first bishop in 635. St Cuthbert was appointed bishop in Lindisfarne in 664, the year of the Synod of Whitby which committed the church in England to allegiance to Rome rather than the Celtic tradition.

Often the lives of these early British Christians are encrusted with colourful and sometimes bizarre legends that to our way of thinking tend to hide, rather than enhance, the historical figures. St Bee, for instance, came from Ireland to Cumbria and founded a monastery there. Legend has it that she was betrothed to a pagan Viking prince. When attempting to escape on the eve of her marriage she went down to the shore but found no boat. She cut a turf and sailed on it across the Irish Sea and landed safely on the Cumbrian shore.

The finest remains of a medieval religious establishment on a headland are at Tynemouth. This was the site of a monastery in the 7th century which was destroyed by the Danes in 800. The monastery here was re-founded in about 1090 and dissolved by Henry 8th in 1539. Extensive medieval ruins remain.

The World of Work

Shipwrecks used to provide the local population with welcome booty. Even if 'wrecking' was not widespread or common, smuggling was a lucrative occupation and was done with a clear conscience as many considered the excise duty payable on imports to be iniquitous (see Cudden Point).

Headlands also provide opportunities to turn an honest penny. Within the headland there may be rocks and minerals of commercial value. Portland Stone from the Isle of Portland is seen in many of our most famous buildings such as St Paul's Cathedral and the Cenotaph. Poorer quality limestone from other headlands, St Aldhelm's for instance, went to less prestigious projects. Attractive objects are carved and turned in Serpentine rock at the Lizard in Cornwall. Clays and shales containing alum ore were discovered in Elizabethan times on the Yorkshire coast. Alum was used as a mordant in the dyeing of textiles which were Britain's principal export. Previously all alum in Europe came from Italy. Alum clays were quarried extensively both north and south of Whitby. The headlands of Saltwick Nab and Kettle Ness were virtually removed in the process. Examples of mineral mining in headlands include the Bronze Age copper mines in Great Orme and tin mines in Cornwall, notably Wheal Coates mine at St Agnes Head.

Several ports are built on headlands providing shelter for commercial fishing vessels and pleasure craft. Keith Inch is the name of the headland at Peterhead, home to one of Britain's largest remaining fishing fleets.

The tourist and leisure industries have left their mark, some would say their scar, on a number of dramatic headlands. Lands End and Tintagel are arguably the most 'developed' of them all, cashing in on their geographical location and Arthurian legends respectively. Many local authorities recognise the value of access to these attractive sections of the coast and provide car parks and other amenities.

Nuclear power stations are frequently sited on the coast. The clean lines of such power stations at Dungeness and Torness add drama to these stretches of coast. I admit that many would take a different view.

Leisure

Headlands are a natural playground providing scope for all. Many enjoy them for coastal scenery and a good walk in the fresh air.

Others may carry fishing rods and try their skill at landing some of the many species of fish around our shores. Others may prefer a golf club in their hands. Several of the best courses in Britain are on headlands, St Andrews, Turnberry, Nefyn and Porthcawl. The 9th tee of the Ailsa course at Turnberry set right on the coast near the lighthouse and ruins of Bruce's castle is one of the most scenic and most photographed in the world.

For those who prefer the spice of danger then rock-climbing on headland cliffs provides thrills aplenty. There are numerous sites where this is a popular sport. Running off a cliff with hang-gliders on their backs appeals to some.

Those with a more cerebral than physical bent may find headlands a rich source of information on history, natural, civil, military and ecclesiastical. There are an infinite number of subjects to inspire the artist and photographer.

The marine and Coastal Access Act of 2009 has allowed access by the public to lengths of the English coast for the first time. There must be certain restrictions to protect the breeding grounds of sea birds, particularly those that nest on shingle.

The Future

Britain has a coastline second to none in the world. Her headlands, as well as being outstandingly beautiful, breathe the very history of the nation. We are fortunate that relatively few have been spoilt by inappropriate 'development' and most have easy access. Change is bound to happen and we cannot turn the coast into a museum. And yet it is imperative that our coastline, with its headlands, is not spoilt by tasteless development. At present we have this wonderful resource to enjoy. We must hand it on to future generations.

THE HEADLANDS

starting at the Thames Estuary
and going round the coast in
a clockwise direction.

North Foreland   ♿   Kent

3 miles from Margate
Grid Ref: TR 396710
Maps: OS Explorer 150, OS Landranger 179.

The headland of North Foreland faces the North Sea and the Thames Estuary. The Thames that a few short miles upstream flows through the heart of London! Surely a headland at the entrance to this river should carry a mighty statue of Britannia with trident in one hand and the other proudly pointing out to sea and Empire; a 'Colossus of Margate'. But where would such a statue stand? The Romans built an enormous triumphal arch 27m high at Rutupiae (modern Richborough) — the gateway to Britain. The concept of a huge white horse at Ebbsfleet (will it ever be built?) visible from train and road reflects the fact that many from the continent come to Britain through the channel tunnel and very few by sea.

White Ness, North Foreland

3

From Kingsgate Bay a coast path leads on past White Ness with its natural arch, and Foreness Point to Margate, a distance of 5km. The cliffs around this coast are of chalk, but not as white and gleaming as the chalk cliffs along the channel coast. The intertidal part of the cliffs and underlying wave cut platform are riddled with piddock burrows. Piddocks are small bivalve molluscs with rather pointed serrated shells. By gripping the rock tightly with a 'foot' they then rotate and bore their way into the chalk. The burrow provides the piddock with shelter from predators throughout its life. A squat structure, Neptune's Tower, at White Ness is a Victorian folly. There are fine offshore stacks at Foreness Point.

North Foreland lighthouse stands beside the road just north of Broadstairs. The first light was established here in AD 1499 to warn sailors of the treacherous Dogger Bank just offshore. This first light was coal-fired. Trinity House purchased the lighthouse in 1832 and electrified it in 1920. In 1998 it was the last of all Trinity House lighthouses to be fully automated.

This area of Kent is still called the Isle of Thanet because it used to be separated from the mainland by the Wansum Channel. Up to Roman times sea-going vessels would cut through the Wansum from the English Channel to the Thames Estuary to avoid the danger of rounding North Foreland. The Romans built forts at either end of the Wansum, Regulbium (Reculver) to the north and Rutupiae (Richborough) to the south. It was not until the Romans had left these shores that the Wansum was filled in, partly by longshore drift of shingle and natural silting up, and partly by the building of sea walls. With global warming and rising sea levels will it become a seaway once again?

Close to Richborough at Ebbsfleet is the traditional site for the landing of Hengist and Horsa in AD 449. Vortigern, who ruled much of southeast England, hired Saxon mercenaries under the command of Hengist and Horsa to protect him from attack from the north. This was the start of the Saxon takeover of England. Ebbsfleet is also thought to be the place where St Augustine arrived in AD 597.

South Foreland   ♿   Kent

2 Miles from Dover
Grid ref: TR 369432
Maps: OS Explorer 138, OS Landranger 179.

The dazzling white cliffs of Dover at South Foreland mark the shortest distance from England to France, a mere 34km (21 miles) away. The view across the Channel to the French coast takes in the ferries, pleasure boats and container vessels on this busiest seaway in the world. Cross channel swimmers set off from the nearby beach at St Margaret's bay. It was from here that Guglielmo Marconi made the first international radio contact with Wimereux, near Boulogne, in April 1898. The previous year he had communicated from here with the Goodwin Lightship, the first ship to shore wireless message.

South Foreland lighthouse

5

The High Foreland Lighthouse (sometimes called Langdon Cliffs Lighthouse or St Mary's Lighthouse) stands back from the cliff edge. The lighthouse, together with cliff-top land, is in the hands of the National Trust and is open to the public, but not every day. Although not functioning as a light any more the mechanism has been restored and open to view. This light was built in 1843 and decommissioned in 1988. Another first is that Michael Faraday himself conducted experiments with electric powered light in this lighthouse, but at that time oil lamps were more reliable. The first time an electric light shone from a lighthouse was from South Foreland on 8th December 1858. The Low Foreland Light can be seen poking above trees near the edge of the cliff. It was built in 1793 and removed from service in the early 20th century. It is not accessible to the public. A little further west along the coast are the remains of a Roman lighthouse in Dover Castle.

Being the closest point to France this stretch of coast was of great defensive importance. Today some concrete remnants of World War 2 defences can still be seen. Underground, though, are extensive tunnels that used to house shelters, plotting rooms, munitions stores and even an underground hospital. South Foreland Battery comprised four 9.2 inch guns with a range of 30,000 yards, not far short of the French coast. During the cold war some of the underground rooms were equipped to measure radiation in the event of a nuclear attack. Today these underground tunnels are not open to the public and to attempt to enter them would be highly dangerous. There is a story that a large wooden gun was constructed at South Foreland. This did not fool the Luftwaffe who responded by dropping a wooden bomb. There are several such apocryphal accounts of wooden bombs being dropped on decoy targets during World War 2.

Access to the lighthouse is from either Dover or St Margaret's at Cliffe along the stunning Saxon Shore Way. From Dover to St Margaret's at Cliffe is about 5km. Circular walks can be planned to incorporate part of the Saxon Shore Way and South Foreland. The Saxon Shore Way runs all the way from Hastings to Gravesend, a distance of 262km (163 miles). There can hardly be a more dramatic section of that trail than here at South Foreland.

Dungeness   ♿   Kent

16 miles from Folkestone
Grid ref: TR 092169
Maps: OS Explorer 125, OS Landranger 189.

There can be no headland in Britain that suffers from so many misconceptions as Dungeness. Many who have never been there think of it as a dreary, windswept place dominated by a nuclear power station. In reality it is full of interest and variety.

How many people know that there is a nature reserve of 1000 acres, home to over 600 species of plants, accounting for an amazing 1/3 of all native species found in Britain? Dungeness is one of the largest vegetated shingle banks in Europe and is of international importance. It juts out into the English Channel like a gigantic canine tooth. It is still growing as storms throw up new ridges of shingle. These are prominent along the shore and across the whole area about 500 ridges can be discerned. Shingle from the west side is swept round the point and deposited on the east side at the rate of 100,000 cubic metres a year by the process of longshore drift. A fleet of trucks continuously moves it back again to prevent erosion of the foundations of the nuclear power stations. Bare shingle is a hostile environment for plants particularly as total rainfall here is low. Plants have developed specialised means of getting and preserving moisture and resisting the ravages of salt spray. Plants that flourish include sea-kale *(Crambe maritime)*, biting stonecrop *(Sedum acre)*, sea spurge *(Euphorbia paralias)* and yellow horned Poppy *(Glaucium flavum)*. A short way from the coast a variety of habitats is found, which is the reason for the rich diversity of plant, insect and bird life found here. The Purple Heron, a rare visitor to Britain, has nested for the first time at Dungeness. Many kilometres of paths crisscross the nature reserve.

Mainly along the eastern shore of the headland is an extensive scattering of small houses that look rather unusual at first sight.

On closer inspection it becomes apparent that many of them started off as railway carriages. They have been extended and painted so that their origins are hardly discernible. This used to be a community of fishermen. Now only a few still ply this trade. Their boats and gear are drawn up on the beach. There is a smokery where locally caught fish smoked in the traditional way are for sale. Many of the houses are holiday accommodation. Artists are attracted here and a small shop sells their handiworsk. Derek Jarman (1942-1994) film director, artist, gardener and gay rights activist lived at Dungeness at Prospect Cottage. Here he created a famous garden of plants, shingle and a multitude of artefacts.

There have been five lighthouses near the tip of the Dungeness headland. The first, built in 1615 was a wooden tower carrying an

Dungeness lighthouse

open coal fire as a beacon. A second lighthouse, this time brick built around 1635 and about 110 feet (33m) high served for over a century. It found itself apparently drifting inland as the shingle headland advanced. A third lighthouse was constructed in 1792 and lit by oil. Trinity House acquired this light and electrified it as early as 1862. This proved too expensive at the time and the light reverted back to oil. The oil-fired lamp gave a surprising 850 candlepower and surrounded by glass prisms was 100 times as bright as its predecessor. All these three lighthouses have been demolished, but there are two later ones that are still standing. The Old Lighthouse (in reality the fourth) is an elegant, tapering, 150 ft (46m) brick tower surmounted by a lantern. This is a fine example of Victorian civil engineering. It is open to the public and can be hired for functions. When the nuclear power station went up in the 1950s it would have partially obscured the light from the lighthouse and it was necessary to build a fifth. This New Lighthouse was built in 1961 and was the first to display a xenon electric arc lamp. Its mode of construction was novel. Above a spiral base it is made of pre-cast concrete rings one above the other. These rings were threaded over vertical steel cables which, when the topmost ring was in position, were tightened, thus compressing the tower and giving it rigidity. Floodlighting the tower has reduced bird mortality.

The Romney, Hythe and Dymchurch Railway is no toy, but a very grown-up 15inch railway. It was the brainchild of two men, Captain J. E. P. Howey, a rich landowner and enthusiast for racing cars and miniature railways and Count Louis Zborowski a racing driver who died in the Italian Grand Prix at Monza in 1924. Howey drove the project on and the line from Hythe to New Romney was opened in 1927. Soon it was extended to Dungeness, an overall distance of 13.5 miles. For the most part it has carried passengers, both commuters and holidaymakers. During World War 2 it was requisitioned by the military who built the only armed and armoured miniature train in the world. It played a part in laying Pluto (the Pipe Line Under The Ocean) that supplied the allied forces with fuel. Today it carries tourists in comfort all the way from Hythe to the Old Lighthouse near Dungeness Point.

Dungeness A, a Magnox generator, was the first of the two nuclear power stations and was operational in 1965. It was decommissioned in 2006. Dungeness B, an advanced gas cooled reactor came on stream in 1983 with an output of 1110 MW. Its life is scheduled to end in 2018. Whatever one's view of nuclear power generation, the sheer size, bright whiteness and clean horizontal and vertical straight lines of these structures cannot fail to impress. Whether a shifting shingle bank was the most sensible site to choose is another matter.

Dungeness Lifeboat Station is on the east side of Dungeness Point. It is equipped with a modern Shannon class lifeboat.

Beachy Head   ♿   East Sussex

3 miles from Eastbourne
Grid ref: TV 594956
Maps: OS Explorer 123, OS Landranger 199.

Beachy Head is one of the most beautiful and iconic headlands in the British Isles. The name is derived from the French 'Beau Chef', Beautiful Head. It lives up to its name and never disappoints.

At 162 metres (530 feet) these are the highest chalk cliffs in Britain. Their dazzling whiteness is a consequence of the rate at which they are being eroded. Each fall from the cliff face exposes more fresh white chalk. An estimated 50,000 to 100,000 tons fell just behind the lighthouse on 10/11 January 1999. More frequently quite small pieces of chalk fall away, particularly in winter after heavy rain. The pounding of the waves quickly break up fallen blocks of rock and then the cliff is exposed to the erosive action of the sea again. The land covered with springy turf rises towards the cliff edge like a launch ramp on an aircraft carrier. When viewed from the sea the cliff is a great white wall with no view of the land behind it. From the top of the cliff the views both east and west are spectacular. To the east lies the town of Eastbourne and on a clear day Dungeness can be seen 40 miles away. To the west is a magnificent line of undulating chalk cliffs and occasionally the Isle of Wight can be made out 70 miles distant.

The chalk was laid down in the Cretaceous Period stretching from 144 to 65 million years ago. During this time much of Ireland, Britain, Northern France and beyond was covered by a fairly shallow warm sea. Coccolithophores, microscopic single-celled algae, thrived in this environment. Each formed a minute coat of Calcium Carbonate. These 'coccoliths' sank and formed the chalk we see today. Chalk is 98% pure calcium carbonate. The rate of deposition was about 1cm every 500 to 1000 years. Chalk occurs up to 500m thick requiring 25 to 50 million years to accumulate. The cliffs to the west of Eastbourne, which include Beachy Head, contain the full sequence of chalk deposition throughout the Cretaceous period. They are the 'type-section' which means they form a standard to which other chalk exposures are compared. A casual inspection of the cliffs reveals more or less horizontal layers of flint embedded in the chalk. Flint is almost pure silica (quartz) and probably formed around sponges living on the sea floor. They occur frequently in chalk and provide a hard building stone in chalk downland areas. Chalk

Late evening light at Beachy Head

is found on the Yorkshire coast (see Flamborough Head) as well as the south of England. The end of the Cretaceous Period saw a major mass extinction which put paid to the dinosaurs.

Beachy Head Countryside Centre is run by volunteers and houses an innovative museum providing a fascinating insight into the history and wildlife of the area.

Although the scene out to sea is peaceful enough today it would have been very different on 10th July 1690. In the War of the Grand Alliance the naval Battle of Beachy Head was fought between the French with a fleet of 70 ships of the line and 5 frigates and an Anglo-Dutch fleet of 56 ships. The French were the victors, but failed to press home their advantage by pursuing the English into the Thames Estuary. The French fleet was finally put out of action two years later at the battle of La Hogue off the Normandy coast.

Beachy may mean Beautiful Head, but the white chalk cliffs contrast with the black statistics of the number of suicides that happen here. Regrettably the cliffs here have seen an increasing number of suicides in recent years. Many who contemplate suicide are persuaded to think again. A telephone box near the top of the headland displays the number of the local branch of Samaritans and the national helpline.

The first lighthouse, Belle Toute, was built near the cliff edge in 1828 about 2.5 km west of Beachy Head. It remained operational until 1899. The light was often obscured by fog at that elevation even when visibility at sea level was good. Because of this it was decided to build a new lighthouse nearer to sea level. Beachy Head Lighthouse was designed by Sir Thomas Matthews and built on the wave-cut platform off Beachy Head itself and was operational by 1902. This was the last of the traditional stone lighthouse towers to be built around the shores of Britain and 3,660 tons of Cornish granite were used in its construction. It was automated in 1983. Cliff erosion threatened Belle Toute. In 1999 using a combination of hydraulic jacks and rollers it was moved to a safer location a little way inland. It is now a private residence.

There is a car park at Beachy Head or the South Downs Way can be followed from Eastbourne almost to Seaford along the cliff tops affording possibly the finest chalk cliff scenery in the country.

Selsey Bill   ♿   West Sussex

4 miles from Chichester
Grid ref: SZ 857921
Maps: OS Explorer 120, OS Landranger 197.

Before the town of Selsey appeared there may well have been seals on the shingle beaches as Selsey means 'Seal Island'. A steep flint-shingle and shell bank swings round the little town of Selsey. Groynes placed at right angles to the shore help to prevent loss of shingle by longshore drift. About 2 km off the tip of Selsey Bill is the Mixon Beacon marking rocks which once were quarried for building stone. Further to the southwest stands Nab Tower. This is a reference point for the Admiralty from which Royal Navy ships report their distance in nautical miles. At night it flashes a white light every 10 seconds.

Selsey Lifeboat Station is on the more sheltered east side of the headland. The lifeboat is kept in a boathouse with slipway at the end of a pier so that it can be launched quickly at any state of the tide. The Royal National Lifeboat Institution was founded in 1824 and Selsey has had a lifeboat since 1861. The early lifeboats were open to the elements and propelled by oars. Over the years lifeboat design has steadily developed to the sophisticated, almost unsinkable boats in service today. The present boat is the *City of London*, a 'Tyne' class lifebo- at. There is also an inflatable inshore lifeboat, the *Peter Cornish*. Visitors are welcome to look round the life- boat station. Each request for help is

Lifeboat Station at Selsey Bill

called a 'shout.' A newsletter lists all the 'shouts' they receive and impressive reading it makes too. It is reassuring to know that the skill and dedication of lifeboat crews are there if required.

Saint Wilfrid of York (AD 634 – 709) was a colourful and energetic character. His life was a switchback series of controversies with secular and ecclesiastical authorities, banishments, appeals to Rome and reinstatements to high office. He was appointed Bishop of York, founded monasteries at Hexham and Ripon, argued successfully at the Synod of Whitby for the adoption of the Roman tradition, and in AD 680 was banished by King Ecgfrith of Northumbria and took refuge in Sussex where Ethelwald, King of the South Saxons made him welcome. He established a monastery at Selsey, possibly at the site of Norton Priory now a nursing home. Tradition has it that the people of the region were destitute and that he taught them how to fish with nets. In AD 685 he was reinstated as Bishop of Hexham and later of York. A bishopric was established in Selsey in AD 709. Twenty-three bishops oversaw the work before the See was moved to Chichester in AD 1070.

The medieval church serving the people of Selsey stood at Church Norton about 2km north of the present town. In 1866 the whole church building except the chancel was moved stone by stone and re-erected as the Parish Church of St. Peter at the north end of Selsey. The chancel remained at the original site as St. Wilfrid's Chapel. Both church buildings are of architectural merit and contain furnishings of note.

The prominent windmill in the town was built in 1820. A windmill had stood there for a century or more before that. It is not open to the public.

There is a car park near the tip of Selsey Bill from where it is a walk of just over 1km round the point to the lifeboat station.

Southsea Castle   ♿   Hampshire

At Southsea
Grid ref: SZ 642980
Maps: OS Explorer OL29, OS Landranger 196.

On the 19th July 1545 King Henry VIII stood proudly on his castle and watched as a formidable fleet of French warships sailed up the Solent to threaten Portsmouth. An English fleet was prepared for them led by King Henry's flagship the Mary Rose. To his horror, even though the weather was calm, she heeled over, water poured through the gun-ports and she rapidly sank leaving just the tops of two masts above the surface. "O my gallant men! They are drowned like ratten" he cried. The loss of life was compounded by the fact that anti-boarding netting was stretched across the mid and aft decks trapping the sailors beneath.Southsea castle was one of many that Henry VIII built around the south coast of England. It was constructed in 1544 to a design attributed to the king himself. The square keep, rectangular gun platforms and angular bastions reflected the most advanced military thinking of the day. The moat is dry and was never intended otherwise. In the 19th century a brick tunnel called a counterscarp was constructed within the outer wall of the moat with openings that provide covering fire into the moat. The counterscarp is reached by a covered passage across the moat, the caponier. The castle has undergone various additions and alterations, but Henry's design still predominates.

Southsea Castle and Lighthouse

In 1828 the lighthouse was built into the western rampart of the castle. It is no longer a functioning navigation light. Portsmouth

City Council owns the lighthouse and it shines again on special occasions.

Close to the castle and in a building that echoes the shape of the castle is the D-Day Museum. This graphically portrays the preparation for the Normandy landings and the events of this largest sea and airborne invasion of all time. The centrepiece is the Overlord Embroidery. At 83m it is the longest work of its kind in the world. It depicts the build up to the invasion and the landings by sea and air with great realism and in meticulous detail. Caen was the first town to be liberated by the allies and next to the D-Day Museum is a Peace Garden donated by the citizens of Caen.

Nearby is an Aquarium complete with underwater tunnel. Also near the castle is The Pyramids, a multifunction leisure centre with swimming pools and concert venues. A traditional esplanade from the pier to the castle and adjacent gardens cater for those who like a quiet stroll by the sea.

The western side of the entrance to Portsmouth Harbour is guarded by Fort Gillkicker.

Hurst Castle   ♿   Hampshire

15 miles from Bournemouth
Grid ref: SZ 319899
Maps: OS Explorer OL22, OS Landranger 196.

Henry VIII built Hurst Castle between 1541 and 1544 to guard the entrance to the Solent. It consists of a 12-sided keep within a curtain wall with three bastions and a moat on the landward side. Two that remain of 10 huge guns from this era are on display. They weigh 38 tons apiece and required a gun-crew of 12 men who could fire an 820lb shell with a range of 6000 yards every 6 minutes. The cannons are muzzle-loaders and the shell was lifted into position with a block and tackle.

Cromwellian forces imprisoned Charles I in Hurst Castle in November 1648 for several weeks. He took exercise by walking on the shingle spit. From here he was transferred to Windsor Castle and on to his execution.

Long west and east wings were added in the reign of Queen Victoria. On the seaward side these are revetted with vast granite blocks between the gun casemates giving a distinctly Egyptian appearance. The castle was manned through both World Wars and equipped with the armaments appropriate to the time. Like many other forts around the coast of Britain it was never called upon to fire on any enemy ship. A display in the castle explains its history and other interesting features of the area.

Last rays of the setting sun on Hurst Castle and Lighthouse

A 26 metre high tower lighthouse stands just beyond the castle. It was built in 1867 and replaced a series of high and low lights which had been obscured by the wings added to Hurst Castle. A low light was built on the wall of the castle and is now not operational and is painted grey so as not to confuse mariners.

The shingle spit that projects from the mainland near Milford-on-Sea and extends more than halfway across the Solent towards the Isle of Wight is dominated by Hurst Castle at its tip. The spit is subject to erosion and has been reinforced with shingle dredged from banks offshore. The building of concrete sea defences at Milford means there is less erosion along that stretch of coast which historically replenished the shingle of Hurst spit. Severe storms such as those of the winter of 2013/2014 seriously erode shingle spits. A series of groynes limit movement of shingle by longshore drift. It is surprising (it surprises me at any rate) that the 16th century castle and its huge 19th century extensions, all built on shingle, have stood for so long and appear perfectly secure today.

The castle can be reached on foot along the 3km shingle bank from Milford-on-Sea or in summer by ferry from Keyhaven. Often walking on shingle is a tiring affair, but the ridge of this shingle bank is easy walking. The walker is rewarded with a range of plants that are adapted to thrive in the harsh, dry, salty conditions of a shingle spit.

Hengistbury Head & Bournemouth

3 miles from Bournemouth
Grid ref: SZ 180906
Maps: OS Explorer OL22, OS Landranger 195.

Twelve thousand years ago the Grand Solent River flowed west to east just to the north of what is now the Isle of Wight along the line of The Solent as we know it today. England was still part of the Continent of Europe and Hengistbury Head was high ground on the side of this great river valley.

Stone Age hunters were already here and left some of their flint tools on Warren Hill, the highest point of Hengistbury Head. These people belonged to the Upper Palaeolithic Period (Old

18

Stone Age) somewhere between 40,000 and 10,000 years ago. No doubt Mesolithic and Neolithic man also roamed over this landscape, but only a few of their artefacts have been found. People were here in the Bronze Age and cremated their

Mudeford Spit from Hengistbury Head

dead and buried the ashes in tumuli together with a variety of grave goods. Any visitor to the headland will cross the Double Dykes. These are Celtic Iron Age (600BC – 400AD) ditches and ramparts protecting the headland from attack from the landward side. When first constructed they would have been even higher and more impressive than they are today. Iron ore was abundant on the headland itself and also occurred as boulders, known as 'doggers', down on the beach. On the northern side of the headland a pre-Roman port and trading centre thrived on trade with the Continent. Pottery shards of amphorae have been found that would have contained wine from Italy. The trade through Hengistbury declined and finally ceased during the Roman occupation of Britain when other ports further to the east were established.

Another massive excavation that crosses the headland is the result of opencast mining for iron-ore in Victorian times. The removal of 'doggers' from the beach in the mid-nineteenth century exposed the soft sandy cliffs to the erosive power of the waves. A significant proportion of the headland, probably as much as half, was washed away before action was taken to prevent it. Groynes were built to conserve the foreshore by preventing longshore drift. A substantial breakwater, the Long Groyne, was constructed from the eastern tip of the headland out towards Beer Pan Rocks.

Today human occupation is confined to Mudeford Spit which runs at right angles to the headland and almost closes the entrance to Christchurch Harbour. Here colourful wooden houses, each with a small boat or two with names like *Lizzy-Anne,* stretch almost to the tip of the spit. A 'land-train' from Southbourne at the base of the headland carries excited children to Mudeford Spit and saves the legs of the people who live there.

Part of the headland and the adjacent Christchurch Harbour are nature reserves with a great variety of habitats. The rare Natterjack toads are found on the headland. They have been introduced to various sites to increase their number. These largely nocturnal creatures are said to be the loudest amphibians in Europe. Sand martins nest in the soft cliffs around the tip of the headland.

From a car park at the base of the headland a wide path climbs up and along to the end of the high part of the headland, then turns sharp left down to Mudeford Spit. A low path back skirts the salt marsh within Christchurch Harbour. The whole round trip to take in the end of the spit makes a fine walk of about 6km (4miles).

The Foreland or Handfast Point
Dorset

3 miles from Swanage
Grid ref: SZ 053824
Maps: OS Explorer OL15, OS Landranger 195.

The fine chalk cliffs of The Foreland, also known as Handfast Point continue out to sea as a line of chalk stacks called Old Harry Rocks. They point straight to The Needles, similar stacks projecting from the Isle of Wight. These fragments are all that remain of a ridge of chalk that linked the Isle of Wight to the mainland before the last ice age. North of this ridge ran the Grand Solent River to flow into the recently formed English Channel to the east of what is now the Isle of Wight.

The Foreland and Old Harry Rocks

A cliff-top walk of 1km from the village of Studland reaches this beautiful headland. Spectacular views of chalk cliffs, stacks and arches are seen along the coast path to the south of The Foreland.

In AD 876 a Viking fleet of, it is said, 120 ships set sail westward from the region of Poole to bring reinforcements to Guthram who was at Exeter. In a great storm the fleet was wrecked on the headland. At that time Mercia, East Anglia and Northumbria were all in Viking hands. The Saxons under Alfred the Great only held Wessex and they were in danger of being overrun by Guthram. The storm came to the rescue of the Saxon kingdom in the nick of time. Legend recounts that Earl Harold was on one of the ships and when he drowned he was turned into a pillar of chalk — hence Old Harry Rocks. Old Harry's Wife was the stack furthest from the shore, but collapsed, poor thing, in 1896. History repeated itself in the time of Elizabeth I when another storm wrecked the Spanish Armada.

The Church of St Nicholas in Studland is Norman, but shows evidence of its Saxon origins probably extending back to the time of St Aldhelm (AD 639 – 709).

Durlston Head   ♿   Dorset

1 mile from Swanage
Grid ref: SZ 035772
Maps: OS Explorer OL15, OS Landranger 195.

George Burt was a Victorian stone merchant, citizen of Swanage and a visionary. He bought land that included Durlston Head, built Durlston Castle and laid out his estate for the public to enjoy. Typical of his era, he intended his guests to be educated and improved as well as refreshed by their visits. His estate is now Durlston Country Park open to the public as he would have wished. One of his most prominent legacies is a magnificent stone globe 10 feet in diameter and weighing over 40 tons. This is in a prominent position on the headland overlooking the sea. The founder of the Mowlem construction company was a relative of George Burt and the globe was made in his workshops at Greenwich. The 15 sections of the globe were assembled on Durlston Head in 1887. Ranged round the globe are large stone tablets inscribed with astronomical data about the earth, the moon and the sun. Here and elsewhere on the estate are other tablets with astronomical inscriptions, excerpts of poetry and quotations from the Bible.

Continuing the educational theme into the modern era are information boards at strategic points around the estate. The information centre at the shop is full of amusing, relevant and interesting facts. Seventy percent of early spider orchids *(Ophrys sphegodes)* in Britain are found on the coastal strip between Durlston Head and St Aldhelm's Head. No fewer that 10 species of orchid grow wild on the estate. Clumps of stinking iris *(Iris foetidissima)* grow beside the path at the tip of the headland. Durlston Head is a good place to watch cetaceans, particularly Bottle Nosed Dolphins, in the English Channel. Along the coast is ample evidence of the once thriving stone-quarrying industry. Further inland, beside a path, is a reconstructed 'quarr'.

The Globe at Durlston Head

These were small family-owned mines for extracting the valuable Purbeck Limestone. Stone was loaded underground onto 'quarr carts' and hauled to the surface by donkeys turning capstans. In the 19th century there were hundreds of these quarrs in the area around Swanage.

The Dorset and East Devon Coast UNESCO World Heritage Site is Britain's first World Heritage Site, chosen for its natural features. It extends from Exmouth in the west to Swanage in the east. The oldest rocks are cliffs at Orcombe Point near Exmouth that date from the Triassic Period. As one travels east along the coast the rocks get younger, Jurassic (206 — 144 million years ago) and then Cretaceous towards Swanage. The Jurassic rocks exposed along this coast are mainly limestones and clays laid down in warm seas and coastal swamps. They are rich in fossil shells, plants and vertebrates, particularly dinosaurs. It is illegal to remove fossils from cliffs. The best time to find fossils is after a severe storm and high tide.

Jurassic rocks are also found in South Wales (see Lavernock Point) and Cleveland and Yorkshire between Redcar and Filey.

The view north takes in Peverill Point with its National Coastwatch Station that marks the south end of Swanage Bay. This headland is just a short walk from the town of Swanage.

There is a car park at Durlston Country Park. On foot it is just 1km, mainly by coast path, from the centre of Swanage.

St Aldhelm's (St Alban's) Head   Dorset

6 miles from Swanage
Grid ref: SY 961753
Maps: OS Explorer OL15, OS Landranger 195.

A circular walk of 7km from the village of Worth Matravers swings round the headland along the South West Coast Path passing several fascinating features along the way. About 5km west of St Aldhelm's Head is the hamlet of Kimmeridge that gives its name to Kimmeridge Clay. Like the other rocks in this vicinity, Kimmeridge Clay was laid down in the Jurassic Period. To the west can be seen slumped cliffs where near vertical beds of limestone and shale have slipped on the underlying clay. This is part of the Dorset and East Devon UNESCO World Heritage Site that runs from Orcombe Rocks near Exmouth to Old Harry Rocks, East Dorset. (See Durlston Head.) The headland itself is composed of Purbeck Limestone which has been extensively quarried. Blocks of stone were lowered directly into barges moored beneath the cliffs.

A stone table and benches and a memorial stone set within a small garden remember Royal Marines killed from 1945 to 1990. Another memorial stands in honour of radar research workers who carried out important research at Worth Matravers and on St Aldhelm's Head during World War 2. The memorial represents two radar dishes in the form of a fire basket, an ancient way of warning of invasion. Sir Bernard Lovell performed the unveiling ceremony n 2001.

Looking out to sea is a National Coastwatch Station where volunteers keep keen eyes trained on the English Channel for any vessel in distress. They are always happy to show people round and explain the work they do.

Set back a few meters from the tip of the headland is the atmospheric and rather mysterious Chapel of St Aldhelm. Legend has it that it was built by a local man in AD 1140 having witnessed his daughter and her newlywed bridegroom drown off the end of the headland. Although dedicated to St Aldhelm the building is of Norman style and date. The plan is square with the corners pointing North, South, East and West. Eight simple arches springing from a central pillar support the roof. Access is by a door in one wall and a small window in another provides the only light. Low earthworks surround the chapel indicating that this may have been a site of Christian worship possibly stretching back to the time of St Aldhelm himself. It is still used for this purpose today.

Here is a headland that cannot seem to decide between two saints. Ordnance Survey maps record both, but name St Aldhelm first. Why should it carry two names? St Aldhelm (AD 639-709) was born in Wessex, educated in Canterbury, became Abbot of Malmesbury and later the first Bishop of Sherborne. He is said to have been fluent in Latin, and was a famous composer of Latin riddles, and also spoke Greek and was able to read Hebrew. St Alban, on the other hand, was a Roman soldier and the first known English martyr who died around AD 304 for sheltering a Christian fugitive during a time of persecution. He is more associated with Hertfordshire than with Wessex. Worthy though he was, he can have little claim to a headland in Dorset.

St Aldhelm's Chapel

In the churchyard of the parish church of St Nicholas in Worth Matravers (also well worth a visit) is the grave of a farmer by the name of Benjamin Jesty. In 1774 he carried out the first recorded vaccination with material from a cowpox vesicle. He vaccinated his wife and two children during a smallpox epidemic. All survived although his wife ran a high fever and had a painful, swollen arm, possibly from the introduction of other pathogens with the cowpox virus. None of them contracted smallpox. It was 22 years later in 1796 that Dr Edward Jenner inoculated James Phipps, an 8 year old boy, with cowpox material from the hand of a dairymaid, Sarah Nelmes. In 1797 a Dr George Pearson who had worked with Dr Jenner published a paper mentioning a farmer in Dorsetshire who had inoculated his wife and children before Dr Jenner's first experiment. Despite hearing this evidence a House of Commons committee in 1802 decided that Dr Jenner "had made the discovery" and awarded him £10,000. Dr Pearson founded the Vaccine Pock Institute in London (a rival to the Royal Jennerian Society) and in 1805 the institute invited Benjamin Jesty to come to London to have his portrait painted. Although there were those who recognised the importance of Benjamin Jesty's action during his lifetime he was never acknowledged by Jenner and is only now beginning to receive the honour he is due.

Portland Bill   ♿   Dorset

8 miles from Weymouth
Grid ref: SY 677683
Maps: OS Explorer OL15, OS Landranger 194.

Thomas Hardy described the Isle of Portland as "carved by time out of a single stone." Portland Stone is termed a 'freestone' meaning that it can be cut in any plane with little danger of it splitting. It is, therefore, highly sought-after for building and for sculpture. Inigo Jones was the first to use Portland

The Isle of Portland

Stone in London when in 1626 he built the Banqueting Hall in Whitehall that survived the fire of London. Christopher Wren used it for many London churches including St Paul's Cathedral. Other notable London structures of Portland stone include Buckingham Palace, the Bank of England and the Cenotaph. The War Graves Commission employs it throughout the world in war cemeteries. Tout Quarry Park in the north part of the Isle of Portland is a disused stone quarry turned information centre and sculpture-park and supplies many details about the stone and its uses.

The famous Portland Stone is, in fact, overlain by Purbeck Beds consisting mainly of limestones, shales and clay spanning the Jurassic/Cretaceous boundary. Extensive quarries are scattered over the Isle. Portland stone is not particularly hard. To the northwest of Portland Bill the sea has scooped out a series of caves in this rock and the roofs of several have collapsed. Pulpit Rock is an impressive stack almost at the tip of the headland. Portland is within the stretch of coast designated a UNESCO World Heritage Site on account of the unique rock sequence with its contained fossils from late Triassic to the Cretaceous Period displayed chronologically from west to east.

The sea a little way off Portland Bill is in a constant state of agitation. This is the Portland Race where tidal currents cross. Many ships have come to grief on the rocks or on Chesil Beach. Two lighthouses were erected on either side of the point in the early 18th century, but the lights were poorly maintained. A new tower replaced one of these at the end of the century. This was the first lighthouse in Britain to be lit by a group of Argand lamps backed by mirrors. These were oil lamps with circular wicks. Air was drawn up through the centre of the wicks. The light they provided was superior to any previous lamp. New high and low lighthouses were built in 1869. The present tall lighthouse, with its prominent central red band, at the tip of Portland Bill was built in 1906 and was fully automated 90 years later. A Tourist Information and Visitor Centre lie at its base. The old low lighthouse is now a bird observatory. About half a mile north of the tip of Portland Bill is a National Coastwatch Station.

While at the tip of Portland Bill note the white obelisk built in 1844 as a daymark to warn shipping of treacherous shelves of rock that project 30 metres out into the English Channel. Just along the coast are numerous huts looking out to sea. These are popular with coast lovers who do not mind being exposed to gale-force winds and no view of a sandy beach.

Marie Stopes bought the Old Higher Lighthouse in 1923 and used it as a refuge from life in London. She was never idle and pursued among her many interests that of palaeontology. She founded the Portland Museum and acted as curator.

The Isle of Portland holds many other sites of interest. At Church Ope Cove on the east shore are the ruins of Rufus Castle and St Andrew's Church. The castle was probably built by Richard, Duke of York, between 1432 and 1460 to fend off the French during the Hundred Years War. It is now in private hands and not open to the public. St Andrew's Church, now ruinous, may have been a site of Christian worship predating the Norman Conquest. It served as the parish church of Portland until 1756.

28

Portland Castle built 1539/1540 at the mainland end of the Isle of Portland overlooking and protecting Portland Harbour is one of Henry VIII's best-preserved coastal castles. English Heritage administers the castle and it is open to the public. At the outbreak of the Civil War it was in Parliamentarian hands, but Royalist soldiers captured it in 1643. A body of Royalists divided into two, half of them disguised as Roundheads who were chased along the shore by those still dressed as Cavaliers. The castle gates were opened to give refuge to the apparent Roundheads who then overran the garrison. Oh, the deceitfulness of warfare! Clever though.

Portland Harbour was once the largest man-made harbour in the world incorporating 6 million tons of stone in its breakwater. Two huge Phoenix Caissons tower above pleasure yachts. They were to be part of Mulberry Harbours at the D-Day Normandy landings.

The Isle of Portland, although reached by road from Weymouth across a bridge, is not strictly speaking an island as it is attached to the mainland by the great arc of Chesil Beach, a shingle bar 13 km long separating the open sea from the Fleet Lagoon. Portland Bill is the southern tip of the Isle of Portland. A coast path runs round the whole of the Isle of Portland a distance of 14km. There is a car park at Portland Bill for whom walking is not an option.

Beer Head   Devon

10 miles from Lyme Regis
Grid ref: SY 227879
Maps: OS Explorer 116, OS Landranger 192.

The origin of the name Beer does not come from a local brew, but from the old English *bere* or *beare* meaning woodland.

A pleasant walk from the village of Beer passes through pasture fields and open grassland with the sea far below. Lines of trees

29

Chalk cliffs of Beer Head

demarcate ancient fields that may even precede the Romans. The result of the dramatic landslip of 1790 at Hooken Cliffs is unmistakable. At that time ten acres of pasture supported by chalk slid to seaward on underlying Triassic Mercia Mudstone. At this point, just west of Beer Head, the path drops down to a shingle beach below Hooken Cliffs and a walk back along the shingle reaches Beer Head itself, a vertical chalk cliff with an overhang. This, with Hooken Cliffs, is the most westerly appearance of Cretaceous chalk in England.

In January 2007 the stricken container ship MSC Napoli was beached just west of Beer head and spilled part of her cargo along the beach providing a bonanza for opportunists.

Hope's Nose   Devon, Torbay

At Torquay
Grid ref: SX 949637
Maps: OS Explorer 110, OS Landranger 202.

This small headland has been preserved for nature, yet could so easily have been overrun by the adjacent town of Torquay. Hope is a common place name in England and means a small enclosed valley or plot of land. A gentle path leads

Winter angling at Hope's Nose

down from the road to flat rocks popular with both amateur and professional anglers. Two rocks off the tip of the headland are called Lead Stone and Ore Stone. Hope's Nose itself has been quarried extensively. The tip is limestone of Devonian age, 350 million years old, containing fossil corals, trilobites and bivalves, but are difficult to identify. Gold is here as well and even more hidden. Much more obvious is dusty miller or silver dust *(Senecio maritima)* that grows here in profusion. This is an attractive woody plant with silvery downy leaves and yellow, daisy-like flowers. Juice from the plant dropped onto the eye is said to cure cataract — not to be recommended.

Berry Head

Devon, Torbay

1.5 miles from Brixham
Grid ref: SX 947566 and SX 937546
Maps: OS Explorer OL20, OS Landranger 202.

The first sight of England for William of Orange as he sailed across the Channel on 5th November 1688 would have been the high cliff of Berry Head. With these cliffs on his port side he would sail into Brixham harbour with a force of 20,000 men. So started the 'Glorious Revolution' that installed the Protestant William and Mary jointly on the throne of England. A statue of William stands at Brixham harbour.

A hundred years or so later England felt genuinely threatened by Napoleon Bonaparte. Vast defences were constructed on Berry Head, Berry Head Fort (North Fort) and the Old Redoubt (South Fort). Strategically placed cannon and extensive perimeter walls

Berry Head lighthouse

still stand that give a clear impression of the sheer size of these fortifications. It was never put to the test. The name Berry comes from the Saxon 'Byri' or 'Byrig' meaning a castle or fortification.

The most prominent building is the lighthouse though it is the squattest in the British Isles. The light was once turned by clockwork powered by a weight dropping 45m down a shaft.

A large see-through flying saucer is a navigation beacon. The property of National Air Traffic Services it gives accurate bearing and range measurements to aircraft within the London Flight Information Region to a distance of 85 nautical miles at a height of 50,000 feet.

Berry Head and Sharkham Point, a 6km walk to the south, are National Nature Reserves. They are home to cirl buntings that are almost confined in Britain to south Devon. Another rarity is the goldilocks aster *(Aster linosyris)*. Apart from these rarities the area sports a great range of wild flowers and birds. The rock is limestone of Devonian age. Quarrying ceased here in 1969.

Brixham is still a thriving fishing port. It is said that Brixham fishermen founded the ports of Grimsby, Hull and Scarborough. A notable resident of Brixham was Rev, Henry Francis Lyte who wrote the hymn 'Abide with me, fast falls the eventide.' Inevitably his residence, now a hotel, was called 'The Lyte House.'

The tip of Berry Head is a 2km walk from Brixham Harbour and there is a car park at the base of the headland.

Start Point   Devon

15 miles from Salcombe
Grid ref: SX 830371
Maps: OS Explorer OL20, OS Landranger 202.

This is one of the most exposed and windy points along the whole English Channel coast and has a feeling of utter remoteness. It pokes its scrawny finger 1km into the sea.

Jagged rocks of Start Point

Jagged outcrops of glistening mica-schist stick upward like dragon's teeth. The name 'Start' derives from the Anglo-Saxon 'steort' meaning 'tail'. The Common Redstart is a bird with a conspicuous red tail and gets its name from the same root.

To the north is a magnificent view of the sweep of Start Bay all the way to the mouth of the River Dart. The sandy shore stretches away for 10km. About 2km along the coast are the ruins of the village of Hallsands which in its heyday at the end of the 19th century supported a population of 159. The houses were built on a ledge of rock below the cliff and hardly above sea level. The Admiralty planned to enlarge the naval dockyard at Plymouth and needed vast quantities of shingle to make concrete. The engineering firm Sir John Jackson Ltd negotiated a contract with the Board of Trade in 1896 to dredge shingle below low-water mark between Hallsands and Beesands to the north. The village was paid £125 annually for damage to their crab pots and fish stocks. Some at the time were worried that there would be more serious consequences following the loss of shingle from the seabed. Within a few years the level of the beach had fallen by several feet and by 1902 following direct action by the villagers all dredging ceased. However, the damage had already been done and in a storm the following winter homes were damaged. Compensation was agreed, but in January 1917 a severe storm did so much damage that a few months later only one house was habitable. Amazingly there was no loss of life. Today the shells of several houses can still be seen nestling below the cliff.

James Walker built the tower of Start Point lighthouse in the Gothic style with its castellated parapet in 1836. Alan Stevenson, one in the family of Scottish lighthouse builders, designed the Dioptric apparatus that was installed here. An adjacent house was home for the lighthouse keepers and small walled gardens provided them with fresh vegetables. A steep path led down the cliff to a small beach from which they were able to launch a fishing boat provided the sea was calm. The light was automated in 1993.

From the village of Chillington on the A379 between Torcross and Kingsbridge a minor road runs south 7km to a car park at the base of Start Point. From there the lighthouse is just 1km further. Alternatively Start Point can be incorporated in a longer walk along the beautiful south Devon coast path.

Prawle Point   Devon

15 miles from Salcombe
Grid ref: SX 772351
Maps: OS Explorer OL20, OS Landranger 202.

This rounded headland of green hornblende schist provides superb coastal views east to Start Point and west to Bolt Head. The word Prawle may mean a lookout hill. In particular to the east there is an extensive raised beach backed by a cliff. A small information centre tells of local natural history. This area is a stronghold for the increasingly rare and localised cirl bunting.

View from Prawle Point with a raised beach in the middle distance

Nearby on the seabed are two important wrecks on English Heritage's protected list. At Moor Sands, Salcombe is one of only two known sites of Bronze Age shipwrecks off the English Coast, the other is at Langdon Bay near Dover. It is thought that artefacts found on the sea floor near Moor Sands represent two Bronze Age shipwrecks. Between 1977 and 1982 eight Bronze Age implements were recovered. All traces of a wooden boat had vanished. Then in 2005 divers found gold jewellery and bronze weapons of a design originating from northern France. Again there was nothing remaining of the boat itself. In 1992 archaeologists discovered a Bronze Age boat from about 1500 BC during excavation for a new road near Dover. This remarkably well-preserved boat is on display at Dover Museum. Probably the best-preserved Bronze Age shipwreck was found at Ulu Burun, Turkey.

The other nearby protected wreck dates from about 1640 AD. Only a small fragment of green oak remained of the structure of the boat. Nine cannon lay in two distinct groups. Most ships of the time had cannon mounted along either side. Barbary pirate ships, however, had cannon mounted fore and aft to make room for slaves manning the oars amidships. Many items of gold jewellery of Moroccan design were found and they had been cut neatly in half, which was a practice of the pirates of the day. A Dutch clay pipe lay among the other artefacts. Sometimes European sailors would skipper pirate ships from the Barbary Coast. It may be that this particular ship had a Dutch captain. These corsairs would have come to our shores for slaves and hostages. It is estimated that over a million individuals were taken into slavery between 1530 AD and 1780 AD from Europe to North Africa. John Ward was an Englishman who became a corsair and rose to run a fleet of pirate vessels employing 500 men. He applied to James I for pardon unsuccessfully and eventually died of plague in Tunis in 1622.

A National Coastwatch Institution (NCI) Lookout Station at the tip of the headland commands a view both out to sea and along the coast in both directions. There is a welcome here for the public to shelter from the weather in the adjacent Information Centre and to visit the station itself. HM Coastguard coordinates all search and rescue operations in British waters, but relies on radio communication and no longer provides visual observation of inshore waters. If windsurfers, divers or canoeists are swept out to sea, or if a yacht capsizes and loses all means of communication, then the only hope of rescue relies on visual surveillance. This is what the NCI provides. It is manned entirely by volunteers and financed by voluntary subscriptions. Currently there are 50 Lookout Stations found mainly around our southern shores. The number is on the increase.

The National Trust own Prawle Point and a National Trust car park is a mere 500m from the point, the most southerly tip of Devon. Or incorporate Prawle Point in a longer walk along the coast path, maybe a circular walk from the village of East Prawle.

Bolt Head

Devon

3 miles from Salcombe
Grid ref: SX 726361
Maps: OS Explorer OL20, OS Landranger 202.

Walk from Salcombe or park in the National Trust car park at Overbecks Museum and Gardens and follow the path for 2km to the end of Bolt Head, also owned by the National Trust. A high path crosses fields and drops down into the deep valley of Starehole Bottom where there are fine mounds of greater tussock sedge *(Carex paniculata)* along the stream. From here a short steep climb leads up to Bolt Head. The headland is somewhat marred by crumbling remains of a World War 2 concrete lookout, but the view, particularly back up Salcombe Harbour, is stunning. Many bushes of butcher's broom *(Ruscus aculeatus)* with their red berries and sharp pointed leaves (which are really flattened stems) grow on the cliffs. As spiky as the butchers broom are the jagged outcrops of mica-schist rock similar to those at Start Point.

Evening light on Bolt Tail

Returning to Salcombe it is possible from Starehole Bottom to take the Courtenay Walk. This is a path cut into the cliffs by the Courtenay family in the 19th century to give access round Sharp Tor, where the best views up the estuary are to be enjoyed. A pleasant circular walk takes in the tranquil headland of Bolt Tail.

Rame Head Cornwall

24 miles from Plymouth
Grid ref: SX 418481 and SX 441488
Maps: OS Explorer 108, OS Landranger 201.

Rame Head and Penlee Point are the western and eastern ends of a headland that guards the entrance to Plymouth and the Royal Naval Dockyards of Devonport. A ferry from Plymouth to Crymell links with a fine coastal path with varied scenery through Mount Edgcumbe Country Park and Kingsand to Penlee Point. The whole area has been and still is of prime strategic importance. Penlee Point, in particular, overlooks the approaches to Plymouth and carried a formidable battery from the Napoleonic era. In Victorian times the battery boasted three disappearing guns. One was the largest in the country, a 13.5" gun weighing in at 69 tons. The barrel landed at Penlee Point Steps in 1892, but it was another two years before it was ready to fire. So-called disappearing guns after firing would drop down into a pit for reloading and would then have been invisible to the enemy. The batteries around the headland were operational till and through World War 2 and Tregantle Battery above Whitsand Bay is still in use. The site of Penlee Battery is now a nature reserve of the same name. Little remains to be seen of the previous defensive works. Other military buildings have been converted to residential use or demolished.

Near the tip of Penlee Point is a folly called Queen Adelaide's Chapel. An apse was cut into the cliff and three arches look out to sea and a fourth along the coast to Rame Head. Princess Adelaide of Saxe-Meiningen married Prince William in 1818. She often stayed at Mount Edgcumbe from where she used to walk to Penlee Point. When William ascended the throne she took the title Queen Consort. Their two daughters died and it was left to William's niece Victoria to succeed him.

Queen Adelaide's Chapel on Penlee Point

Penlee has had a lifeboat since 1913. The cargo ship *Union Star*, on its maiden voyage, lost power in hurricane force winds on 19th December 1981. An attempt to rescue the crew by helicopter failed because of the severity of the wind. The Penlee lifeboat managed to get alongside and four of the crew jumped on board. The lifeboat attempted to rescue the remainder but was itself wrecked. The *Union Star* went down and there were no survivors from ship or lifeboat. All eight members of the lifeboat crew came from the village of Mousehole and received posthumous medals for bravery.

A car park at Rame Head lies alongside a National Coastwatch Station where visitors are welcome. The approach to the end of Rame Head involves crossing a ditch and rampart of an Iron Age fort. A short climb leads to the highest point topped by the tiny, partly ruined Chapel of St Michael. This simple 14th century chapel may mark the site of an earlier Christian hermitage. Beacons were once lit here as a warning to shipping. That role has been taken over by the Eddystone Lighthouse 8 miles out to sea.

There are car parks at both Rame Head and Penlee Point.

Gribbin Head   Cornwall

4 miles from Fowey
Grid ref: SX 098495
Maps: OS Explorer 107, OS Landranger 214.

Gribbin Head, known locally as The Gribbin is a grassy headland dominated by a tall, red and white striped daymark. Before the daymark was built in 1832 sailors were apt to confuse Gribbin Head with St Anthony's Head near Falmouth. The National Trust owns the headland and daymark. The daymark is open to visitors on certain days. Over the entrance door is an unexpectedly crudely carved and punctuation-free inscription, which reads "For the safety of commerce and the preservation of mariners this beacon was erected in the year of our Lord 1832 by the corporation of Trinity House of Deptford Strond the most noble John Jeffreys Pratt Marquis Camden KG Master Capt John Woolmore KCH Deputy master".

The nearest car park is at Menabilly Barton only 1km away. Menabilly House was the home of Daphne du Maurier who used the house as a model for Manderley in her novel *Rebecca*.

Why not design a circular walk from Fowey to the east or Polkerris to the west across the base of the

Daymark at Gribbin Head

headland and back along the switchback coast path? St Catherine's Castle between Gribbin Head and Fowey is a small coastal fort built by Henry VIII to protect the harbour at Fowey.

Dodman Point   ♿   Cornwall

11 miles from St Austell
Grid ref: SX 002393
Maps: OS Explorer 105, OS Landranger 204.

Everything about Dodman Point, or The Dodman, as it is known locally is larger than life. The first to be seen is a truly massive embankment crossing the path from the car park. This is an Iron Age ditch and rampart known as the Bulwark 2000ft (616m) long and 20ft (6m) high defining one of the largest promontory forts in Britain. After more than 2000 years of erosion

The Dodman

this is still an impressive structure. Bronze Age man left his mark on The Dodman in the form of two burial barrows. Medieval strip field systems are evident.

A triangulation point shows that the highest part of the Dodman is 114m above sea level making this the highest headland on the south Cornish coast. The rocks are pale grey slates and phyllites of Devonian age. They are not particularly resistant to erosion and in the past the headland may have projected another mile into the sea.

Almost on the edge of the cliff at the tip of the headland is a huge granite cross erected in 1896 by Rev. Martin of Caerhays. This has served as a navigational aid to shipping, but Rev. Martin's main motive was religious as the inscription indicates: "In the firm hope of the Second Coming of our Lord Jesus Christ and for the encouragement of those who strive to serve HIM this cross is erected AD 1896".

Not far from the cross and beside the path is a small watchhouse with adjacent structure that was once an 18th century Admiralty lookout. Observers here could give early warning to Plymouth of shipping sailing up the English Channel.

The Dodman is National Trust property. There is a car park at Penare 2km south of Gorran Haven. Avoid the road from Boswinger to Penare as it is very steep and narrow. From the car park follow a well-signed path to The Dodman.

Nare Head   ♿   Cornwall

14 miles from Truro
Grid ref: SW 916370
Maps: OS Explorer 105, OS Landranger 204.

In June Nare Head is a natural garden carpeted with flowers: foxgloves *(Digitalis purpurea)*, field scabious *(Knautia arvensis)*, pignut *(Conopodium majus)*, tormentil *(Potentilla erecta)*, bird's-foot-trefoil *(Lotus corniculatus)*, thrift *(Armeria maritime)*,

Nare Head and Gull Rock

bluebell *(Hyacinthoides nonscriptus)*, speedwell *(Veronica persica)* and many others. Attractive rocky outcrops enhance the scene. Fine views are seen along the coast in both directions. Off the tip of the headland stands Gull Rock, an important nesting site for seabirds.

Nare Head is a mass of solidified lava spewed out from an ancient volcano. Pillow lava can be seen indicating an underwater eruption.

Curious green-painted structures mark the site of an underground observation station of the Royal Observer Corps active during the cold war. Established in 1963 its role was to observe any nuclear attack on Britain and to measure radioactive fallout. It was finally closed down in 1991.

A car park at Penmare Farm near Veryan is just 1km from the tip of the headland. A tarmac path from the car park allows wheelchair users to climb up and enjoy the superb views along the coast. The National Trust owns Nare Head.

This Nare Head is not to be confused with Nare Point between Falmouth and The Lizard where there is a National Coastwatch Station.

Zone Point and
St Anthony Head   ♿   Cornwall

13 miles from Truro
Grid ref: SW 851311 and SW 847312
Maps: OS Explorer 105, OS Landranger 204.

St Anthony Head and Pendennis Point guard the entrance to Carrick Roads, one of Britain's finest natural harbours. In times of war or the threat of war this safe anchorage has been of strategic importance to the Royal Navy. From the 18th century there have been plans from time to time to build a massive series of wharfs and docks along the east shore of Carrick Roads. These would provide deep-water anchorage at all states of the tide without the need to build any sea defences. The remoteness of this beautiful estuary has saved it from such development.

St Anthony Head lighthouse and Zone Point

The estuaries of three rivers, Fal, Carnon and Percuil, flow into Carrick Roads. These, together with Carrick Roads itself, are good examples of drowned valleys known as 'rias' that are found along the southern shores of Cornwall and Devon.

The lighthouse was built in 1835 and was originally fuelled by paraffin. The road to the lighthouse passes the old paraffin store which looks like an oversized dog-kennel. The light was electrified in 1954 and automated in 1987.

Extensive defences on St Anthony Head have been preserved and to a large extent restored. Much is accessible by wheelchair. In 1805 24-pounder guns were mounted just above the lighthouse. The main fortifications were built with protective rampart and ditch to seaward in 1885. At that time the battery housed 64-pounder muzzle loading guns. Just 20 years later the battery was rebuilt and 6inch guns of the latest design were installed. The battery remained operational throughout the two World Wars and was not finally cleared of all ordnance till 1957, two years before the National Trust acquired the site. There is still much to see to interest the military historian and there are information boards to read.

St Anthony Head and Zone Point at the southern end of the Roseland Peninsula are only 0.5km apart. Roseland takes its name from the Cornish *ros* meaning 'promontory'. Between the two headlands is a small beach inaccessible by land because of high cliffs. Atlantic grey seals with pups use this as a safe refuge just as they do at Godrevy Point on the north Cornish coast. Zone Point, just a short step to the east, is a peaceful grass-covered headland with few signs of human activity where guns and warfare seem a thousand miles away.

Castle Point — St Mawes   ♿   Cornwall

11 miles from Truro
Grid ref: SW 841327 Maps: OS Explorer 105,
OS Landranger 204.

St Mawes Castle is the best preserved of all Henry VIII's coastal forts. It occupies virtually the whole headland guarding the entrance to the great natural harbour of Carrick Roads. It is owned by English Heritage and is open to the public. The very stones speak volumes for the power of the monarch and the skill of Tudor stonemasons. The construction is a giant cloverleaf with central round tower embraced by three round bastions, one on each side and one in front facing the sea. The whole castle was once surrounded by a moat. It would have

St Mawes Castle

bristled with guns covering the sea approach to Falmouth. Having a fairly low profile it would have afforded a relatively small target for guns on enemy ships if they were ever able to sail within range. The quality of the stonework and attention to detail is remarkable. There is no doubt that, in addition to the defence of the realm, one motive for building the castle was the glorification of the monarch. This is shown by inscriptions in stone such as one over the main entrance that reads *Semper honos Henrice tuus laudesque manebunt,* "Henry, thy honour and praises will remain for ever."

The land in front of the castle was carved into a series of terraces descending down to the shore in Napoleonic times. These provided better shelter for twelve cannon placed behind sloping earth ramparts termed The Grand Sea Battery. They, in their turn, were replaced as technology moved on.

On the east side of Castle Point is the small, picturesque harbour of St Mawes.

Pendennis Point   ♿   Cornwall

At Falmouth
Grid ref: SW 826315
Maps: OS Explorer 103 and 105, OS Landranger 204.

Of all the coastal forts built by Henry VIII Pendennis Castle is one of the finest. It is the most westerly of all, maintained by English Heritage and open to the public. It houses a Discovery Centre with vivid representation of life in the fort over the last five centuries. Right at the tip of the headland and only just above the high-tide mark is the oldest of all the fortifications on Pendennis Point. This is The Blockhouse (Little Dennis) built on Henry's orders in 1538 to house cannon until the fort proper was ready for use. Pendennis Castle is on higher ground with a more commanding view. It consists of a guardhouse

Pendennis Point and Castle with Falmouth beyond

(largely replaced in the 20th century), a central round tower with guns mounted on three levels and a surrounding perimeter wall. This fort was vulnerable to cannon fire from enemy ships and later in the same century under Elizabeth I the extensive ramparts with arrow-shaped bastions at the corners were constructed. Grass-covered earth slopes rising up from a surrounding ditch were designed to absorb the impact of cannon balls.

Pendennis Castle was Royalist in the Civil War and endured a 5-month siege in 1646, being one of the last royalist fortresses to fall to Parliamentarian forces.

Half Moon Battery was constructed below the ramparts in 1793. A century later it was equipped with three 6-inch breech-loading 'disappearing' guns. These would be raised for firing then lowered out of site of the enemy for reloading. Half Moon Battery remained operational throughout World War 2. Remains of other defensive works and gun emplacements can be seen around the headland.

Just below Half Moon Battery is the H M Coastguard Maritime Rescue Coordination Centre.

At the base of the headland is the town of Falmouth and its docks. This has been and still is an important centre for ship repairing and capable of accommodating ships up to 100,000 tons.

Across Falmouth Bay stands Rosemullion Head at the mouth of Helford River. From there, they say, you may see Morgawr, a sea-monster. You have to be patient as the last supposed sighting was in 1976. The headland is worth a visit for the walk and the views.

The Lizard   🔖   Cornwall

12 miles from Helston
Grid ref: SW 695116
Maps: OS Explorer 103, OS Landranger 203.

The name 'Lizard' comes from the Cornish *Lys Ardh* meaning 'The High Place'. The village of Lizard is surrounded by sea on three sides with Lizard Point to the southwest, Bass Point to the southeast and between them the lighthouse and a string of rocks disappearing out to sea as if the most southerly point of mainland Britain is reluctant to give way to the ocean. The Lizard is National Trust property.

Currents and tides around The Lizard make this one of the most dangerous points around the Cornish coast. Many ships have met their end here. Polpeor Cove is a tiny cove with a sandy beach where there is an old lifeboat station. This was one of the first lifeboats in Cornwall. Originally it was kept on top of the cliff and later was housed down by the shore. The Royal National Lifeboat Institution closed it down in 1961 when the lifeboat moved to near Church Cove on the east side of The Lizard. The Lizard lifeboat is proud to hold an important national record. On March 17th 1907 the 12,000 tonne liner *Suevic* belonging to the White Star Line ran aground on rocks off Lizard Point. It was dark, foggy and the sea was running high. With just four lifeboats

The Lizard. The most southerly point of the British mainland

from Lizard, Cadgwith, Coverack and Porthleven propelled only by oars 456 people were rescued. Among them were two stowaways who disappeared as soon as they reached land. This record still stands as the largest number rescued from one ship by lifeboats round the shores of Britain. At bass Point adjacent to the coast path is a National Coastwatch Station and a little further along at Kilcobben Cove is the RNLI Lizard Lifeboat Station operational since 2012. Visitors are welcome at both sites to see the measures taken to make our coastal waters as safe as possible.

The wrecks around The Lizard include the *Royal Anne*, a frigate of 42 guns, bound for Barbados which foundered on rocks in1721 taking with her John, 3rd Lord Belhaven and Stenton on his way to take up the governorship of Barbados.

The first light to be established on The Lizard was built in 1619 by Sir John Killigrew. Ship owners failed to pay their dues and this threatened to bankrupt Killigrew who was forced to dismantle the light. It was not until 1751 that a light shone again to warn sailors of the treacherous rocks. Thomas Fonnereau built two light towers on either side of a cottage. The lights at that time were fires. If the fires dimmed an overseer in the cottage would blow a cow-horn to tell the bellows operators to work harder. The two towers remain, but there is now a solitary light from the eastern tower. This was automated in 1998. It flashes a white light every three seconds with an intensity of 800,000 Candelas and a range of 26 miles making it one of the most powerful lighthouses in the world. This light marks the transition from the Atlantic Ocean to the English Channel.

Prominent above Bass Point is a square white building now a private house, but formerly a Lloyds Signal Station. Sailing ships from all over the globe would give their identity by flags, the signal station would then telegraph the owners and signal back instructions to sail to a particular port. Delays in this process led to several ships being wrecked along this dangerous coast. Nearby are two huts, restored by The National Trust, where Guglielmo Marconi conducted important experiments in radio communication. From here he established radio contact with the Isle of Wight. From a much larger station at Poldhu Cove near Mullion he sent the first radio signal, the letter S, across the Atlantic. A short way inland the huge dishes of Goonhilly Satellite Earth Station can be seen. At one time this was the largest satellite tracking station in the world and was where the first transatlantic television transmission was received. Much of the site and the visitor centre are currently closed. There are plans to convert part of the facilities to a Space Science Centre. Links with other radio astronomy centres will bring Goonhilly into the forefront of deep space exploration and research.

The Lizard is famous for its green serpentine rock, which is seen best at the picturesque Kynance Cove a couple of kilometres to the west. This rock is easily worked and turned and will take a high polish. Local craftsmen use it to make souvenirs, model lighthouses, lamp-stands and the like.

The cliffs here, and in several other places in the southwest, are smothered in the Purple Dew Plant which is closely related to the Hottentot Fig of South Africa. Although somewhat unwelcome as an alien species it cannot be denied that it adds a splash of colour.

Cudden Point   Cornwall

7 miles from Penzance
Grid ref: SW 549275
Maps: OS Explorer 102, OS Landranger 205.

Cudden Point gives fine views across Mounts Bay and in the opposite direction to The Lizard. At Rosudgeon 5km east of Marazion take a minor road signed to Prussia Cove. This leads to a small car park and a footpath runs down to the sea. Turn west along the coast path to Cudden Point.

What is the connection with Prussia? John Carter, brother of Harry, in the 18th century, acquired the nickname 'King of Prussia' while a boy. He became a successful smuggler and lived at the cove named after him. There are in fact three coves that comprise Prussia Cove: from west to east, Piskie's Cove, Bessy's Cove and King's Cove. In the 18th century these were quite off the beaten track and an ideal place to land contraband. Parallel grooves can be seen in the flat rocks of Bessy's Cove. These ruts enabled carts to be taken out to boats drawn onto the beach even when covered by the tide. (Similar rutways are found on the Yorkshire coast for quite legally loading alum onto ships drawn up on the shore. See Old Peak). At the time of the Carters there was 'honour among thieves.' On one occasion contraband items that John Carter had promised his 'customers' were intercepted by excise men and locked in a warehouse. John Carter broke into the warehouse, took the goods he considered to be his property and left all other items untouched. He would never let his customers down. Harry Carter's autobiography, *Harry Carter, Cornish Smuggler. An Autobiography 1749 – 1809* is a rare opportunity to read a first hand account of life at that time from the pen of a common working man, let alone a smuggler. On his retirement he became a preacher and pillar of the Methodist Church.

Just before Cudden Point is Little Cudden Point on which are the footings of a small rectangular building. A plaque attached to a rock reads "We have a building of God a house not made with hands eternal in the heavens" and "Where the Spirit of the Lord is there is liberty." This area is now a private burial ground. Is it pure coincidence that the first quotation is from the Bible (2 Corinthians chapter 5 verse 1) and also appears in Harry Carter's autobiography?

Prussia Cove is the site of the International Musicians Seminar held twice a year under the directorship of the cellist Steven Isserlis.

St Michael's Mount ♿ Cornwall

3 miles from Penzance
Grid ref: SW 514297
Maps: OS Explorer 102, OS Landranger 203.

This must be the most photographed scene in Cornwall. Through a light mist the Mount appears to float ethereally over the sea. The wide curve of Mounts Bay is the oyster and St Michael's Mount the pearl.

Tin was being exported from Cornwall in pre-Roman times. It was shipped across the Channel and then taken overland through Gaul to the Mediterranean. Diodorus Siculus writing in the 1st century BC refers to tin being shipped from a site called Ictis, which was an island at high tide and a promontory at low tide. Some have equated this with St Michael's Mount, but it is a big assumption that the coastline was the same then as now.

An even less likely tale is that the giant Cormoran, who terrorised the area, built the Mount of granite. He was killed by the wiles of a local lad called Jack — Jack-the-Giant-Killer.

The history of St Michael's Mount is succinctly described in an illustrated booklet written by John St Aubyn. Verifiable history begins after the Norman Conquest. A priory church on the Mount was consecrated in 1144 as a daughter church of Mont

Nightfall at St Michael's Mount

St Michel on the other side of the Channel. The subsequent history of the priory was chequered. The building was destroyed by an earthquake in 1275 and rebuilt during the following century. The Black Death devastated the community in 1349 leaving only the prior and two monks to continue the work. Its links with Mont St Michel were finally severed when it was granted to Syon Abbey at Twickenham in 1424. It was an important destination for pilgrims in the Middle Ages and ships sailed from there to Spain with pilgrims en route to Santiago de Compostela. The priory church became a private chapel when St Michael's Mount was a family home in the 17th Century. It is open to visitors and services are still held there in a building that would be familiar to the monks of the Middle Ages.

The history of the Mount as a military fortification is equally turbulent. Towards the close of the 12th Century it was seized by force and fortified on behalf of John, Earl of Cornwall, who later became King John. Three hundred years later the Earl of Oxford, who was on the losing side of the War of the Roses, captured the Mount. King Edward IV laid siege and it fell after 26 weeks.

The Earl of Oxford was imprisoned in Hamme Castle near Calais, but escaped to join Henry Tudor, Earl of Richmond, who was crowned King Henry VII after the battle of Bosworth Field. In 1549 it fell briefly into the hands of Cornish rebels who objected to having the Prayer Book in English, a language which some of them could not understand. During the Civil War Francis Basset, a Cornish landowner, strengthened the fortifications in the name of the King. He died in 1645 and his brother Sir Arthur Basset took command of the garrison. Following the fall of Cornwall to Parliamentarians under General Fairfax St Michael's Mount was again besieged. After putting up an honourable defence Sir Arthur Basset surrendered and was afforded free passage to the Isles of Scilly which were still loyal to the King. Since that time the only invaders of St Michael's Mount have been hordes of tourists.

Since 1659 the Mount has been the home of the St Aubyn family who generously bequeathed it to the National Trust in 1954. They still live there for part of the year. Many of the rooms and much of the gardens are open for the public to enjoy.

It is an island for about half the tidal range, so it is imperative to know the state of the tide before walking there along the causeway from Marazion. Don't despair, there is a ferry.

Logan Rock — Cornwall

8 miles from Penzance
Grid ref: SW 397219
Maps: OS Explorer 102, OS Landranger 203.

This small headland is built of great blocks of granite. A natural pillar of granite like a slipped obelisk near the tip of the headland is graced with the name of Horrace. The headland is famous, though, for a rocking stone or 'logan'. This is a roughly cubical block of granite weighing about 80 tons. At one time it could be rocked with the slightest pressure exerted at the correct spot. In April 1824 a Lieutenant Goldsmith of the Royal Navy together with some accomplices and the aid of crowbars sent the rock crashing down the cliff. The local inhabitants were so incensed by this act of vandalism that had robbed them of a tourist attraction that the Royal Navy using blocks and tackles restored it to its original position at a cost of £130. Sadly it no longer wobbles.

The headland can be reached along a footpath from the small village of Treen. It was the site of an Iron Age promontory fort.

Headland of Logan Rock

Gwennap Head   Cornwall

10 miles from Penzance
Grid ref: SW 366215
Maps: OS Explorer 102, OS Landranger 203.

Here are the most dramatic granite cliffs in the country. Frost, wind and rain have sculpted the rock into blocks and columns stacked high one on the other. These cliffs are popular with climbers and birdwatchers and stand 60m (200 feet) above the sea. Blowholes, caves and tunnels have been formed by the erosive action of the waves. The Cornish name for Gwennap Head is *Tol-Pedn-Penwith*, the

Granite of Gwennap Head

'Holed Headland of Penwith' whereas *Gwennap* is named after a local saint.

In the Permian Period (290— 251 million years ago) all the continents were joined into a super-continent called Pangea. Britain was surrounded by dry land at that time. During the Permian period semi-liquid magma rose up into the overlying rocks of what would become the southwest peninsula and solidified as granite. Erosion of overlying rock has exposed the granite both inland and at points around the coast where it forms spectacular headlands.

This is the most south-westerly point of mainland Britain. Two conical daymarks warn shipping of dangerous submerged rocks offshore while sharp eyes in a National Coastwatch Station look out for boats in distress.

A car park at the hamlet of Porthgwarra is less than 1km along the coast path from the headland.

Land's End   &♿;   Cornwall

9 miles from Penzance
Grid ref: SW 342251
Maps: OS Explorer 102, OS Landranger 203.

D oes the most famous headland in Britain deserve its reputation? It's all a matter of taste. If the presence of a single other soul spoils the experience for you then Land's End will disappoint. The A30 road used to run from Central London all the way to Land's End, but nowadays part has been replaced by the M3 motorway. Many are the visitors that drive it.

The tourist facilities are mainly arranged around a courtyard and comprise a variety of restaurants, shops and entertainments for all ages. Nearby is the *First and Last House* restaurant to the north and Greeb Farm to the south. Here there are craft workshops and animals for children to see. Edward Williams makes

Land's End

59

jewellery here and keeps *Bighead* the pirate cat under his counter. When asked how old the cat is he replies "He was born in 1742 or thereabouts. He's not been awake long enough to die." Maybe he's spent too long awake since I saw him.

The granite cliff coastline is unspoilt. The 33m high Longships lighthouse marks a treacherous line of rocks about 2km offshore. On a clear day the Wolf Rock lighthouse and the Isles of Scilly can be seen.

Between Land's End and the Isles of Scilly the fabled land of Lyonesse is supposed to lie submerged beneath the sea. Only one man survived when it was overwhelmed by a tidal wave, Trevillian, a horseman whose horse outran the wave. This land with cities and churches with high spires once linked the Isles of Scilly to the mainland.

This is the starting point for end-to-enders heading for John O' Groats. Land's End and John O' Groats are neither the most southerly nor most northerly points. Why not walk from The Lizard to Dunnet Head (most southerly to most northerly) or Gwennap Head to Duncansby Head (most south-westerly to most north-easterly)? But who would ever understand or appreciate your achievement? And it doesn't have quite the same ring to it.

Cape Cornwall   ♿   Cornwall

8 miles from Penzance
Grid ref: SW 350318
Maps: OS Explorer 102, OS Landranger 203.

This dramatic National Trust headland is one of only two in Britain honoured with the title of Cape, the other being Cape Wrath. The cape is a hill surmounted by a high, ornate chimneystack built in the mid 19th century as a flue for tin smelting. The draw was so strong that another stack was built at a lower level. Just to the east is a steep-sided valley with buildings

60

Old tin mine at Cape Cornwall

Rocks called The Brisons, or Charles de Gaulle in his bath

relating to the mining industry. The mine galleries extended out deep beneath the seabed. It takes some imagination to think of this peaceful spot echoing to the noise of heavy industry.

The headland, like many in Cornwall, is granite of Permian age that intruded into older Devonian slates. The heat from the granite altered the slates (thermal metamorphism). Mineral-bearing hot liquid was forced through the slates providing Cornishmen 250 million years later with an honest living digging out the tin.

Near the car park is a small ruined building with a cross surmounting its gable end. This is an old barn, but is reputed to be the site of St Helen's Oratory dating back to the 4th century and is one of the earliest Christian sites in Cornwall.

Across the headland are the banks and ditches of an Iron Age cliff castle. On the seaward side of the headland is a National Coastwatch Station with a room giving local information about, for instance, the wreck of the *Malta* on nearby rocks in 1889 and the rescue of passengers and crew. Just off the headland are rocks known as 'The Brisons', which, at the right time of the tide, bear an uncanny resemblance to General Charles de Gaulle in his bath!

Narrow sea inlets called *zawns* cut into the north Cornish coast between Cape Cornwall and St Ives and there are many small headlands that are worth seeing, such as Pendeen Watch and Gurnard's Head.

Zennor Head   Cornwall

7 miles from Penzance
Grid ref: SW 450395
Maps: OS Explorer 102, OS Landranger 203.

Legend has it that a young man in Zennor village, Matthew Trewhella, was an accomplished singer. A mermaid who lived in Pendour Cove, beside Zennor Head, heard him

Zennor Head

singing and fell in love. He was equally besotted with her and followed her under the waves never to be seen again. Sometimes his voice can be heard singing from his resting place. A carved mermaid graces a 14th century bench end in St Senara Church in Zennor. The name Zennor is derived from Senara.

The National Trust headland is approached from Zennor village. The end is a jumble of huge stone blocks apparently thrown down at random. One has fallen into a cleft making a 'window' looking out to sea.

The ancient field walls have interesting curved shapes. Where the ground is flat they are walls, but on sloping ground they are ha-has. Were they built that way, or has soil washed down and been arrested by the walls?

The Island — St Ives   ♿ Cornwall

At St Ives
Grid ref: SW 520412
Maps: OS Explorer 102, OS Landranger 203.

The town of St Ives takes its name from St Ia, an Irish missionary to Cornwall in about 460. Today St Ives is a Mecca for artists and surfers. The headland that springs from the town, separating the harbour from Porthmeor beach is known locally as 'The Island'. It is really a headland and well and truly part of the mainland. This was not always the case. This high grassy mound is crowned with the Chapel of St Nicholas. As St Nicholas is the patron saint of sailors many chapels around the coast are dedicated to him. The present chapel on The Island is an ancient structure dating from the 15th century, but was partially dismantled in 1904 and restored in 1911 and again in 1971. It is

The Island, St Ives

used for worship on Thursdays at 11am. Different denominations take the service in rotation.

Also on The Island are a National Coastwatch Station and the remnants of a coastal battery. The Royal Commission on the Defence of the United Kingdom in 1860 recommended the building of numerous coastal defences to counter the threat from France. These became known as Palmerston Forts. The Battery on the Island was one such defensive structure. It would protect the harbour from enemy vessels that might then be able to attack the naval base at Falmouth from landward. Guns placed here could cover Porthmeor beach, the harbour and approaches to the town. The fort did not enjoy a long life and was decommissioned in 1895.

St Ives lifeboat station is at the base of the "island". It is designated as a Discover Station that open their doors to the public in the summer.

The town houses the Tate St Ives Gallery and the Barbara Hepworth Museum and Sculpture Garden.

Not so many are aware that this was once a mining town. The uranium that Marie Curie used in her experiments came from a mine in St Ives.

Godrevy Point   ♿   Cornwall

10 miles from St Ives
Grid ref: SW 579433 and SW 592437
Maps: OS Explorer 102, OS Landranger 203.

The view of Godrevy Island with its lighthouse just off the end of the headland is unforgettable. The National Trust owns this outstandingly beautiful stretch of coast. This lighthouse plays the title role in Virginia Woolf's novel *To the Lighthouse*.

So often it has taken a major disaster for the authorities to be persuaded that a lighthouse is really required. The steamer *Nile*

Godrevy Point and Godrevy Island

ran on the rocks here with the loss of all crew and passengers on 30th November 1859. The light, designed by James Walker, was established in 1859 and automated at the exceptionally early date of 1939. In 1995 it was converted to solar power.

Just to the east of the point is a small cove. There is no way down the high cliffs which means that this cove is left for the resident colony of grey seals to breed unmolested. Grey seals breed late in the year from October to December.

Navax Point is just 1km along the cliff-top coast path. From there the view east along the rugged coast seems to stretch to infinity.

About 6km north of Hale there are three National Trust car parks towards Godrevy Point.

St Agnes Head   ♿   Cornwall

7 miles from Redruth
Grid ref: SW 698515
Maps: OS Explorer 104, OS Landranger 203.

Wheal Coates lies close by St Agnes Head. 'Wheal' is Cornish for 'mine'. The buildings have a grandeur that is enhanced by their dramatic position by the sea. Tin had been mined here since medieval times. Channels and depressions in the ground are a result of opencast mining of this period. In Victorian times deep shaft mining was carried out, even extending out under the sea. Water was continuously pumped out of the mine with the famous Cornish beam-engines kept in special engine houses. The three buildings on the site are all engine houses for powering the winding gear, pumping water out of the mine and stamping the ore. The Towanroath engine house on this site is one of the most photographed of all buildings relating to the Cornish tin-mining industry. Information boards give details of the activities at this mine. When Cornish tin mining fell into decline miners emigrated all over the world in search of work. It was said that wherever

Wheal Coates Mine,
St Agnes Head

67

there was a hole in the ground you would find a Cornishman at the bottom of it.

The headland is a flat-topped plateau covered in gorse *(Ulex europaeus)* and heather *(Calluna vulgaris)*. There are views west along Porthtowan beach and east to Trevose Head. It is possible to park at the head 2km west of St Agnes village or plan a circular walk from St Agnes village. Just off the Coast Path stands a small white building that is the St Agnes Head National Coastwatch Station. Visitors are welcome.

Penhale Point   Cornwall

6 miles from Newquay
Grid ref: SW 756591
Maps: OS Explorer 104, OS Landranger 200.

To north, east and south of this headland the theme is sand. Here are some of the highest sand dunes in the country. Holywell beach to the north featured in the opening scenes of the James Bond film *Die Another Day*. Huge dunes rise up behind Holywell beach and Perran beach to the south. The ancient Oratory of St Piran, together with surrounding graves, have been entirely engulfed by the dunes. The nearby parish church was dismantled and moved in 1805 as it, too, was being threatened by the advancing sands.

St Piran, or Perran, is the patron saint of tin miners and of Cornwall. Little is known about him. It is probable that he came from Ireland and founded the oratory covered by the sands. There is a legend that he lit a fire on a slab of rock that contained tin ore. The heat melted the tin that rose to the surface as a white cross. A white cross on a black background was his standard and was adopted as the flag of Cornwall.

The path from the National Trust car park in the village of Holywell, midway between Newquay and Perranporth, leads to

Penhale Point

Holywell beach then up onto the headland. Ramparts and ditches of an Iron Age fort, disused mine shafts and curious paraphernalia of the Ministry of Defence are spread over the headland. During World War 2 a decoy airfield was built here to divert attention from the airfield further west at Trevellas. Just offshore are Carter's or Gull Rocks looking like an iceberg that has been cleft in two with an axe wielded by a Cornish giant.

Pentire Point West   Cornwall

4 miles from Newquay
Grid ref: SW 772612
Maps: OS Explorer 104, OS Landranger 200.

This headland is rural as opposed to the almost urban Pentire Point East. The headlands to the west are wilder still. It was bequeathed to the National Trust in 1960.

Kelsey Head, Pentire Point West,
Pentire Point East and Towan Head

An information board states that it is one of the best sites in Cornwall for arable weeds: poppies *(Papaver rhoeas)*, corn marigolds *(Chrysanthemum segetum)*, small-flowered catchfly *(Silene gallica)*, speedwell *(Veronica persica)*, purple loosestrife *(Lythrum salicaria)* and ragged robin *(Lychnis flos-cuculi)*. Beyond the fields is open grassland sloping gently down to a chaotic jumble of crumpled rocks and a violent, restless sea. The contrast between the pastoral and nature in the raw could not be more pronounced.

Park in the hamlet of West Pentire which is less than 1km from the end of the headland. The more energetic could walk the coast path to take in Kelsey Head or Penhale Point as well making walks of about 5km and 10km respectively.

Towan Head   ♿   Cornwall

At Newquay
Grid ref: SW 799630
Maps: OS Explorer 104, OS Landranger 200.

Towan Head is part of Newquay and the west end of Newquay Bay and, yet, it has a certain remoteness especially on a stormy day. Even on a calm day the waves around the head can be substantial. Because of this, Fistral Bay on the exposed west side of the headland is one of the most popular surfing beaches in Cornwall.

At the base of the headland is a conspicuous white building dating from the 14th century. This is the Huer's Hut. It was used as a lookout. When the Huer spotted a shoal of pilchards in the bay he would raise a 'hue and cry' and could signal to the fishermen how to position their boats so as to surround the

Huer's hut at Towan Head

71

shoal with their nets. It is possible that it was originally built as a hermitage.

The old lifeboat house and slipway are still present. This was the steepest lifeboat slipway in Britain with a gradient of 1:2.25. Being on the lifeboat as it was launched must have been quite an experience, but not as extreme as meeting the Atlantic rollers round the end of the headland.

An unusual piece of architecture is the public toilet block near the car park. Built in a low spiral it resembles one of Henry VIII coastal forts.

Trevelgue Head   Cornwall

1 mile from Newquay
Grid ref: SW 823631
Maps: OS Explorer 104, OS Landranger 200.

Trevelgue Head's claim to fame is that it is one of the most important Iron Age promontory forts in Britain. However, human occupation of the headland extends right back to Mesolithic times. Flint fragments have been found from 8,000 years ago. It also bore a significant Bronze Age settlement. Burial mounds with cremated remains and also a Bronze Age foundry have been excavated. Iron Age man was active here from sometime between 400 and 100 BC and on into the Roman period. The headland was defended from attack on the landward side by no fewer than eight ramparts and ditches. The ramparts were built of stone and earth and would have been surmounted by wooden palisades. This must have been one of the most impregnable promontory forts in Britain. Despite erosion over more than two millennia they are still impressively high. The path along the headland cuts through these defences. Archaeologists have found evidence of iron smelting on the headland and the foundations of

Trevelgue Head

Iron Age round houses. One large house 14.5m in diameter is thought to have been a meeting-house rather than a dwelling. A very rare feature is that terraced fields from this period have also been identified. It was probably the headquarters of an important chieftain as high quality pottery fragments and glass beads have been found on the site. Occupation extended into the Roman period as evidenced by the find of Roman coins.

This small headland lies beside one of Newquay's popular beaches on the east side of the town and provides a pleasant walk when the delights of bathing and beach cricket have been exhausted.

Park Head   Cornwall

6 miles from Padstow
Grid ref: SW 840709
Maps: OS Explorer 106, OS Landranger 200.

Bedruthan Steps, leading down to a famous beach with its high rock stacks, is a popular destination on the north Cornish coast. At the north end of this beach is the National Trust headland of Park Head. The headland, in common with the majority of headlands along this coast, was the site of an Iron Age promontory fort and banks and ditches can still be clearly seen.

Park Head

Park Head is composed of Greenstone, a hard igneous rock that is more resistant to sea erosion than the slates to north and south. The views along this rugged coast are breathtaking. To the south are the stacks of Bedruthen Steps with Newquay beyond. Northward lies Trevose Head and its lighthouse.

Turn off the B3276 between Porthcothan and Trenance signed to Pentire Farm and Park Head. Ten or so cars can park at the farm. It is possible to do a circular walk taking in Park Head and Porth Mear and back along a narrow valley cut by a stream.

74

Trevose Head   Cornwall

4 miles from Padstow
Grid ref: SW 848762
Maps: OS Explorer 106, OS Landranger 200.

This is a major headland of hard igneous rock that marks a change in the direction of the coast from approximately North-South to East-West. To the south is the fine stretch of sand of Booby's Bay and Constantine Bay. The surf can be magnificent, but currents are strong and only experienced surfers should risk this beach.

From the car park on the headland walk southwest towards the coast, but beware! The Round Hole is a huge deep hole in the ground. It is a partially collapsed cave. Waves crash into it far below. This is definitely not somewhere to venture in the dark. Alternatively construct a circular walk from one of the nearby

Trevose Head

villages taking in Trevose Head and a handful of beautiful beaches en route.

Dinas Head, the most westerly part of Trevose Head, is reached across a saddle of land on which stands a rocket post. Dinas Head points towards the offshore rocks, the Bull and further away the Quies. Rocket posts were erected round the coast. From them the coastguard would fire a rocket trailing a thin line over the stricken ship. The crew would pull a heavier line over to the ship and the two ends would be made fast to the ship and to the rocket post. The crew and passengers could then be hauled to safety by breeches buoy. How often were ships wrecked within range of a convenient rocket post?

The lighthouse was built in 1847 and has been in operation ever since. This is the high light. There used to be a low light as well which was extinguished in 1882. It was automated in 1995 and is not open to the public. The old keepers' cottages are now holiday lets.

The Padstow Lifeboat Station is at Mother Ivy's Bay on the east side of Trevose Head. The public are welcome from 10am – 4pm and there is even a lift for disabled visitors.

Stepper Point — Cornwall

3 miles from Padstow
Grid ref: SW 915785
Maps: OS Explorer 106, OS Landranger 200.

The air is constantly filled with the song of larks. No herbicides or pesticides are used on fields on this headland so wild flowers, invertebrates and birds thrive.

The access is along the coast path from Padstow past the granite war-memorial cross high above the Camel estuary. Far below there appears to be a landing craft loaded with soldiers heading for the Normandy beaches. It is the ferry from

Stepper Point and the Camel Estuary

Rock full of holidaymakers. If the tide is out there is a shortcut across the sands of Harbour Cove and climb the low cliffs back to the path. At the point is a solar-powered light and nearby a tall daymark tower reminiscent of the chimney of a Cornish tin mine.

The National Coastwatch station is well worth a visit. It replaces a previous manned coastguard station. It became operational in 2002. The volunteer staff are always welcoming and keen to point out to visitors the work of the station.

St John's Well is reported to be at Stepper Point. It seems now to be just a seasonal spring and takes some finding.

Pentire Point and Rumps Point

Cornwall

8 miles from Wadebridge
Grid ref: SW 923804 and SW 934812
Maps: OS Explorer 106, OS Landranger 200.

The scenery here is some of the best in Cornwall, or even the whole of England. These two points are at the corners of one headland just north of Polzeath owned by the National Trust.

Pentire Point is the more westerly of the two. There are fine views up the Camel Estuary. At the most northerly part of Pentire Point a memorial plaque is set into the natural rock by a seat. This is to Laurence Binion (1869-1943) who composed *For the Fallen* on these cliffs in 1914.

Bluebells on Rumps Point

'They shall not grow old, as we that are left grow old:
Age shall not weary them, nor the years contemn.
At the going down of the sun and in the morning
We will remember them.'

Pillow lava rock at Pentire Point is quite distinctive. Lava was extruded from vents beneath the sea and cooled rapidly to form hard rock that is well described by its name.

Rumps Point is composed of two small hills joined to each other and to the mainland by a narrow isthmus across which are three banks and ditches of what must have been a formidable Iron Age 'cliff-castle'. Huts were situated between the two hills and behind the ramparts. Excavation revealed pottery from the Mediterranean and wine amphorae. A deep inlet of the sea between the two hills seems intent on prizing them apart. The more westerly of the hills is the higher and rockier. Wild flowers grow in profusion. Bluebells are often thought to be just woodland flowers, but here great drifts of them flourish on open slopes exposed to Atlantic gales. Just off the point are The Mouls, composed, like Rumps Point, of Greenstone, a type of Dolerite.

On the 30th May 1995 the *Maria Assumpta*, which was at the time the world's oldest square-rigged ship, ran onto the rocks at Rumps Point with the loss of three lives. The skipper had taken her between The Mouls and the mainland close to a lee shore. At that very moment her diesel engines failed and the wind and currents drove her onto the rocks. Mark Litchfield who was the Captain and owner was convicted of manslaughter.

Construct a circular walk from Polzeath overland to Pentireglaze and the coast of Port Quin Bay then back along the coast path via Rumps Point and Pentire Point, a distance of 10km. Alternatively it is possible to park close just 1km from Rumps Point at Pentire Farm where there is space for 6 cars. Both Pentire Point and Rumps Point are signposted.

Tintagel Head

Cornwall

At Tintagel
Grid ref: SX 047892
Maps: OS Explorer 111, OS Landranger 200.

Tintagel Head has genuine history and manufactured legend, the village of Tintagel contains authentic old buildings and modern tackiness and the coastline is magnificently rugged, but dominated by an outsize cliff-top hotel. The area is a curious mixture of the genuine and the fake.

The name 'Tintagel' or 'Din Tagell' means 'Fortress of the Narrow Entrance' and indeed it is. Today the headland is reached over a narrow footbridge spanning the chasm that separates it from the 'mainland'. On the more sheltered east side are the partially excavated remains of houses dating back to as early as the beginning of the 5th century AD. It was here that a large

Tintagel headland

collection of pottery fragments of eastern Mediterranean design was found. The conclusion is that Tintagel was an important trading port and, probably, the stronghold of a powerful chieftain. There is no evidence that it was ever a monastic site.

There are extensive remains of a medieval castle. These are unusual in that the castle consisted of two separate parts: a great hall and courtyard on the 'island' and two more extensive courtyards perched on a cliff on the adjoining 'mainland'. This castle is principally of 13th century construction.

Geoffrey of Monmouth wrote in 1136 that King Uther Pendragon fell in love with Igraine, wife of Gorlois Duke of Cornwall. Gorlois hid his wife at Tintagel. The wizard Merlin turned Uther into the likeness of Gorlois who gained access to the fortress of Tintagel and Igriane. She bore him a son, Arthur. Thus the legend began and upon this legend has been built the exploits of King Arthur and his knights. A rich basis this has been for the tourist industry at Tintagel.

Another courtly legend is rooted in Tintagel, that of Tristan and Yseult. King Mark of Cornwall was supposed to hold court at Tintagel. Tristan, nephew of King Mark, was wounded in battle and was cured by Yseult the beautiful daughter of the king of Ireland. King Mark planned to marry Yseult, but Tristan and Yseult drank a love potion..........and so the legend continued to its tragic conclusion. This was the inspiration for Richard Wagner's opera *Tristan und Isolde*.

The rock of the headland is predominantly slate of Devonian age. This rock has been dramatically deformed and faulted by later earth movements such that in places older rock has been thrust over younger. Caves are frequent and Merlin's Cave passes right through the headland under the remains of the medieval castle. Walk to the end of Barras Nose for a view across to Tintagel headland. A charge is levied to cross to 'The Island', the path is steep and care must be taken, but it is well worth going.

Which is it that leaves the more enduring impression of Tintagel Head, the rich history or the fanciful legends?

The adjacent headland of Willapark provides fine views of Tintagel headland. Steep steps with a hand rail lead down to the tiny sandy beach and natural arch of Bossiney Haven.

Hartland Point   ♿   Devon

16 miles from Bideford
Grid ref: SS 230277
Maps: OS Explorer 126, OS Landranger 190.

The term 'point' does not do this headland justice as it marks an important change in direction of the coastline from north-south to east-west and stands at the entrance to the Bristol Channel. A similar change in direction occurs at Bull Point further up the coast.

There is a car park at the point. The point itself is a high narrow cliff with a lighthouse on a flat projection near its base and is not accessible to the public. The lighthouse was designed by the great English lighthouse builder Sir James Douglass and was opened by the Bishop of Exeter in 1874. Originally the light

Hartland Point

was turned by a clockwork mechanism that required winding every two and a half hours. Soon after it was built it became apparent that the sea was eroding the land on which it stood. Attempts to prevent this by bringing down rock from the cliff behind the lighthouse were short-lived. Eventually, in 1925, a strong sea wall was built which has stopped further erosion. The light was automated in 1984. Once there were cottages around the lighthouse for four keepers and their families. These were demolished to make way for a helipad.

Many ships have come to grief along this coast. A notice board refers to the coaster *Johanna* that ran aground close to the lighthouse on the last day of 1982 and nearby is a memorial to those who died when the hospital ship *Glenart Castle* was torpedoed near here in 1918. On that occasion it was man rather than nature that claimed their lives.

Baggy Point   Devon

10 miles from Ilfracombe
Grid ref: SS 419406
Maps: OS Explorer 139, OS Landranger 180.

The coast path leads from a National Trust car park in Croyde to the end of the headland and beyond. This is a broad headland of farmland fringed by fine cliffs that afford challenging rock climbs. The rocks are mainly Devonian sandstones of varying coarseness. To the north is the sweep of Woolacombe Sands stretching away to Morte Point.

The area gave inspiration to the author Henry Williamson. He is best remembered for *Tarka the Otter*, but he wrote many other books that he considered much more important. His subjects included his observations of nature, farming and his experiences in the First World War.

Baggy Point

Morte Point   Devon

7 miles from Ilfracombe
Grid ref: SS 441456
Maps: OS Explorer 139, OS Landranger 180.

Jagged, vicious rocks point skyward along the length of Morte Point like the plates along the back of a Stegosaurus. They glisten with a silver sheen. More sharp pointed rocks are seen offshore or lurk beneath the surface. Morte Stone is the largest. Death Stone it has been as many ships have come to grief here. This National Trust headland has a savage beauty unequalled along the whole Devon coast.

The silvery shiny rock is Morte Slate from the Upper Devonian Period about 380 million years ago. It was Devon rocks that gave the name to the Devonian Period (417 — 354 million years ago).

Morte Point from Woolacombe Sands

Rocks of this age are not confined to Devon. Old Red Sandstone is also of Devonian age, made from the erosion of the massive Caledonian mountain range, and is found in South Wales, extends up into the Welsh Marches and appears again in northeast Scotland where it forms several dramatic headlands.

Atlantic grey seals are often seen off Morte Point, most frequently on the north side. On the south side of the headland is a small sandy beach, Grunta Beach, so called because a ship was wrecked here carrying a cargo of pigs that swam ashore, grunting as they came.

Access to Morte Point is by a 1.5km footpath from Mortehoe or the coast path, part of the Tarka Trail, from Woolacombe 3km away.

Bull Point

Devon

6 miles from Ilfracombe
Grid ref: SS 461469
Maps: OS Explorer 139, OS Landranger 180.

The lighthouse is a squat tower with nearby cottages that are now holiday lets. A lighthouse was first built here in 1879. In 1972 15 metres of cliff crashed into the sea and a further 15 m slumped causing extensive damage to the engine room. A temporary light had to serve for two years until the present tower was constructed. The optical equipment in the old tower was not damaged by the landslip and was transferred intact to the new tower where it continues to shine to this day.

Bull Point is a 2km walk along the South West Coast Path from Mortehoe. Here the coast turns from south – north to west – east similar to Hartland Point. The slate rock has a silver sparkle as at nearby Morte Point. Lundy Island lies just over 30km to westward.

Bull Point and lighthouse

Foreland Point   ♿   Devon

2 miles from Lynmouth
Grid ref: SS 754512
Maps: OS Explorer OL9, OS Landranger 180.

The steep hills of this headland make it unique. Three hills rise from 200 to 300 metres separated by deep steep-sided combes. Some slopes are grassy and others are covered with scree. Red deer may be seen grazing on the hillsides.

In 2003 Marine Current Turbines Ltd built the worlds first experimental undersea turbine powered by the strong tidal currents in the Bristol Channel just 1km off the tip of the headland. The currents here exceed 5 knots and, unlike wind, are totally predictable. The turbine being anchored to the seabed is out of sight and causes no environmental damage. Britain is ideally equipped to develop such systems as there are many sites around her shores where tidal flows are fast. Sites of tidal turbines

Foreland Point

producing electricity now include Anglesey and Strangford Lough, Northern Ireland.

Lynmouth Foreland Lighthouse is not an ancient light having been in operation only since 1900 and was automated in 1994.

There is parking at the Sandpiper Inn at Countisbury, 2km east of Lynmouth, or half a kilometre further east again along the A39. Paths lead north towards the headland. A tarmac road zigzags down into one of the combes and goes right on to the lighthouse at the tip of the headland. A path on the west side gives views of Lynton and Lynmouth. The round walk to the lighthouse and back by the other path is just 5km, some of it very steep. The narrow path round the end of the headland above the lighthouse needs extreme caution. Where the path crosses scree footsteps sound like breaking glass in a bottle-recycling bank.

Hurlstone Point   Somerset

7 miles from Minehead
Grid ref: SS 899492
Maps: OS Explorer OL9, OS Landranger 181.

High outcrops of rock form the end of the headland. To the east is the expanse of Selworthy Sand. To the west is a long shingle bar between low-lying land and the sea. A stream called Horner Water passes beneath the shingle into the sea. The spot may be marked by a little tongue of shingle projecting into the sea. Sometimes after very heavy rain the stream breaches the shingle bar and the sea rushes in with a great roar.

A curious castellated square tower at the end of the headland is a disused coastal lookout station.

Take the coast path from the car park in Bossington through woods beside the flat land behind the shingle bar and up onto the headland.

Brean Down

Somerset

11 miles from Weston-Super-Mare
Grid ref: ST 280593
Maps: OS Explorer 153, OS Landranger 182.

Brean Down points like an arrow at the island of Steep Holm 5km away in the Bristol Channel. This is not surprising as both Brean Down and Steep Holm are extensions of the Mendip Hills. Brean is composed of Carboniferous limestone dipping to the north with a steep escarpment to the south. Brean Down is almost an island itself and is joined to the mainland merely by sand. The views extend to Weston-super-Mare, the two bridges across the Bristol Channel, the Welsh coast and the islands of Steep Holm and Flat Holm.

The National Trust owns Brean Down. There is a car park at the base of the headland 2.5km north of the little village of Brean.

Brean Down

Nearby is a bird garden where many exotic species can be seen. A walk of 2km reaches the tip of the headland. Steep steps climb up to the ridge of Brean Down. To the right lie the remains of an Iron Age fort. To the left once stood a Romano-Celtic temple built in 340 AD but destroyed by barbarians a mere 27 years later.

Paths lead across ancient field boundaries to the tip of the headland where a Palmerston Fort was built in 1870. This was to counter the threat from the French, in particular from their iron-side *La Gloire*. She was the first ironclad battleship to be built. Never a shot was fired in anger. A shot was fired by 'accident', though, on 4th July 1900 when Gunner Haines fired through a ventilation shaft into Expense Magazine number 3 that contained three tons of powder. The explosion caused immense damage so that the fort was soon closed down. The only casualty was Gunner Haines and this was probably a rather spectacular suicide. The fort was rearmed in the Second World War and served as a testing ground for secret weapons.

Plans were made to construct a transatlantic port at Brean Down. A foundation stone was laid with much pomp and celebration on 5th November 1864. By the next day the stone had been washed away and was later found off Steep Holm! Despite further attempts to revive the project it was finally abandoned within the decade.

On 18th May 1897 when Guglielmo Marconi was only 23 years old he successfully transmitted a wireless message from Lavernock Point on the Welsh coast to Brean Down. A distance of 14km and the longest distance transmission at that time.

The steep cliffs on the south side of Brean Down provide a habitat for the rare white rock-rose *(Helianthemum apenninum)*. This is the most northerly site in the world for this plant which is only found at two other locations in Britain.

Sand Point

North Somerset

5 miles from Weston-Super-Mare
Grid ref: ST 320659
Maps: OS Explorer 153, OS Landranger 182.

The name Sand Point is misleading. Sandy it is not. It is decidedly rocky, thin and straight as an arrow. The path to the end of the headland goes through rolling limestone pasture that has been grazed since the Middle Ages. Near the trig point are a round barrow and a disc barrow probably dating from the early Bronze Age about 1800 BC. The rocks towards the tip of Sand Point are particularly jagged. Sand point is popular with sea anglers, rock climbers and bird watchers looking out for passage migrants.

On a small shingle beach on the north side the rocks are interesting. Here a volcanic tuff is sandwiched between beds of

Needle sharp Sand Point

limestone. Pillow lava is also to be seen. An information board at the car park states that this is one of only three sites in England where volcanic rock lies between beds of limestone.

Nearby St Thomas's Head is inaccessible to the public. Just south of St Thomas's Head are the remains of Woodspring Priory. The Augustinian Woodspring (or Worspring) Priory was founded in the early 13th century. The original church was rebuilt in the perpendicular style in the 15th century. The priory was dissolved by Henry VIII and fell into disuse. Stone was taken for farm buildings. The Landmark Trust took control of the buildings in 1969 and opened them to the public. Although little remains of the former glory the isolated peaceful environment gives it a particular charm.

There is a car park at the base of the headland just 4km north of Weston-super-Mare. Don't climb the steep steps, but follow the path west to the tip of the headland. The National Trust owns Sand Point.

Lavernock Point
The Vale of Glamorgan

2 miles from Penarth
Grid ref: ST 187681
Maps: OS Explorer 151, OS Landranger 171.

The cliffs at Lavernock Point are Lower Liassic limestone and mudstone. This dates from the beginning of the Jurassic Period (206 — 144 million years ago). The bedding planes are so well marked and horizontal that it almost looks as if they were manmade. These are some of the finest cliffs of this age in the world. At the time these limestones were laid down Ammonites had recently evolved and inhabited the shallow seas. Dinosaurs were the dominant animals on land and aquatic dinosaurs such as Ichthyosaurs and Plesiosaurs swam the seas.

Jurassic cliffs at Lavernock Point

Guglielmo Marconi did not invent radio communication as is popularly believed. Others had experimented with wireless waves for 50 years before Marconi made his first transmissions at his home in Italy in 1895. He came to Britain and in March 1897 transmitted about 6km across Salisbury Plain. The first transmission across water was on 18th May 1897 from Lavernock Point to the island of Flat Holm in the Bristol Channel about 5km away. The Morse code message was 'Are you ready?'. After this success he transmitted from Lavernock right across the Bristol Channel to Brean Down. Although many physicists had experimented with radio waves it was Marconi who had the drive and business acumen to develop the concept and make it a commercial success.

Part of Lavernock Point is a nature reserve and SSSI. Limestone grassland and scrub form a habitat for unusual plants and insects. The site is a resting point for migrating birds in Spring and Autumn. Hidden in the reserve are the remains of a World War 2 coastal battery.

If you are tempted to visit Sully Island, a couple of kilometres to the west, be very careful of the treacherous tides.

There is limited roadside parking near the church at Lavernock Point. Alternatively walk for 3km along the coast path from the centre of Penarth.

Headlands at Barry   ♿   The Vale of Glamorgan

(Nell's Point, Friar's Point and Cold Knap Point)
Grid refs: ST 120662, ST 111659 and ST 103660
Maps: OS Explorer 151, OS Landranger 171.

The most easterly is Nell's Point on Barry Island now well and truly part of the mainland. All the excitement of the funfair at Barry Island is just a stones-throw away. It marks the east end of the fine sands of Whitmore Bay. Through both world wars it carried a coastal battery the remains of which are still to be seen. Now there is a National Coastwatch Station on the headland where volunteers keep a sharp lookout for boats, sailboarders and others in trouble. Take the time to call in and talk to them about their work, or better still support this worthwhile service by joining as a volunteer or making a donation.

Friar's Point, a narrow finger-like projection at the west end of Whitmore Bay and still part of Barry Island, is the most scenic of the three headlands. Barry Rotary Club organises a firework display on Friar's Point each year on bonfire night. Friars Point Hay Meadow, managed by the Vale of Glamorgan Council, is famous for its profusion of cowslips in the Spring. Flint tool from the Mesolithic Period have been retrieved from Friar's Point.

Cold Knap Point, like Barry Island, was once detached from the mainland. It is flanked with pebbly beaches. This is a popular venue for surfboarders as they can be launched and retrieved at low tide, a rarity throughout the Bristol Channel. At the base of the headland are the remains of a Roman villa and a boating lake shaped like a Welsh harp made familiar to many through the poem 'Cold Knap Lake' by Gillian Clarke.

Each headland is about 1km from the next and all can easily be reached on foot from Barry Island where there is a car park.

Nash Point The Vale of Glamorgan

14 miles from Barry
Grid ref: SS 914683
Maps: OS Explorer 151, OS Landranger 170.

Nash Point stands at the centre of the 14 miles of Glamorgan Heritage Coast that extends from Porthcawl to Gileston Beach, Aberthaw. The rock of the cliffs dates from the Lias, the earliest division of the Jurassic Period 200 million years ago and contains fossil ichthyosaurs, ammonites and gryphea. Ichthyosaurs, the name means 'fish-lizards', were aquatic dinosaurs. Ammonites are related to present-day octopi and squids. Their spiral shells are quite distinctive and they

Stormy day at Nash Point

95

are used to date the rocks in which they are found. Gryphea (Devil's Toenails) were bivalve molluscs.

The paddle steamer *Frolic* ran onto Nash Sands in March 1831 and sank with the loss of all hands, 78 in total. This was sufficient for Trinity House to commission James Walker, its Engineer-in-Chief, to design and build two lighthouses on the point. James Walker also built lights on Start Point, The Needles, Bishop Rock and Wolf Rock. His experience rivalled that of his fellow-Scotsmen, the Stevensons. The two lights, the low light and the high light, set 302 metres apart enabled ships to avoid the treacherous sands. The low light was extinguished in the early 20th century and the high light modernised. It was one of the last to be fully automated in 1998. Two enormous foghorns are preserved, but no longer sounded.

A board on Nash Point recounts how in 1962 the *BP Driver* ran onto the rocks below Nash Point. The coastguard boat rescued nine of the crew, but the captain refused to leave the stricken ship. The coastguard offered his hand in a gesture of goodwill, but then did not let go and hauled him into the safety of the rescue boat. Minutes later the *BP Driver* rolled under the waves.

The cliffs at Nash Point are breached by Marcross Brook. On the northern side of the brook stands the remains of an impressive Iron Age fort. No fewer than four ditches and ramparts guarded this 'cliff-castle'. Much of the fort has been eroded by the waves and disappeared into the sea.

What a contrast is rural Nash Point to Breaksea Point to the East that is wholly occupied by Aberthaw Power Station. For anyone interested in getting close to a power station there is a path round the point.

There is a car park at Nash Point, but a coast path runs from Llantwit Major westward past St Donat's and Nash Point to Marcross or on to the hamlet of Broughton. A number of circular walks can be planned to include Nash Point.

Trwyn y Witch ♿ The Vale of Glamorgan

6 miles from Bridgend
Grid ref: SS 884726 Maps: OS Explorer 151,
OS Landranger 170.

There have been a house and gardens on the headland since Tudor times. The gardens are open to the public and consist of four contrasting 'rooms' with different themes. The first is a Tudor garden, the second an orchard, the third commemorates plant hunters and the fourth is Victorian. The first walled paddock was built in 1543. Little remains of the house.

Swirling rock patterns at Trwyn y Witch

The last house on the site was built in the reign of Queen Victoria and demolished in 1962.

The headland is composed of limestone of early Jurassic age. The wave-cut platform to the south of the headland shows amazing patterns in the rock. The headland is accessible, partly wooded and partly grass. Two large Iron Age ramparts and ditches run across from one side to the other. The sea has eroded much of the land since the Iron Age fort was built. It is possible that Caractacus mustered his forces here to confront the Romans.

Several low mounds are 'pillow mounds'. These were constructed out of stones and earth in medieval times to form rabbit warrens. Men known as 'warreners' managed these warrens and farmed the rabbits for their meat and fur.

Park by the beach at Dunraven Bay near St Brides Major just 0.5km from the headland. Alternatively St Brides Major is only another 2km away by footpath.

Sker Point   Bridgend

3 miles from Porthcawl
Grid ref: SS 788798
Maps: OS Explorer 151, OS Landranger 170.

The headland, just 3km north of Porthcawl, is a desolate, windswept place. On either side of the low rocks of the headland are vast expanses of sand: Rest Bay and the Royal Porthcawl Golf Club towards Porthcawl and Kenfig Sands backed by extensive dunes beyond the point. In the distance across Kenfig Sands are the steel works at Port Talbot, but they are far enough away to hardly be noticed. The sense of isolation is accentuated by the presence of a solitary building. This is Sker House. The Cistercian monks of Neath Abbey founded it in the 12th century as a grange. The Turbevilles, a staunch Roman Catholic family, gave refuge there to Catholics priests during the

Lonely Sker House

protestant reign of Queen Elizabeth 1. Father Phillip Evans was arrested at Sker, tried in Cardiff with another priest, Father John Lloyd. They were both sentenced to death on the charge of being Catholic priests and entering Wales illegally. They were executed in May 1679. Both men were canonised in 1970. The house fell into disrepair. The Buildings at Risk Trust and the Architectural Heritage Fund have been instrumental in restoring the building. It is now privately owned. Once again it stands gaunt against the sky.

Tragedy stalks this place. In 1947 the S.S. Santampa ran onto rocks off Sker Point in a great storm. The entire crew of 39 and all 8 men of the Mumbles lifeboat lost their lives.

The Maid of Sker is a novel by R. D. Blackmore published three years after his more famous work Lorna Doone.

To reach Sker Point walk along the coast for 2km from the north end of Porthcawl where there is a car park by the Royal Porthcawl Golf Course.

Mumbles Head ♿ Swansea

5 miles from Swansea
Grid ref: SS 634872
Maps: OS Explorer 164 and 165, OS Landranger 159.

Mumbles Head consists of two rocky islands connected to the mainland at low water with a lighthouse on the further island. The name Mumbles may be derived from the French 'Mamelles' meaning 'teats', an example of the fertile Gallic imagination.

The mainland portion of the headland is busy with promenades, shops, playgrounds, a Victorian pier with a sailing club and a lifeboat station (see Sker Point). The first fee-paying passenger railway in the world ran the five miles from Swansea to Mumbles. When it started on the 25th March 1807 the carriages were horse-drawn. Experiments were performed with sails mounted on the carriages.

Mumbles Head

100

These reduced the journey time provided the wind was favourable. In the early 1860s steam locomotives disguised to look like carriages were in use. Its heyday was during the Edwardian years when a single train might carry 1800 people. The line was electrified with overhead wires in 1929. Having survived Hitler's bombs the railway finally succumbed to the grim realities of economics. Much to the sorrow of local residents and visitors the last train ran on 5th January 1960. One positive outcome is that Swansea Council acquired the land and had the good sense to convert it into a promenade and cycleway linking Swansea with Mumbles Head.

The Swansea Harbour Trustees authorised the building of a lighthouse as long ago as 1792. A local builder, William Jernegan, undertook the work. The half-built structure collapsed and the tower was not completed till 1794. At the start the tower carried two open coal-fire lights one above the other. Soon these were replaced with a single oil fired lamp. The present lamp is solar-powered, automated and controlled from the Trinity House Operation Control Centre in Harwich. The tower still shows the original two-tiered structure that carried the two coal fires. The buildings around the base of the tower are coastal defences from the mid-19th century.

The Mumbles lifeboat station, near the tip of the headland, has disabled access and is open to the public during summer months.

Oxwich Point   Swansea

12 miles from Swansea
Grid ref: SS 512851
Maps: OS Explorer 164, OS Landranger 159.

Oxwich Point is a headland of contrasting halves. The north-east side is thickly wooded, whereas the south-west aspect is open to the sky and there are high inland cliffs. The difference could not be greater. The path from the village of

Oxwich Point from Port Eynon

Oxwich goes through woods carpeted with bluebells *(Hyacinthoides non-scriptus)*, violets *(Viola riviniana)* and primroses *(Primula vulgaris)* and alive with birdsong. It passes the church of St Illtyd. The tiny chancel may mark the site of a 6th century Celtic cell. St Illtyd lived in the late 5th and early 6th centuries. Many sites in South Wales are dedicated to him. He probably founded a seat of learning at Llantwit Major.

There are many ways down to the water's edge and the rocky shore provides natural tables and chairs for picnics. A small branch path leads to an Iron Age fort with banks and ditches. There are splendid views across Oxwich Bay.

The main path rounds the point where the woods give way to gorse *(Ulex europaeus)*, squill *(Scilla verna)*, yellow rock-roses *(Helianthemum chamaecistus)* and orchids. Port-Eynon Point can be seen across Port-Eynon Bay to the west. Inland limestone cliffs tower high above some way from the sea. The path takes advantage of an extensive raised beach below the crags. It then climbs obliquely up the cliff to the plateau above and swings right at a mobile home park to Oxwich village. Oxwich Castle is a fine, but ruined, mock-fortified 16th century mansion open to the public.

Oxwich Nature Reserve at the base of the headland behind the sands of Oxwich Bay contains several habitats including salt marsh and reed beds with a corresponding rich variety of plant, insect and bird life. It is an important site for reed warblers, sedge warblers and grasshopper warblers. Bitterns can sometimes be heard and more rarely seen.

The round walk from Oxwich village is 5km.

Port Eynon Point Swansea

16 miles from Swansea
Grid ref: SS470844
Maps: OS Explorer 164, OS Landranger 159.

The A4118 from Swansea plunges steeply down into the picturesque village of Port Eynon. The beach is popular with surfers. Walk along the shore to what looks like quite a large ruined house. This is all that remains of a 16th century salt house. Salt was extracted from the sea by evaporation, stored and distributed from here. Look out for Horton and Port Eynon Lifeboat Station. In the summer it may be open to the public to learn of the amazing work that lifeboatmen do.

From the salt house a steep path climbs up the headland. Be careful for it seems to go straight to the cliff edge. Keep to the right and up to an upright memorial stone erected by the Gower Society in memory of Gwent Jones (1910 – 1962) and Stephen Lee (1889 – 1962). Gwent Jones was a local doctor, philanthropist and founder of the Gower Society. Stephen Lee retired to the Gower from Oxford where he was a mathematics

Port Eynon Point

don at Magdalen College. He worked tirelessly for local causes such as the preservation of footpaths for which we should be grateful even today. The cliffs on the west side of the headland are dramatic. If coming down the same way do not follow strips of scree that look like paths but end in impenetrable thorn thickets. A better way up and down might be to take a more inland route from Port Eynon and follow the ridge of the headland to the memorial stone.

On the west side is Culver Hole, a cleft in the cliff blocked off by a stone wall. Culver is an old English word for a pigeon or dove and Culver Hole is a medieval dove cote. There must have been easier more accessible places to build a pigeon house. Subsequently smugglers could well have used it to store their contraband.

Worms Head (Penrhyn-Gwyr)

Swansea

36 miles from Swansea
Grid ref: SS 383877
Maps: OS Explorer 164, OS Landranger 159.

This is the Welsh Dragon couchant! Its undulating spine snakes its way 3 km into the sea. At any moment it may wake and thrash its great tail round the concavity of Rhossili Bay. The name comes from the Norse 'wurm' meaning serpent or dragon. The same word gives rise to Great Orme and Little Orme in North Wales. There must be a family of Welsh dragons.

Much of the headland can only be accessed 2 1/2 hours either side of low water. On the island side a bell stands so that anyone

Worms Head from Rhossili Beach

Natural arch on Worms Head

stranded by the tide can ring the bell to be rescued. It is highly dangerous to attempt to cross if the incoming tide is beginning to cover the intervening rocks. There have been fatalities as the tide-race is strong. Dylan Thomas was stranded here by the tide for half the night. The walk to Inner Head takes about 20 minutes across flat rocks covered with mussels. There are numerous rock pools and fissures in the limestone teeming with marine life. A rarity found here and only in a few other sites in Pembrokeshire and Cornwall is the cushion starfish *(Asterina phylactica)*. Once onto Inner Head a path leads on to a difficult scramble across the rocks of Low Neck then over the dramatic Devil's Bridge, a natural arch in the steeply dipping beds of Carboniferous Limestone, to Outer Head. To the north are steep cliffs where kittiwakes, fulmars, razorbills and guillemots breed. Access to this part of Worms Head is forbidden in the breeding season. The mainland part of the headland is now grazed. As a consequence choughs have returned as they require short grass through which they can probe for food with their curved red bills.

There are magnificent views of the 5 km long beach of Rhossili Bay, surely one of the finest in Britain, terminating in the small headland of Burry Holms which is an island at high tide. Down at the near end of the beach, half submerged in the sand, are the ribs of the *Helvetica* which met its end here in 1887. Behind the beach is the Old Red Sandstone mass of Rhossili Down which at 193m is the highest point on the Gower Peninsula.

106

For those who do not relish the exertion of crossing the rocks at low tide to the further part of the headland the gentle 3km walk from the village of Rhossili to the end of the main headland and back is a delight. Just before the tidal part of the headland is a National Coastwatch Station. You will receive a welcome there. It is always interesting to see what goes on and hear more of the work of the National Coastwatch Institution.

Castle Hill, Tenby   ♿   Pembrokeshire

At Tenby
Grid ref: SN 138005
Maps: OS Explorer OL36, OS Landranger 158.

> There is a fortress on the foreland height
> I know at Tenby, safe above the sea,
> Beyond the reach of ninth successive wave
> When surging ocean tide puts forth its might.
> Fine are its men when savouring their ease –
> Merry, with neither insult to displease
> Nor lack of welcome; better far a slave
> In Dyfed than a Deudraeth yeoman free!

Thus sang an anonymous 9th century bard, but in Welsh of course. The poem comes from the Book of Taliesin (975 AD) translated by B D Price.

Nothing remains of a 9th century castle which would have been a wooden structure with surrounding earthworks. There are isolated sections of a medieval castle on the promontory known as Castle Hill. A 13th century tower and portion of wall with a barbican are all that remain. A narrow easily defended isthmus connects the headland with the mainland and the town

Castle Hill Tenby

of Tenby. The castle changed hands on several occasions during the civil war.

In a far better state of preservation than the castle are the 13th to 15th century town walls that stretch from shore to shore originally enclosing the whole town and protecting it from attack from the landward side. These were pierced by three gates and strengthened by twelve towers. Almost all the wall together with one gate and seven towers still stand today.

During the 17th and 18th centuries Tenby fell on hard times. In 1784 John Wesley visited Tenby and wrote "There is no such town in England – two thirds of the ancient town are either in ruins or vanished away." The year 1790 marked a change in fortune. It was then that the first bathing machine was installed. Tenby was reached by boat from Bristol and the Channel ports as the journey by road was long and hazardous and it would be another 60 years or so before the railway arrived. The fashion for sea bathing, together with the closure of Europe to English tourists by Napoleon Bonaparte, brought prosperity and gave the town its current Georgian streetscape. Tenby gained the title of 'The Naples of Wales.' Today the English and Welsh influences complement each other in this "Little England beyond Wales."

The Tenby Museum and Art Gallery is sited on the headland of Castle Hill and incorporates part of the medieval castle. It contains a clear and informative account of the history of Tenby from Palaeolithic times to the present day. The art gallery displays works by Tenby's most famous artists, Augustus John and his sister Gwen. Other artists represented include E J Head who founded the art school that Augustus John attended, John Piper, Nina Hamnett, Julius Caesar Ibbetson and modern local artists. Many consider Gwen John's work to be finer and more sensitive than her brother's. Certainly she was as reserved and introspective as he was flamboyant. She studied at the Slade School of Art and later moved to Paris where she fell under the spell of Auguste Rodin. She was his model for several portrait heads and for his unfinished 'Monument to Whistler'.

A new lifeboat station has been built on the headland. The current boat is the tenth to have served since the Shipwrecked Fishermen and Mariners' Benevolent Society installed the first boat at a cost of £125 in 1852.

Prominent upon the headland is a large statue to Prince Albert. Inscribed on the plinth are the words in Welsh 'Albert Dda', meaning 'Albert the Good'.

Tenby daffodils are a subspecies with short stiff stems that grow wild over Castle Hill.

At the far end of South Beach is Giltar Point. Augustus John was thought to be only of average ability when he dived off Giltar Point, hit his head, and "emerged a bloody genius." Other mediocre artists should not try this. The jagged Monkstone Point is reached along the coast path just 3 km north of Tenby.

Lydstep Point Pembrokeshire

4 miles from Tenby
Grid ref: SS 094975
Maps: OS Explorer OL36, OS Landranger 158.

Here the high precipitous cliffs are some of the most dramatic in Wales. They consist of beds of Carboniferous Limestone dipping almost vertically and provide nesting sites for fulmars and other seabirds. Choughs now nest here. They are the national emblem of Cornwall and used to be seen frequently around the rugged coasts of Wales and the Southwest Peninsula. They became very rare, but are making something of a comeback. They are a delight to watch with their red curved bills, red legs and tumbling flight. A path along the north side of the headland gives views of the fine sandy beach of Lydstep Haven and, unfortunately, a large caravan park as well. The south path

Vertical rock strata at Lydstep Point

110

reveals the more spectacular cliff scenery. These cliffs are popular with rock-climbers, coasteerers and anglers. The coast to the west is riddled with caves.

The headland belongs to the National Trust who have provided a car park just south of the village of Lydstep and about 500m from the end of the headland. The town of Tenby is a delightful 7km walk away along the Pembrokeshire Coast Path. In the opposite direction is Manorbier Castle. This was the birthplace of Gerald of Wales (Geraldus Cambrensis) the great Welsh churchman, historian and writer of the early Middle Ages. On Priest's Nose, the headland at Manorbier, is King's Quoit a Neolithic burial chamber.

Further to the west stands Trewent Point that has many similarities to Lydstep Point.

Stackpole Head — Pembrokeshire

5 miles from Pembroke
Grid ref: SR 995942
Maps: OS Explorer OL36, OS Landranger 158.

According to Wikipedia Barafundle Bay has featured in The Times and Country Life as one of the top ten most beautiful bays in the world. I can well believe it. Stackpole Head forms the southern limit of Barafundle Bay. All round the headland are high cliffs of Carboniferous limestone with caves and natural arches. There are superb views of Old Red Sandstone cliffs to the north and Lundy Island is on the horizon.

This headland is popular with rock climbers. There are strict rules designed to keep the cliffs from damage; no bolting is allowed and plants and soil must not be removed from fissures to provide a better hold, a practice known as 'gardening'. The cliffs provide nesting sites for seabirds, peregrines and choughs. Rare lichens grow in this limestone habitat.

Stackpole Head with a natural arch

The Stackpole Estate is part of Pembrokeshire National Park and is managed by the National Trust and part of it is a Site of Special Scientific Interest. Park at the tiny harbour of Stackpole Quay and walk along the coast path then across the sands of Barafundle Bay and up onto Stackpole Head a distance of just 2km.

St Govan's Head — Pembrokeshire

8 miles from Pembroke
Grid ref: SR 974927
Maps: OS Explorer OL36, OS Landranger 158.

Whether St Govan was a real person is open to doubt. There are stories of an Irishman called Govan or Gobhan or Gobban in the 6th century possibly the abbot of Dairinis, Co. Wexford. Legend has it that while chased

112

St Govan's Chapel

by pirates, a fissure in the cliff opened to hide him then closed over him until the pirates had left. In gratitude he lived as a hermit at that very spot and his followers later built a chapel there. Outside the chapel is a large boulder known as Bell Rock. Pirates stole a silver bell from a church tower and when a great storm wrecked their ship angels retrieved the bell and inserted it into the centre of the boulder. When St Govan struck the boulder it would ring with a tone many times louder than the original bell. Whatever the true story might be it is certain that the chapel that now nestles low down in a cleft in the cliff was built as a place of Christian worship many centuries ago, probably in the 11th century and part may date back to the 6th century. The roof is in keeping with the style seen in Pembrokeshire in the 13th century. The chapel spans the cleft, so it is necessary to go through the building to reach the sea. Outside the chapel is a well which is now dry.

St Govan's Head stands 1km east of his chapel. This is a high Carboniferous limestone headland with cliffs frequented by rock-climbers. Evidence remains of its use during World War 2 as a gunnery and bombing range. There are three concentric circles of limestone pieces bisected by an arrow. This was a bombing target. There are several low, turf-covered rooms pointing out to sea from which emerge small railway tracks. These housed winches that pulled targets along the tracks for tank firing exercises. The whole scene is blissfully peaceful today. On the east side of the headland is a deep valley running down to an attractive little cove with a sandy beach sheltered from the wind. This is New Quay.

Cars can be parked at St Govan's Chapel. Better still walk a round trip from Bosherston along the minor road to St Govan's Chapel, round the headland and back via the beach of Broad Haven, a distance of 6km.

St Ann's Head   Pembrokeshire

11 miles from Milford Haven
Grid ref: SM 807028
Maps: OS Explorer OL36, OS Landranger 157.

S t Ann's Head stands at the entrance to one of the finest deep-water natural harbours in Britain. The ability of Milford Haven to accommodate the largest oil tankers has led to its development as an oil terminal with refinery. It is now also the entry port for liquefied natural gas. The refinery is tucked round a corner out of sight and the town of Milford Haven is sufficiently far away not to spoil the rural atmosphere of St Ann's Head. The rock formation at Cobbler's Hole near the tip of the headland shows spectacular folding of the strata.

Many ships have come to grief on rocks around this headland from the earliest days of seafaring to the oil tanker, Sea Empress, which spilt 72,000 tons of crude in 1996. Crow Rock lying 7 miles to the southwest held particular terror for sailors. The first coal-burning light was built here in the late 17th century, but its life was short. Joseph Allen built two coal-fired lighthouses in 1714 which acted as leading lights to enable sailors to steer clear

114

St Ann's Head lighthouse

of Crow Rock. The Low Light is the one that is currently operational. It was rebuilt in 1841 and automated in 1998. The High Light is part of a holiday accommodation complex and houses a small museum.

Henry Tudor with 2000 men landed at Mill Bay on the east side of St Ann's Head in 1485, marched on to win the Battle of Bosworth Field and be crowned King Henry VII of England thus marking the end of the Plantagenet and beginning of the Tudor Dynasty. Blockhouses were built on either side of the entrance to Milford Haven to protect the approach to this important harbour. (See East Blockhouse Point.)

Y Bocs is the Welsh name for a monster wave that forms occasionally over a reef to the southwest of St Ann's Head. Although it does not last long the ride is said to be one of the most exhilarating in Europe and one of the most dangerous.

There is a small NT car park 1.5km short of the lighthouse. Alternatively follow a circular 7.5km walk right round this glorious headland. From the car park walk a few metres towards the lighthouse then turn right to the Pembrokeshire Coast Path. Follow this round the headland past West Blockhouse Point and

Watwick Point to Castlebeach Bay. Turn inland through a wooded valley then left along the road to complete the circle.

Across the entrance to the deep waters of Milford Haven is East Blockhouse Point. This headland carries World War 2 defences, and the teetering ruins of a 16th century gun tower part of which has fallen into the sea.

Wooltack Point (Deer Park)
Pembrokeshire

11 miles from Milford Haven
Grid ref: SM 754094
Maps: OS Explorer OL36, OS Landranger 421.

The end of the headland called the Deer Park is almost cut off from the mainland by a deep gully due to a fault in the rock strata. A high wall with an imposing gateway was built across the neck of the headland so that deer could be kept here, but they never were. The tip of Deer Park is Wooltack Point. The whole area is in the hands of the National Trust. A small open ferry runs from Martin's Haven at the north end of the gully to the nature reserve of Skomer Island famous as a breeding ground for puffins and Manx shearwaters. The scientific name for the puffin is *Fratercula arctica* and Manx shearwaters are bizarrely named *Puffinus puffinus*. Over half a million seabirds nest on Skomer and the shearwater population is the largest in the world at over 150,000 nesting pairs. Shearwaters nest in burrows. They spend all day out at sea and return at dusk. The colonies are noisy at night with their ghostly calls. They are summer nesting visitors spending the winters off the coast of South America. They are among the longest lived birds on earth surviving for well over 50 years. During their long lives they may fly up to 1 million kilometres on migration alone.

116

Wooltack Point and Skomer Island

The waters round Skomer Island are a Maritime Nature Reserve. An excellent digital exhibition of the reserve is found on the road down to Martin's Haven. Just below this display beside the road stands a stone marked with a cross and ring. This dates from 7th to 9th centuries. It was found just above high water and is evidence of the importance of sea communications to the early Celtic church.

An Iron Age rampart runs along the top of the gully just within the wall that demarcates the Deer Park. On the south side of the Deer Park a long cat-slide of rock slips down to the sea. Elsewhere there are cliffs, inaccessible little coves and a natural arch. A National Coastwatch station occupies a previous coastguard lookout post on the highest ground. Volunteers man it at peak times. Choughs wheel and roll along the cliffs landing from time to time to probe in the short grass for insects with their long curved red bills.

There is a car park near Martin's Haven. From there a circular footpath of just 1.5km goes round the headland a bit like a miniature Dinas Head.

Pen Dal-aderyn   Pembrokeshire

3 miles from St David's
Grid ref: SM 715233
Maps: OS Explorer OL35, OS Landranger 157.

At Porthstinian there is a private house, a lifeboat station the ruins of the Chapel of St Justinian and a small car park. A ferry runs from Porthstinian in summer months to the nature reserve of Ramsey Island.

St Justinian, a 6th century saint, lived on Ramsey Island, but little is known of his life. St David is purported to have been impressed by his holiness and came to him for confession. It is possible that his servants, who could not maintain the austere standards he set, murdered him.

Pen Dal-aderyn is the most westerly point on the Welsh mainland. The coastal views are stunning with Ramsey Island just

Porthstinian near Pen Dal-aderyn

118

a kilometre away. There is a severe tide race between the island and the mainland sufficient to form waves that are a challenge to white water kayakers. The strength of the tidal flow makes this an ideal location for an experimental underwater turbine. This would generate electricity in an entirely predictable way and would only cease generation when there is slack water at the turn of the tides.

A walk of 2.5km from Porthstinian along the Pembrokeshire Coast Path reaches the headland. You could continue along the coast path and strike inland at Porthlysgi Bay to make a round trip of 8km.

St David's Head (Penmaen Dewi) Pembrokeshire

3 miles from St David's
Grid ref: SM 722279
Maps: OS Explorer OL35, OS Landranger 157.

Rhygyfarch, son of a Bishop of St David's in the 11th century, wrote a biography of Dewi Sant, or St David as he is known to the English. He wrote this about 500 years after the death of the saint. If Rhygyfarch is to be trusted then we know a lot about St David, but if he fabricated the biography to support the case for the Welsh church struggling to be independent of Canterbury, then we know next to nothing. Virtually all we know for certain is that he lived in the 6th century, was Bishop of Menevia (later to be called St David's) and was canonised by Pope Callistus II in 1120.

Human activity on St David's Head goes back much further than St David. Coetan Arthur (Arthur's Quoit) forms a striking silhouette on the skyline. A short climb up a steep path reaches this partly collapsed Neolithic burial chamber constructed about

119

Coetan Arthur at St David's Head

6,000 years ago. The huge capstone now rests on just one upright. A substantial Iron Age double stone rampart and ditch crosses the headland from one side to the other. The stone footings of huts within this promontory fort can easily be seen.

St David's Head is composed of a hard intrusive gabbro providing challenging climbs. All along this coast the headlands are of hard igneous rock and the bays have been eroded out of softer rock such as shale.

The National Trust own St David's Head. There is a car park at the fine surfing beach of Whitesands Bay. From here follow the coast path about 2km to the tip of the headland. Sections of the path are quite steep. A very easy to miss side path goes straight up to Coetan Arthur. If you miss this continue up to the ridge and double back along the ridge to the burial chamber.

Penbwchdy   Pembrokeshire

6 miles from Fishguard
Grid ref: SM 877373
Maps: OS Explorer OL35, OS Landranger 157.

The sharp tip of Penbwchdy points due west giving extensive views along the coast in both directions. The hard dolerite rock is the reason the headland has not been eroded away. The beautiful bay of Pwll Deri to the north has been cut by wave action from soft slates.

Just above the bay, beside the path leading to the headland, is a memorial stone to the Welsh poet, Dewi Enrys (1879 – 1959). The stone carries a couplet from one of his best-loved poems entitled 'Pwllderi'.

Park at a small National Trust car park on the east side of a little hill 'Garn Fawr', walk down to the coast path and another 2km to the headland.

Strumble Head   &   Pembrokeshire

7 miles from Fishguard
Grid ref: SM 899415
Maps: OS Explorer OL35, OS Landranger 157.

This is a popular destination for a picnic and walk along the cliffs. This rugged coast looks like giant paws with short toes standing in the sea. From the car park at Strumble Head it is a pleasant walk along the coast path to the headland of Pen Caer less than 1km away.

Here is one of the best places in Britain to watch for cetaceans. (See Chanonry Point on the Moray Firth for another.)

121

Strumble Head and lighthouse

An information board records the species that may be seen: bottle nose dolphin, common dolphin, Risso's dolphin and harbour porpoise. Sunfish are seen frequently in August and September. These are the largest bony fish in the world and may reach a length of 4 metres. Their position is given away by a flock of gulls hovering overhead probably hoping to peck off a parasite or two.

The rock here is basaltic lava extruded from underwater volcanoes of Ordovician age formed about 460 million years ago. Columns of this rock can be seen on the island that bears the lighthouse. Pillow lavas are also prominent. The Ordovician Period was one of intense volcanic activity. Many of the rocks in Britain dating from this period are volcanic tuffs, lavas and intruded igneous rock. Strumble Head is the nearest Wales gets to Ireland.

The lighthouse stands on a small island, Ynys Meicel or St Michael's Island, reached by an iron bridge. It is not open to the public. In the 19th century no fewer than 60 vessels were wrecked around Strumble Head. Trinity House established the first light in 1908. The original 4.5 ton light was rotated by clockwork with a massive weight that dropped down the height of the tower. It needed winding twice a day. The light was converted to electricity in 1965 and fully automated in 1980.

There is a car park at Strumble Head, or the headland can be incorporated into a walk along the glorious Pembrokeshire Coast Path.

Carregwastad Point Pembrokeshire

3 miles from Fishguard
Grid ref: SM 926406
Maps: OS Explorer OL35, OS Landranger 157.

No self-respecting Welshman would forgive me if I omitted this small, unimposing headland. The name Carregwastad is certainly imposing meaning Everlasting Stone.

Park in the little village of Llanwnda. Follow a muddy track becoming a footpath down to the coast path, down into a deep valley, across a stream and up the other side to Carregwastad Point. A stone on the headland is inscribed in Welsh and English 'Memorial Stone of the Landing of the French. February 22nd 1797.'

This headland is a most unpromising site for an invasion. The cliffs are not vertical, but rocks tumble down into the sea all round the point. Yet this marks the site of the last and most bizarre invasion of Britain. In 1797 a French force of about 1400 men, some regular soldiers and some prisoners from Parisian jails, under the command of William Tate, an Irish-American, landed at Carregwastad Point. They hoped that the disaffected Welsh would join them in an insurrection against the English. The episode was not without casualties on both sides. The most famous incident was the capture of 12 Frenchmen single-handedly by Jemima Nicholas. She earned the epithet Jemima Fawr, Jemima the Great. Booze in the local farmhouses proved too great a temptation for the undisciplined ragtag force and Captain Tate had no

Portion of the Millenial Tapestry depicting
the French invasion at Carregwastad Point

option but to surrender two days later to Lord Cawdor who had
stationed himself at the Royal Oak in Fishguard. A splendid mil-
lennial tapestry, reminiscent of the one in Bayeux, commemorates
these events. This can be seen in the museum in Fishguard.

Pen Anglas, a headland that marks the entrance to Fishguard
Bay, slides gently into the sea just 3km to the east along the coast
path. Hexagonal columns of dolerite rock are reminiscent of the
Giant's Causeway in County Antrim.

Dinas Head — Pembrokeshire

5 miles from Fishguard
Grid ref: SN 005412
Maps: OS Explorer OL35, OS Landranger 145 and 157.

Dinas Head, a National Trust headland, is almost an
island. Cutting across the neck of the headland is a deep
valley only a few metres above sea level. This valley was

Dinas Head

probably carved by melt-water at the end of the last ice age. At one end is the hamlet of Cwm-yr-Eglwys and the other the sandy beach of Pwllgwaelod. The headland rises to 141m giving extensive views across Fishguard Bay on one side and Newport Bay on the other and even right across Cardigan Bay to Snowdonia.

At Cwm-yr-Eglwys all that remains of the Church of St Brynach is part of the west wall with a belfry and a low arched doorway of 12th century Celtic design. The rest was destroyed in a great storm in 1859 that wrecked well over 100 ships around the coast of Wales alone. An iron scale model of a coastal trading brig stands as a memorial to those who died in that storm. These brigs had a shallow draught and flat bottom to allow them to be beached near high tide, loaded by horse and cart and floated on the next high tide. A local blacksmith crafted the model to mark the millennium.

The Pembrokeshire Coast Path runs for 4km right round the headland passing the ramparts and ditches of an Iron Age promontory fort and Needle Rock, a fine sea stack.

Cemaes Head Pembrokeshire

5 miles from Cardigan
Grid ref: SN 131501
Maps: OS Explorer OL35, OS Landranger 145.

The view back from this headland up the estuary of the River Teifi is superb and compares well with views of the Mawddach Estuary at the northern end of Cardigan Bay or the Camel Estuary in Cornwall.

The B4546 runs from St Dogmaels along the west bank of the Teifi estuary. It becomes an unclassified road leading towards Cemaes Head. It is possible to park in a field with an honesty box just before a campsite. Walk on along the coast path to the headland. The views back up the estuary are superb.

The spread of bracken at Cemaes Head and elsewhere along this coast is a problem. Grazing by ponies or crushing the stems

Cemaes Head

with rollers drawn by mules where the slopes are too steep for tractors are ways of controlling this invasive plant. Herbicides are ineffective and damage local flora.

Ynys Lochtyn — Ceredigion

10 miles from New Quay
Grid ref: SN 314555
Maps: OS Explorer 198, OS Landranger 145.

The Welsh word 'ynys' means 'island' and indeed this finger-like projection into Cardigan Bay does end as an island. The best view of Ynys Lochtyn is from Pen-y-Badell, a small hill at the base of the headland. The earthworks of the Iron Age fort on the hill are easily seen. From here the headland thrusts its sinuous form into the sea culminating in the knight's move

The complex geometry of Ynys Lochtyn

shape of the island at its tip. Small wonder that Ynys Lochtyn was chosen as the symbol for this heritage coast. Both the headland and Pen-y-Badell are in the hands of the National Trust.

Access to Ynys Lochtyn is from the village of Llangranog just 1km away where a plaque declares that 'Sir Edward Elgar found inspiration for some of his music here in Llangranog'. A page of one of Elgar's sketchbooks is headed *Ynys Lochtyn* on which he noted some of his musical ideas including that of a descending minor third. It is indeed an inspiring place.

Tonfanau Headland   ♿   Gwynedd

3 miles from Tywyn
Grid ref: SH 560037
Maps: OS Explorer OL23, OS Landranger 135.

Tonfanau is a halt on the stunning coastal track between Tywyn and Barmouth. You can take the train or drive. At Rhoslefain 8km north of Tywyn turn onto a minor road a further 2.5km to Tonfanau. Walk across an abandoned spread-out army installation to the sea where the Afon Dysynni has deposited silt to form a little estuary.

In 1972 Idi Amin forcibly expelled Asian people from Uganda. Thirty thousand found refuge in Britain of which 3,000 were housed for six months over the winter in ex-army camp at Tonfanau. This must have been a sharp contrast to the tropical sunshine of Uganda.

The principal activity at Tonfanau is motorcycle racing on a 1 mile (1.6km) road circuit. The mess left by sheep overnight has to be cleaned up before racing starts.

Miniature cliffs of Tonfanau

Criccieth Castle ♿ Gwynedd

At Criccieth
Grid ref: SH 500376
Maps: OS Explorer 254, OS Landranger 123 and 124.

Criddieth Castle and the rock from which it rises stand proudly above the town. The stone of the castle was hewn from the rock and supplemented by boulders from the beach. The rock is rhyolite, a hard igneous rock derived from volcanic activity in the Ordovician Period.

The castle was not built by the English to quell the Welsh, but was a truly Welsh fortress built by Llewelyn ab Iorwerth (Llewelyn the Great) in the early 13th century. The castle was enlarged by the addition of new curtain walls and towers by Llewelyn ap Gruffudd. It fell to the English in1283. Edward 1st undertook

Cricceith Castle

further rebuilding of the castle towards the end of the 13ᵗʰ century. Little has been added since then.

The peaceful scene of families relaxing on the beach is in sharp contrast to the violence experienced on the rock above them.

Cricceith Lifeboat Station, just behind the beach, is classed as a Discover Station equipped with an Atlantic 85 and an Arancia Inshore Rescue Boat.

Across Tremadog Bay is the large campsite of Shell Island. This is a low headland that is an island accessed by a causeway except at peak high tides. From here are superb views of the Lleyn Peninsula and the Snowdon range.

Pen-ychain · Gwynedd

4 miles from Pwlleli
Grid ref: SH 436353
Maps: OS Explorer 254, OS Landranger 123.

This is a delightful little headland. Don't miss it, a fine place for a picnic on a sunny day. They do happen in Wales. There are fine views of Snowdonia. There used to be a

Pen ychain

large Butlins Holiday Park here and the headland was known as Butlin Point. Many holidaymakers would come by train to Penychain station. A large caravan park has replaced Butlins, but trains will still stop on request.

It is possible to park beside the A497 opposite the road running down to Penychain station. Walk down past the station then beyond Penychain and Penrhyn farms to the coast.

Trwyn Llanbedrog　　　　Gwynedd

At Llanbedrog
Grid ref: SH 337308
Maps: OS Explorer 253, OS Landranger 123.

The small town of Llanbedrog shelters beneath the granite porphyry mass of Mynydd Tir-y-Cwmwd that forms this high headland. From Llanbedrog the easiest way is to follow any of several footpaths behind the church that lead up

The Iron Man, Llanbedrog

onto the hill. The steps up from the beach are steep, but afford a shorter route. This path passes a striking figure, the Iron Man, often called the Tin Man after a previous figure on the same site. Hugh Jones, a local blacksmith constructed it to a design by Berwyn Jones, another local resident.

The whole headland is the shape of the shell of a giant tortoise. It is mainly covered with heather *(Calluna vulgaris)* and gorse *(Ulex europaeus)* and peppered with protruding lumps of bedrock also tortoise shaped.

While at Llanbedrog do not miss the superb art gallery of Oriel Plas Glyn-y-Weddw.

Trwyn Llech-y-doll   Gwynedd

3 miles from Abersoch
Grid ref: SH 302235
Maps: OS Explorer 253, OS Landranger 123.

Cilan Uchaf farm provides parking for a fee at the end of the minor road south from Abersoch. Follow fishing signs across several fields to a path that runs along the coast. A large stone in a field marks a burial chamber.

Trwyn Llech-y-doll

From a vantage point the fine cliffs of Trwyn Llech-y-doll are seen far below. In the cliffs there is an unconformity where Ordovician sandstones overlie Cambrian sandstones. Cambrian rocks are the oldest that contain fossils of hard-shelled creatures. The slates of North Wales belong to this period. Fossil trilobite burrows in rocks at Trwyn Llech-y-doll are identical to those found in Newfoundland and Spain indicating that although widely separated now they were once close together and part of a single land mass. Burrows such as these are called trace fossils as they indicate the presence of living organisms rather than remains of the creatures themselves.

Walk westward with high cliffs on your left hand — beware! The cliffs give way to gently rounded grassy slopes of Trwyn Cilan. This change marks the boundary between middle and lower Cambrian rocks. Beware again! The slope towards the sea gets steeper and steeper ending in sheer cliffs. These cliffs are seen best from the sea.

The headland of Trwyn yr Wylfa 3km to the east provides views of the two islands, St Tudwal's Island West and St Tudwal's Island East. St Tudwal was a Welsh monk who founded a monastery in Brittany. For some time he lived as a hermit on the more easterly of his two islands where there are the remains of a priory. He died in 564.

Trwyn Talfarach — Gwynedd

8 miles from Abersoch
Grid ref: SH 214257
Maps: OS Explorer 253, OS Landranger 123.

This National Trust headland stands high above the sea. The highest point, Mynydd Penarfynydd, reaches 177m above sea level giving stunning views along the coast including

View from Trwyn Talfarach. Bardsey Island in the distance

Bardsey Island off the tip of the Lleyn Peninsula. Porth Alwm can be seen to the west. Here there are extensive disused mine workings, not for alum, but for manganese. The 6km long sandy beach of Porth Neigwl or Hell's Mouth is seen to the east.

Park at and patronise the tea-rooms at Ty Croes Mawr 1km south-west of the village of Rhiw. Walk through Penarfynydd farm and follow the footpath along the hill to an outcrop of rock and gaze down at the sea far below. The more energetic can construct circular walks from Rhiw to take in the headland.

Braich y Pwll   ♿   Gwynedd

13 miles from Abersoch
Grid ref: SH 136258
Maps: OS Explorer 253, OS Landranger 123.

The Lleyn Peninsula is one of the major peninsulas around the coast of Britain. Braich y Pwll at the tip of that peninsula is, therefore, in a dramatic location. It does not disappoint in any way. The views in all directions are superb: left and right along the rugged coast, ahead to Bardsey Island and back to the mountains of Snowdonia. The rock here is Precambrian (Monian Supergroup), some of the oldest rock found in Britain formed more than 600 million years ago, but younger than the Precambrian rocks of northwest Scotland.

The National Trust owns the headland and provides a car park. It is also possible to drive, or walk, to the top of Mynydd Mawr for the view. Although the name means 'Great Mountain' it is really a short and not too arduous walk to the top. Previously there was a coastguard lookout station at the summit.

A path leads from the National Trust car park along a beautiful valley between smooth grassy slopes down to the sea. This is the route that countless pilgrims have taken to embark for Bardsey Island. Maen Melyn Llyn, a large standing stone,

Bardsey Island from Braich y Pwll

either erected by ancient people or possibly natural, stands near the shore. St Mary's Well refers to a narrow inlet of the sea which, at certain states of the tide fills with fresh water, presumably from underground springs. Needless to say this phenomenon has been described as a miracle. An information board refers to a 1000 year old inscription found nearby, that records the burial of a wise priest with a multitude of the brethren, 'Senacus Presbiter cum multitudinem fratum'. The letters were joined up and could easily be mistaken for the Roman numerals for 20,000. A legend sprang up that Bardsey Island was the last resting place for 20,000 saints. Certainly Bardsey Island (Ynys Enlli in Welsh) was a site for Christian pilgrimage. The crossing by sea was a hazardous one on account of the strong currents known as the Bardsey Races.

Braich y Pwll is the only place on the British mainland where the Spotted Rock Rose *(Tuberaria guttata)* can be seen growing in the wild.

Horace Love Pritchard, who died in 1927, was an inhabitant of Bardsey Island and bore the title of 'King'. He even wore a crown. Winford Vaughan Thomas in his book 'Wales' graphically describes this formidable character and his diet of crabs and beer.

Penrhyn Mawr — Gwynedd

12 miles from Abersoch
Grid ref: SH 168322
Maps: OS Explorer 253, OS Landranger 123.

The small, but beautiful, beach at Porth Iago, a true gem, has a car park. It takes a little finding on the north coast towards the western end of the Lleyn Peninsula. The beach of fine sand faces south-west and in the right weather conditions there is good surfing to be had.

A footpath from the beach runs round the headland. The defences of an Iron Age cliff castle can be seen. Just offshore is the small island of Maen Mellt. Fulmars nest on the ledges of the low cliffs.

Beach and headland of Penrhyn Mawr

Trwyn Porth Dinllaen   Gwynedd

2 miles from Nefyn
Grid ref: SH 276421
Maps: OS Explorer 253, OS Landranger 123.

This is a magnificent headland. The two sides of this finger of land are totally different. The west side is wild and rocky and is buffeted by gales. The east side is more sheltered, has sandy beaches and the tiny community of Porth Dinllaen which sports a welcome inn. Near the end of the headland is a small breakwater, harbour and lifeboat station. On high ground at the tip of the headland stands a National Coastwatch Station. These are always worth visiting. Banks and ditches of an Iron Age promontory fort are found halfway along the headland.

The finger-like Trwyn Porth Dinllaen

The Old Course of Nefyn Golf Club extends along the length of the headland. The Times golf correspondent listed his ten favourite courses and this was one of them. Another three of his top ten are also on or very near headlands: Royal Porthcawl, Turnberry and St Andrews.

Why is there a lifeboat station at this remote spot? In 1863 a great storm wrecked about 18 vessels that had taken shelter in Porth Dinllaen Bay. A local man, Robert Rees of Morfa Nefyn together with four others managed to rescue 28 men. This incident was the trigger. A boat was purchased with a donation from Lady Cotton Sheppard after whom the first boat was named. The service became operational in1864. The present boat was purchased from a gift from the Miss Hetty Mabel Rampton Charitable Trust and is named the 'Hetty Rampton'. The first cost about £250 and the present one about £560,000. Adjacent to the golf clubhouse is a well-presented little museum of the lifeboat station.

From Morfa Nefyn where there is a National Trust car park it is possible to walk to the end of the headland by a low route along the beach or a high route along a stone track beside the golf course, just 3km for the round trip.

Great Orme   ♿   Conwy

2 miles from Llandudno
Grid ref: SH 757845
Maps: OS Explorer OL17, OS Landranger 115.

This magnificent headland has just about everything expected of a headland except a feeling of isolation. It is too near the town of Llandudno for that. Great Orme means Great Worm or Dragon. The derivation is from the Norse, as in the adjacent Little Orme and also Worm's Head on the Gower Peninsula. So Wales has a family of dragon headlands.

Cliffs of Great Orme

Of the many interesting features on Great Orme space only permits brief mention of its main attractions.

The North Wales Path runs round the headland for 7km away from built up areas and numerous footpaths form a network over the headland. Great Orme is a massive block of Carboniferous limestone about 3km long and 1.5km wide and rising to 207m above the sea. The scenery is typical of a limestone landscape with even an area of limestone pavement.

Bronze Age Copper Mines. These are unique and Great Orme's greatest treasure. Three-thousand five-hundred years ago men with tools made of bone and stone dug several kilometres of tunnels through the rock of the headland. The tunnels seem to meander at random, but they followed the rich veins of copper ore. They have yielded 3,000 stone hammers and 30,000 animal bone diggers. A hard layer of rock prevented Bronze Age miners from going down deeper. It was thought that the Romans mined copper here, but there is no hard evidence for that presumption. The Victorians, however, dynamited the floor of the mine and extracted ore from below the Bronze Age mines. The nearest source of tin to be amalgamated with copper to form bronze came from Cornwall. Where Great Orme copper travelled to is unknown, but it could well have been exported to the Mediterranean as well as the Atlantic seaboard. Some of the tunnels are open to the public and walking through them makes one respect those who mined the copper several millennia ago.

Cromlech Burial Chamber. Near the copper mines stands an even older structure, a Neolithic burial chamber.

Great Orme Tramway. This is the oldest cable-hauled tramway in Britain having made its first journey in1902 and was opened to the public the following year. Tragedy struck in 1934 when a tow-bar on one of the cars snapped and the car hurtled downhill out of control and crashed into a wall. Two were killed and many were seriously injured. Today all cars have automatic emergency brakes. The trams are operated by winchmen at the halfway station. The upper section of the tramway reaches the highest point of the headland.

Great Orme Aerial Cable Cars. This, the longest aerial cable car in Britain, carries passengers from Happy Valley also to the summit of Great Orme.

Summit Complex. At the summit is a collection of buildings housing a restaurant, a shop and a visitor centre with displays that include a scale model of the whole headland. A small garden has been planted

Statue of wild goat on Great Orme

141

with rare plants found on Great Orme. This headland has a species of cotoneaster (*Cotoneaster integerrimus*) that grows wild nowhere else in Britain.

St Tudno's Church. St Tudno was a 6th century missionary who reputedly lived in a cave on Great Orme and founded a church here. He gave his name to the town of Llandudno. Open-air services are held outside the 13th-15th century church during summer months.

Happy Valley, Dry Ski Slope and Alpine Toboggan Run. This park on the eastern side of Great Orme has interest and activities for all ages.

Pen Dinas Hillfort. Above Happy Valley at the landward end of Great Orme is the Iron Age hill fort of Pen Dinas with four concentric ramparts and ditches and evidence of many round houses. A large boulder known as Tudno's Cradle was once used to determine guilt or innocence of the accused. If the suspected felon stood on the stone and it did not wobble he was deemed to be guilty and was thrown over the cliff. From here there are fine views of Llandudno and Little Orme.

Goats Great Orme is home to a flock of white Kashmiri goats. These magnificent animals have roamed the headland for more than a century. They are truly wild and the kids, in particular, should not be touched as they might then be rejected by their mothers. The mascot of the Royal Welsh Fusiliers belongs to the same species.

The Coastline. Marine Drive built in 1878 runs round the headland. Great Orme from the sea gives a totally different experience. The crowds and clamour are left behind. High cliffs and caves and solitude take over. Countless ships have met their end on these cliffs. The most famous incident was the wreck of the brig *Hornby* on New Year's Day 1824. In the middle of the night it ran into the high cliff, known today as Hornby Cliff, with such force that John Williams was flung from the bowsprit onto a ledge on the cliff. He was the sole survivor. By some superhuman effort he managed to scale the cliff in darkness much to the astonishment of the local people. He then gave up seafaring and worked as a miner in the Great Orme copper mines and would tell of his amazing escape to all who would listen.

Little Orme   Conwy

2 miles from Llandudno
Grid ref: SH 816828
Maps: OS Explorer OL17, OS Landranger 116.

This is Great Orme's baby sister on the east side of Llandudno. After the bustle of Great Orme and the resort of Llandudno the peace and tranquillity of Little Orme is

Little Orme from Great Orme across Llandudno Bay

welcome. Known in Welsh as 'Rhiwledyn' it rises 141m above the sea. To call this headland little is just to compare it with Great Orme. In fact the cliffs of Little Orme are high and a challenge to experienced rock climbers.

This headland is a nature reserve. Yellow rock-roses *(Helianthemum chamaecistus)* flower in profusion. A shag 'rookery' at the base of the cliffs can be smelt a long way off. There are a number of inland limestone cliffs, one with quite an overhang. Fine views are to be had in all directions. Lines of large stones reveal the pattern of ancient field boundaries.

The first book to be printed in Wales was *Y Drych Cristianogawl* (The Christian Mirror). The probable date was 1586/7. This was during the reign of Elizabeth I when Catholics were persecuted. In April 1587 the printing press was found hidden in a cave on Little Orme. It is possible that the book was actually printed in the cave. Those responsible were Robert Pue, a local squire and several others including Father William Davies who suffered the death of martyrs in 1593.

It is possible to park in a side street near the entrance path to Little Orme. Or follow the North Wales Path from Llandudno (3km) or Colwyn Bay (5km). Both are mainly along roads at this section. Little Orme is well worth the effort.

Point of Ayr   ♿   Flintshire

5 miles from Prestatyn
Grid ref: SJ 126850
Maps: OS Explorer 265, OS Landranger 116.

Here is a headland of contrasts. The first impression from the car park at Talacre Beach about 7km east of Prestatyn is of bingo, burgers and bouncy castles.

Walk a few metres and there is a superb sandy beach ideal for building sandcastles. Behind the beach is The Warren, an expanse

144

On the beach at Point of Ayr

of dunes and marsh which is a nature reserve and SSSI. The point itself is composed of salt marsh and mudflats rich with wading birds. A hide is provided. It is best to observe these waders at high tide when the rising waters push them towards the hide. At high water it is seen that the eastern tip of the headland is hook shaped. This is typical of sand and shingle spits like Spurn Head at the mouth of the Humber and Blakeney Point in Norfolk. It is due to the process of 'longshore drift', wave action moving loose material along the coast.

Rising from the beach and surrounded by water at high tide is Point of Ayr lighthouse. It was built in 1776, but has not shone since 1883. Quicksands around the base of the lighthouse demand some care. A notice board gives advice as to what to do if sinking!

Just behind the bird sanctuary at the point is the BHP Petroleum gas processing plant. Gas is piped to it from the Celtic gas-field in the Irish Sea.

One area that is now totally invisible because all trace has been removed is the Point of Ayr Colliery. The shafts were within a few metres of the sea and coal was mined from beneath the

Dee estuary. In 1996 this was the last deep coal mine in Wales to close. There are still coal reserves there if needed in the future.

Hilbre Point — Merseyside, Wirral

At Hoylake
Grid ref: SJ 203885
Maps: OS Explorer 266, OS Landranger 108.

Vast expanses of sand are found along the coast all the way from north Wales to the Lake District. Hilbre Point, at the western corner of the Wirral Peninsula, is typical. Extensive sands surround the point and link it at low tide with Hilbre Island 2km offshore. Do not attempt to cross these sands; they are not safe. The rock of the point is New Red Sandstone of Permo-Triassic age and shows distinct cross-bedding.

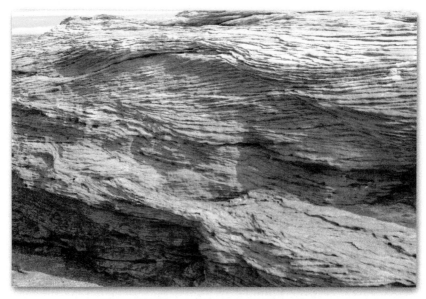

Cross-bedding in rocks at Hilbre Point

A house near the point incorporates what appears to be a lighthouse. This is a folly. There used to be a lighthouse in Hoylake. It was first built in 1764 and rebuilt a century later in 1865. It is now part of another private house and no longer functional.

The Royal Liverpool Golf Club is the second oldest seaside course in England. It was founded in 1869, just five years after the Royal North Devon Golf Club at Westward Ho! Stanley Road that runs from Hoylake along the north boundary of the golf course gives access to Hilbre Point.

It is possible to walk or cycle from Hilbre Point along the coast eastward to Perch Rock, New Brighton and southward all the way down the west coast of the Wirral Peninsula, much of it along the Wirral Way.

Perch Rock   ♿   Merseyside, Wirrall

1 mile from Wallasey
Grid ref: SJ 310945
Maps: OS Explorer 266, OS Landranger 108.

The headland of Perch Rock stands at the entrance to the Mersey and guards the approach to Liverpool. Its strategic importance is self-evident. A fort was planned here to protect Liverpool from Napoleon, but by the time a design had been approved Napoleon was dead! Construction began in 1826 and continued for four years. In common with many coastal batteries its main role has been deterrent rather than offensive. During its life as a military establishment it has undergone many modifications. It was finally decommissioned after the Second World War and was partially dismantled. A private purchaser obtained the fort in 1997 and has restored it to something approaching its original condition. The fort contains a number of permanent exhibitions of local military importance.

147

Entrance to the fort at Perch Rock

The name 'Perch Rock' derives from a wooden structure, or perch, carrying a light erected back in 1683 to guide ships into Rock Channel at the mouth of the Mersey. The present tower was built in 1827-1830 and stands 27m above a wave-washed rock platform. It was decommissioned in 1973 and is now in private ownership. For so many emigrants to the New World the view of this lighthouse was the last they saw of their homeland.

Formby Point   ♿ Merseyside, Sefton

2 miles from Formby
Grid ref: SD 269070
Maps: OS Explorer 285, OS Landranger 108.

Point is an exaggeration. It is decidedly blunt. A vast sandy beach curves round equally vast sand dunes backed by pinewoods. The area is National Trust property and

Sand dunes at Formby Point

nature trails run through the pinewoods that are home to red squirrels.

The beach is mainly sandy, but there are patches of mud that are exposed by the waves and then washed away. This mud was laid down about 4000 years ago. Sometimes it contains hoof-prints of red deer, auroch (extinct cattle from which domestic breeds are descended) and tracks of other animals, birds and even humans. These were Stone Age hunter-gatherers living at about the time of the building of Stonehenge.

Walk the Sefton Coastal Footpath 13km from Southport to Formby or wander the tracks through the Ainsdale National Nature Reserve just north of Formby Point.

Something of the extent of the sand further north along this coast can be appreciated from Rossall Point at Fleetwood. A concrete promenade, part of the Lancashire Coastal Way and Wyre Way, hugs the coast round the point. Here there are vast expanses of sand. Wooden groynes project out from the shore to prevent excessive longshore drift. Visit the newest National Coastwatch Station operational since 2014.

Sunderland Point   Lancashire

6 miles from Morecambe
Grid ref: SD 423553
Maps: OS Explorer 296, OS Landranger 102.

Full many a Sand-bird chirps upon the Sod
And many a moonlight Elfin round him trips
Full many a Summer's Sunbeam warms the Clod
And many a teeming cloud upon him drips.
But still he sleeps — till the awakening Sounds
Of the Archangel's Trump now life impart
Then the GREAT JUDGE his approbation founds
Not on man's COLOUR but his worth of heart.

This sentimental yet poignant verse marks 'Samboo's Grave' to be found on the seaward western side of the headland. A merchant on his way to Lancaster left a slave boy at Sunderland where he tragically contracted a disease to which he, presumably, had no immunity and died there in 1736. Not being a Christian he was not permitted a burial in consecrated ground. His tiny grave, marked by a cross and an inscribed stone, lies in a remote and isolated spot. It and Samboo are not forgotten. The grave is attended by visitors and decorated with flowers and painted stones.

Sunderland Point was once a thriving international port trading in rum, cotton, sugar and slaves, but was soon overtaken by Glasson on the opposite bank of the River Lune and by Lancaster further upstream. They were all important ports for the import of cotton.

Sunderland means 'separated land'. The tiny settlement of Sunderland Point is 7km south of Heysham. It can be reached by road across salt marshes from Overton, but not during the higher half of the tide. There is no other access by road. As the tide was rising I met a motorist there who was trying to get to Runcorn avoiding the M6!

150

Samboo's grave at Sunderland Point

The tip of the point can be reached partly along footpaths and finally along a boulder-strewn foreshore either 1km from Sunderland or 2km from a car park to the northwest near Hawthorne House Farm.

Heysham Head   ♿   Lancashire

At Heysham, 2 miles from Morecambe
Grid ref: SD 408617
Maps: OS Explorer 296, OS Landranger 96 and 97.

The pretty village of Heysham clusters round its narrow Main Street. A path leads up from Main Street, past St Peter's church dating back to the 8th century, and up onto the National Trust headland of Heysham Head.

151

Ancient graves at Heysham Head

Here stand the remains of St Patrick's Chapel that may have been built in the 8th century and fell into ruin 200 years later. The dates are uncertain. A unique feature is a group of six graves cut side by side into exposed bedrock. Four are large enough to take adult burials, but two must have been for children. Two other rock-hewn graves can be found on the other side of the chapel. This collection of graves is the oldest Christian monument in the northwest of England although its exact date is unknown.

There are only two sea cliffs in Lancashire and Heysham Head is one of them. The lower strata are of Millstone Grit laid down in a great river delta about 250 million years ago. This is overlain by another type of sandstone deposited in desert conditions 180 million years ago. A walk of less than 1km along these cliffs leads to the sands of Half Moon Bay.

J M W Turner painted 'Heysham and Cumberland Mountains' in which artistic licence allowed both Heysham Head and the mountains to be portrayed on an Alpine scale. It was on Heysham Head that the puppets Pinky and Perky were given their first public airing.

To be confusing Heysham North Round Head lies 2km south of Heysham Head and can be reached by footpath along Half Moon Bay. This headland forms the entrance to Heysham harbour from where ferries run to Douglas and Belfast. Only the north side has public access. At the end there is a round area of stone blocks and giant cobbles. On the south side of the harbour are two nuclear power stations. There is a car park at the south end of Half Moon Bay. Walk 1.5km or drive along North Shore Road, but the car must be left about 200m short of the tip of the headland.

On the north side of the road to the head is a 9m high sandstone tower on rocks called Near Naze. This was once a lighthouse, but was superseded by the light on the southern side of the harbour entrance. The Near Naze light was built in 1904 and only shone for twelve years. On the same rocks a little further from the shore is the stump of another light. This once carried a 21m high cast iron tower. It has not been functional for many years.

The foreshore when I visited was a feeding ground for several hundred oystercatchers and a flock of turnstones.

Humphrey Head   Cumbria

4 miles from Grange-over-Sands
Grid ref: SD 392732
Maps: OS Explorer OL7, OS Landranger 97.

Humphrey Head is a finger of limestone, very steep on the west side and gently sloping down to the east. Sand surrounds the headland as far as the eye can see except at high spring tides. The finger points south across Morecambe Bay to Heysham and Morecambe.

About 6km south of Grange-over-Sands there is a small car park at the end of a road signed to Humphrey Head. This is on the west side of the headland. The point of the headland can be reached by walking below the western cliffs. It is also possible to

Wide sands at Humphrey Head

climb a very steep path up the cliff, only to be attempted by the sure-footed in dry weather, then down the gradual grassy slope to the point. The limestone rock and maritime environment mean that rare lime-loving plants can thrive here. The east side of the headland is wooded.

Legend has it that the last wolf in England was killed on Humphrey Head. It is not even known in which century this happened. It could be 13th or even the 15th century. Wolves survived longer in Scotland and probably died out there in the 17th century. The oft-quoted reference to a man called MacQueen killing a wolf in 1743 may well be fictitious.

Walney Island
South End   ♿   Cumbria

6 miles from Barrow-in-Furness
Grid ref: SD 230621
Maps: OS Explorer OL6, OS Landranger 96.

The nature reserve at the south end of Walney Island could be aptly named Gull City. It provides accommodation to over 30,000 pairs of ground-nesting gulls, the largest

Viper's Bugloss at Walney Island South End.
Piel Castle in the distance

colony of gulls in Europe. Most are herring gulls, but with an appreciable number of lesser black-backed and a few greater black-backed gulls. This is the most southerly site in Britain where eider ducks breed. There are paths through the reserve and a number of hides at key sites. Wheelchairs have access to one of the hides. It is worth visiting the area for the drifts of viper's-bugloss *(Echium vulgare)* extending towards the end of the spit pointing to Piel Island. Butterflies fly up with every footstep. The lighthouse marks the furthest extent that the public is allowed.

The first lighthouse here was built of wood in 1791. This was before Barrow-in Furness docks were constructed and the light was for the benefit of ships heading for what is now the tiny port of Glasson that served the city of Lancaster. The lighthouse burnt down in 1803 and a more robust tower was built of stone the following year. An adjoining house was built for the keeper and his family. It was later divided into two dwellings. The light was electrified in 1953. The lighthouse was home to Britain's only female principal lighthouse keeper in the whole history of British lighthouses. Her name was Peggy Swarbrick. She was promoted to principal in 1975 and retired at the age of 74. The light was not automated until 2003.

Gravel is extracted from South End, but not during the nesting season. An oyster farm occupies some of the gravel pits. The oysters are grown here, first in heated tanks, then in cold until they are sold on to complete their growth in tanks in the sea elsewhere in Britain. They are ready to eat when three years old.

Walney Island is joined to the mainland by sand at low tide and is, therefore, included as a headland. It is possible to walk across at low tide. Ancient steppingstones indicate that this was the normal way across before there was a bridge. The steppingstones are appropriately named 'Widow's Crossing". It is better to go by the bridge. Walney Island is pickaxe shaped, with south and north ends similar in shape to the much larger Rhinns of Galloway.

From Barrow-in-Furness cross to Walney Island and drive south past a caravan park to a small car park at the nature reserve. There is a car park in Vickerstown near the bridge from Barrow and other car parks to the south. From Vickerstown to the South End is a 10km walk along the Cistercian Way.

Walney Island
North End   Cumbria

4 miles from Barrow-in-Furness
Grid ref: SD 182736
Maps: OS Explorer OL6, OS Landranger 96.

The name Walney may mean *Killer Whale Island* from Old Norse, or alternatively *Quaking Sands Island* from Old English.

The north end of Walney Island is a nature reserve similar to the south end. The Walney geranium grows here as well as at other sites on Walney Island, notably at Biggar Bank. This is a pale

156

pink variety of the bloody crane's-bill *(Geranium sanguineum)*. The reserve contains many different habitats: sand dunes, dune heath, vegetated shingle, salt marsh and inter-tidal mudflats. It is home to the rarest of Britain's six native amphibians, the Natterjack toad. Their numbers nationwide declined dramatically during the 20th century due to loss of habitat. They live in salt marsh, sand dunes and heath. Half of Britain's Natterjacks live in Cumbria and this site is of national importance. The daytime visitor to North End may not see any as they are nocturnal hunters.

Drive over the bridge from Barrow. 'Widow's Crossing' is a way across on steppingstones at low tide. The name would indicate that this is not recommended. There is a car park near Walney Airfield. A 3km walk past the airfield leads to the North End.

St Bee's Head   Cumbria

4 miles from Whitehaven
Grid ref: NX 940145
Maps: OS Explorer 303, OS Landranger 89.

But like not unto any one of these
Is that tall crag, that northward guards the bay,
And stands, a watchful sentry, night and day
Above the pleasant downs of old St Bee's

Straight-levelled as the bayonet's dread array,
His shelves abide the charge. Come one, come all!
The blustering surges at his feet shall fall
And writhe and sob their puny lives away!

The last two stanzas of 'St Bee's Head' by T. E. Brown (1830-1897)

St. Bee's Head is grand by any standard. *Jollie's Cumberland Guide and Directory* of 1811 states "From this eminence there is a sea-view seldom equalled, and surpassed by

Evening at St Bee's Head

none in the kingdom." It can be approached along the coast path from either St. Bees (4km fairly strenuous walk) or Whitehaven (5km). A stone block by the beach at St. Bee's indicates the start of the Coast-to-Coast path. From here a path climbs up to South Head. At first the cliffs have rounded tops and are broken up by cliff-falls. Further north towards North Head the cliffs are sheer and reach a magnificent 80m high. The rock is New Red Sandstone. This was laid down in the arid conditions of the Triassic Period (251 — 206 million years ago). Here and there are *erratics,* granite boulders brought here by ice during the last Ice Age. St. Bee's head is cut by a small stream that runs along the bottom of a steep, narrow valley reaching the sea at Fleswick Bay. Semiprecious gemstones can be found on the dark shingle beach. The cliffs are a major breeding site for seabirds in the north of England and are the only place in England that black guillemots breed.

St. Bee's Head marks a 'watershed' for coastal currents. South of the head beach material is swept south toward Walney Island and north of the headland it is taken north to the Solway Firth. This is of significance should there be a discharge of radioactive material from Sellafield.

The first lighthouse on North Head was built in 1718. It was a squat affair 9m high and 5m in diameter. A coal fire burnt on top to provide light to warn sailors. On windy nights the light was rather unreliable. By 1822 this was the only coal fired light in Britain, but it then burnt down to be

West door to the Priory Church of St Bee's

replaced by the tower that stands to the present day. Joseph Nelson designed the tower and the light was automated in 1987.

St Bee's lifeboat station is virtually on the beach at St Bee's. It houses an Atlantic 85 lifeboat. The station being designated a Discover Station my be open to the public in the summer.

So who was St. Bee? St. Bee or St. Bega is shrouded in mystery and there is more legend associated with her than history. She was reputed to be the daughter of an Irish king engaged to marry the son of the king of Norway. The night before the wedding she escaped down to the shore, but finding no boat she cut a turf and sailed on it across the sea to what is now St. Bee's Head. She is reputed to have founded a nunnery and is remembered for her championing of the poor. A Benedictine Priory was founded at St. Bee's in the 12th century and dedicated to St. Mary and St. Bee. Only the church remains with its magnificent west door. Of even greater fame is the Willis organ installed in1899. It is the last organ to have been built by 'Father' Henry Willis the founder of the firm that bears his name.

St. Bee's Man was a body found in a lead coffin during excavation at the Priory in 1981. The body was in a remarkably good state of preservation so that an autopsy revealed that he had died a violent death sometime between 1290 and 1500 AD. Under certain conditions of temperature and humidity the fat in the body undergoes a chemical change to produce 'adipocere', sometimes called 'grave wax' which preserves the body from further decay. This could explain medieval accounts of the bodies of saints being miraculously and perfectly preserved free of decay many years after their deaths.

Southerness Point   ♿   Dumfries and Galloway

15 miles from Dumfries
Grid ref: NX 977543
Maps: OS Explorer 313, OS Landranger 84.

The lighthouse at Southerness Point built on a wave-cut platform on the beach is the oldest on the Scottish mainland. The merchants of Dumfries arranged for it to be built in 1748. It is a striking building even though the light doesn't shine. Its base is square. The landward corner rises to the top of the tower, the other three are replaced by a circular balcony carrying the lantern.

Richard Oswald of Auchencruive founded the village of Southerness in the late 18th century in the hope that coal would be found there. His dream was never realised. Oswald had amassed a fortune through trading in slaves, sugar and tobacco. Campsites and caravan parks now dominate the village. The Paul Jones

Southerness Point lighthouse

Hotel is named after the famous, or infamous, John Paul Jones who was born in 1747 in a cottage on the Arbigland Estate just 3km up the coast. His birthplace is open to the public and houses a small museum. He joined the Merchant Navy as a boy. In the American War of Independence he took the side of the colonists and in the USA he is revered as the founder of the US Navy. The church at nearby Kirkbean has a font presented by the US Navy in his memory. He is less honoured in this country on account of his part in the attack on Whitehaven in 1778 and the Battle of Flamborough Head. Later he transferred his allegiance to Catherine the Great. Where was his respect for his roots?

The mountains of the Lake District form the skyline across the Solway Firth. Walk along the beach by all means, but keep to the shoreline for safety. Remember the tide comes in very fast across these extensive sandbanks.

Castlehill Point

Dumfries and Galloway

7 miles from Dalbeatie
Grid ref: NX 853523
Maps: OS Explorer 313, OS Landranger 84.

The viewpoint of Castlehill Point is reached along a 1.5km footpath from the pretty village of Rockcliffe. After 3 minutes walk there is a sign to Castlehill Point ½ mile; this is wishful thinking. Along the way is Nelson's grave, not Horatio, but Joseph. Joseph Nelson's body was washed ashore in January 1791 from the wreck of a smuggling ship from the Isle of Man. His widow in Whitehaven provided the stone to mark where his body was buried.

Castlehill Point in the distance

Remains of an Iron Age fort are clearly seen at the point. The headland rises 31m above the sea giving extensive views. St Bee's Head lies on the horizon nearly 40km away. Fishermen ply their trade of stake net fishing on the mudflats far below. The coast path to the east leads to a disused millstone quarry and at 1km the ruins of a 16th century laird's house at Gutcher's Isle.

Almorness Point
Dumfries and Galloway

6 miles from Dalbeatie
Grid ref: NX 840515
Maps: OS Explorer 313, OS Landranger 84.

A small hill 62m high called Moyle at the end of the headland affords 360° views of this incredibly indented and complex yet gentle coastline with the inlets of Rough Firth, Orchardton Bay and Auchencairn Bay, and promontories, islands and sandbanks all spread out below. Inland are the hills and woods of Dumfriesshire. The headlands along this coast are of granite like the mass of Criffel that rises to 569m behind Southerness Point. The distant mountains of Cumbria beckon across the Solway Firth.

Take a minor road from Palnackie as far as possible to a small car park just before Almorness House. Walk on towards Almorness House, then through a gate and follow a wide, stony track through mixed woods. Where it branches keep left down to Horse Isles Bay. This is a beautiful crescent-shaped sandy bay with reeds growing in the salt water. Walk to the far end of the beach and along a narrow footpath across a boggy area towards another smaller sandy bay called White Port. Before the path drops down to the beach bear right along an indistinct path to the summit of Moyle.

163

The road to Almorness House passes Orchardton Tower, the only circular, fortified farmhouse in Scotland. One John Cairns built it in 1450. It is possible to climb to the top of this remarkably well preserved building and to imagine the troubled times when it was necessary to protect property from marauding raiders.

Balcary Point Dumfries and Galloway

10 miles from Dalbeatie
Grid ref: NX 828492
Maps: OS Explorer 313, OS Landranger 84.

Leave the A711 at Auchencairn and take the minor road to Balcary Bay Hotel. From the car park near the hotel a footpath is signed to Balcary Point and Rescarrel. This passes over pasture, through woods and emerges onto the open headland. From the car park to the headland is about one kilometre. A short distance offshore is Hestan Island with its lighthouse. Daft Ann from Auchencairn reputedly tried to reach Hestan Island by placing stepping-stones in front of her, but drowned in the attempt. The rocks at the south end of Hestan Island are called Daft Ann's Steps. In which case it seems she must have reached the island and was not so daft after all! Just round the tip of the headland are fine cliffs and an offshore stack called Lot's Wife.

Approaching storm at Balcary Point

164

Smuggling used to be a profitable line of business along this coast. Smugglers were so blatant that they reputedly built a manor house on the shores of Balcary Bay where they could store their loot. The cellars of Balcary Bay Hotel have walls that are five feet thick with doors that open towards the sea and were probably at one time stuffed with contraband.

Ree of Ross · Dumfries and Galloway

7 miles from Kirkcudbright
Grid ref: NX 652433
Maps: OS Explorer 312, OS Landranger 83.

The dominant feature of this headland is the small island off its tip. This is Little Ross Island with a lighthouse, a beacon and a small cottage with a grass track leading up

Cliffs at the Ree of Ross

to it. This beautiful scene is difficult to reconcile with the events of 1960. Two assistant lighthouse keepers, Robert Dickson and Hugh Clark were manning the lighthouse. A local man and his son landed on Little Ross Island for a picnic and heard a telephone ringing continuously in the cottage. They entered the cottage and found Hugh Clark's body, but no sign of Robert Dickson. Dickson was later arrested, convicted of the murder and sentenced to hang. He was reprieved, but took his own life in prison. The light was automated in 1961, but just too late to save Hugh Clark or Robert Dickson.

The headland of the Ree of Ross stands on the west side of the entrance to Kirkcudbright Bay. About 7km southwest of Kirkcudbright along the B727 turn left along a minor road that leads to Ross Bay. It is possible to park beside the road on the south side of Ross Bay. A wicket gate and public footpath notice at Blackstone indicates a public right of way. The track crosses pastureland and at the second wall turns right beneath a small wood towards the hill of Meikle Ross. Strike left up and over the smaller hill of the Ree of Ross. From the car and back would be 2.5km.

Further along the coast to the west, on the western side of the entrance to Fleet Bay is the delightful little headland of Ringdoo Point. Here is one of the best beaches in Dumfries and Galloway. Part of the beach is made entirely of shells many of which are unbroken. This is a popular place for swimming and water sports. Access is from the A75 along a minor road past Mossyard farm to a campsite where there is a small car park. A 300m path reaches the beach near the point.

Eggerness Point

Dumfries and Galloway

9 miles from Wigtown
Grid ref: NX 492465
Maps: OS Explorer 311, OS Landranger 83.

Walk from the village of Garlieston eastward along a road and continue along a footpath to the right towards the shore. (Think of the paperwork that went into providing this footpath. An information board states that it is a Dumfries and Galloway Countryside Path; South of Scotland European Partnership Objective 2; Southwest Scotland Visitor Access Project part financed by the European Union. How complicated life has become! But we are grateful to them all.) The path passes through woods close to the shore then up along hayfields and pasture. To reach the point itself it is necessary to battle through the wood and onto a boulder-strewn foreshore. The walk from Garlieston to the end of Eggerness Point is about 2km.

Lord Garlies designed the village of Garlieston on a grid pattern in 1760. In the past it echoed to the sounds of shipbuilding. Rope and sailcloth were made in the mill and exported worldwide. Nearby at Rigg Bay Mulberry harbours were assembled before the D-Day Normandy landings. A museum in Garlieston houses an informative Mulberry Harbour Exhibition.

Isle of Whithorn ♿ Dumfries and Galloway

4 miles from Whithorn
Grid ref: NX 480360
Maps: OS Explorer 311, OS Landranger 83.

E very stone of this headland (although called an isle it is really a headland) breathes history. The short walk from the car park to the end of the headland crosses ridges and furrows, clear evidence of farming in medieval times. Just beyond the ridge and furrow the path cuts through three banks and ditches of an Iron Age promontory fort.

St Ninian is reputed to have crossed the Solway Firth and landed at the Isle of Whithorn in 397AD, coming from Carlisle at

Isle of Whithorn

168

the request of people on the Scottish side of the firth. Little is known for certain about his life. The Venerable Bede described him as a Briton, a deeply revered bishop and a man of great sanctity. Other sources relate that he travelled to Rome to train and returned to Whithorn. He built a Candida Casa, a shining or white house, at Whithorn Priory. This could well be how Whithorn got its name. A small chapel stands on the headland. The walls and gable ends survive, but the roof has gone. This chapel was probably built around 1300. Pilgrims visiting the priory and shrine of St Ninian would arrive by sea, land at the little harbour and before walking the 5km or so to the priory would stop at the chapel to give thanks for their safe journey. A 'Witness Cairn' was set up in 1997 to commemorate the arrival of St Ninian 1600 years previously. Excavations at the village of Whithorn in the 1980s provided many artefacts revealing evidence of a sophisticated society that traded with the Mediterranean in the period after St Ninian arrived. The Visitor Centre in the village of Whithorn, near the ruins of the cathedral and the Northumbrian Monastery, graphically displays the history of the area. The museum contains what is described as the finest collection of early Christian carved stones in Scotland.

St Ninian's Cave is west of Burrow Head and about 7km south of the village of Whithorn. There is a car park from which a delightful wooded path through Physgill Glen leads to the shore 1km away. Several ancient crosses carved into the walls of the cave are difficult to identify. Others have been removed to the museum in Whithorn. Mass is held here each year on the last Sunday in August. Blackthorn *(Prunus spinosa)* and hawthorn *(Crataegus monogyna)* grow as creeping plants in the shingle rather than as the more familiar bushes.

Two memorials stand on the Isle of Whithorn to the crew of seven men who lost their lives when the scallop dredger *Solway Harvester* sank in atrocious weather conditions in the Irish Sea in January 2000. Several of the crew came from Whithorn.

Burrow Head Dumfries and Galloway

6 miles from Whithorn
Grid ref: NX 457341
Maps: OS Explorer 311, OS Landranger 83.

Burrow Head was the site of the burning of the Wicker Man in the final scene of the 1973 cult horror film of the same name. Other scenes were shot in the village of Whithorn and various nearby locations.

Burrow Head marks the southern point of The Machars meaning flat land. The headland is bounded by high cliffs which extend along the coast in both directions. The headland can be reached from Burrow Head Holiday Village just 1km away where it is possible to park, but kindly inform staff at reception. Particular care should be taken as the path runs very close to the cliff edge. The cliffs are cut by geos and pierced by caves. A 100ft high sea-stack stands near the holiday village.

Massive Burrow Head

170

A cliff-top path runs about 4km from St Ninian's Cave to Burrow Head and eastward for another kilometre.

Mull of Galloway   ♿   Dumfries and Galloway

22 miles from Stranraer
Grid ref: NX 159306
Maps: OS Explorer 309, OS Landranger 82.

This is surely a five star headland, the most southerly point in Scotland. The Rhins, a pickaxe shaped projection about 40km north to south, form the western limits of Galloway. The southern end turns sharply east to form the Mull of Galloway.

Mull of Galloway with the view across
Luce Bay to the Galloway coast

Mull of Galloway lighthouse among the heather

The Mull itself is high and surrounded with cliffs, but where it joins the South Rhins the land is low-lying and narrow, almost making the Mull an island. At one time sailors used to haul their boats across this isthmus from the open sea to Luce Bay to avoid the treacherous currents around the headland. These angry swirling currents are seen clearly from the tip of the headland as the tide rushes in and out of Luce Bay. The Antrim hills in Ireland, the Isle of Man and the Cumbrian coast are all visible on a clear day.

Excellent facilities are provided for the many visitors who come each year. The area is large enough, though, not to feel crowded and a short walk along the cliff top quickly restores a sense of remoteness and isolation. A Visitor Centre gives a clear and lively account of the natural features of the mull. Video cameras transmit views of seabirds nesting on the cliffs. During the summer an RSPB warden is available to answer questions about the abundant local wildlife. The Gallie Craig Coffee House (closed in winter) with its cliff-top terrace and eco-friendly turf roof provides food and drink with stunning views.

Robert Stevenson designed and built the lighthouse between 1828 and 1830. It is possible to climb the lighthouse at weekends in the summer. The surrounding three cottages, originally for the lighthouse keeper, his two assistants and their families, are now holiday apartments. At first the light was a paraffin lamp giving 29,000 candlepower. The present light gives 1,700,000 candlepower. The lighthouse was fully automated in 1988 and together with all other lighthouses round the Scottish coast is controlled from the headquarters of the Northern Lighthouse Board in Edinburgh. The foghorn that can be reached by a flight of steps partway down the cliff was finally silenced in the 1980s.

A series of three Iron Age banks and ditches across the mull protects an area of 57 hectares making this the largest Iron Age promontory fort in Scotland. From the Mull of Galloway the Roman general Julius Agricola may have gazed across to the hills of Ireland. His dream to conquer Ireland and thus make Britain more secure from attack was never realised.

The rocks of the headland are Silurian greywackes, a type of sandstone with varying grain size and a clay component, about 430 million years old. The collision of tectonic plates crumpled the land so that now the rock strata are aligned nearly vertically. Rocks of Silurian age occur in a broad band forming much of the Southern Uplands of Scotland from the Mull of Galloway on the west to near St Abb's Head on the east.

There is a legend that the Picts who inhabited the Mull of Galloway, before they were driven to the northeast coast of Scotland, brewed the finest fraoch (heather ale) to be found anywhere. Niall, King of Ulster, with the aid of a traitorous Pictish druid, invaded and fought the Picts to discover the recipe. Every Pict was killed except for one old man and his severely wounded son. A bargain was struck that if one of the two revealed the recipe his life would be spared. The old man, seeing that his son was mortally wounded, said that he would recite the recipe to one man, the traitor druid. The son was duly thrown to his death off the cliff. The old man took the druid to the cliff-top, maybe he told him the recipe or maybe not, but it was lost for ever as he hurled himself and the druid into the crashing surf below. Fraoch is still available, but who knows whether it is as good as the Pictish brew?

Ardwell Point   Dumfries and Galloway

12 miles from Stranraer
Grid ref: NX 067450
Maps: OS Explorer 309, OS Landranger 82.

From the A716 that runs down the east coast of South Rhinns take an unclassified road signed to Clachanmore. At the crossroads go straight ahead, do not turn left to another Ardwell that is on the east coast. Ardwell Point is on the west. There is a car park at Ardwell Bay. Follow a coastal path south just a few hundred metres to the rocky point.

A little further along the path is what looks from the distance to be a large cairn of rocks on a spit of land between two geos. Closer inspection reveals the ruins of a once imposing broch dating from about 100 BC. Brochs were approximately circular dry-stone structures with inner and outer walls enclosing a staircase. They are the most complex dry-stone structures in existence and are found only in Scotland and the Northern Isles. This one on Ardwell Point, called Doon Castle, has largely collapsed. Sufficient remains to show clearly the circular structure and, unusually, two entrance passageways, one facing the sea and the other on the opposite side of the broch. Some of the massive stones are more than a metre in length.

Corsewall Point ♿   Dumfries and Galloway

11 miles from Stranraer
Grid ref: NW 980727
Maps: OS Explorer 309, OS Landranger 82.

Corsewall Point stands at the north-westerly point of the North Rhinns peninsula. The lighthouse was built by Robert Stevenson in 1817 and was automated in1994. It is reported that Concorde flew over it in November 1970 on a trial flight and broke several windows. Although the lighthouse is still fully functional it, together with the surrounding buildings, has been tastefully converted into a hotel. The coastal views are superb. At sea numerous craft including the ferries between Cairnryan – Larne and Stranraer – Belfast ply to and fro.

Corsewall Point lighthouse and hotel

Turnberry Point   ♿   South Ayrshire

5 miles from Girvan
Grid ref: NS 195069
Maps: OS Explorer 326, OS Landranger 70 and 76.

Here golf is king. Of the three courses, Ailsa, Arran and Kintyre, many golfers rank Ailsa among the finest in Britain if not the world. On this course in 1977 Tom Watson won the Open in a thrilling duel with Jack Nicklaus which has gone down as one of the most memorable in golfing history. The long façade of the luxurious Turnberry Hotel gazes down over the courses. Out at sea the eye is drawn like a magnet to the mass of Ailsa Craig. Two footpaths cross the golf courses to the point, lighthouse and castle. Due care must be taken when crossing fairways and if there is doubt as to the way to follow it is necessary to ask.

Turnberry Hotel

During World War 1 the area of the golf courses was a training ground for the Royal Flying Corps, the forerunner of the Royal Air Force. In World War 2 it was again an airfield of Royal Air Force Coastal Command. For a second time buildings and runways were removed and the courses rebuilt. The remains of a runway are still present and form part of a path to the point.

Little remains of Turnberry Castle except a few low walls and a fragment of vaulting. The cliff-top site is magnificent. Although the cliffs are not high they make up for this by their ruggedness. The castle is one of two or three contenders for the birthplace of Robert the Bruce on 11th July 1274. His father was 6th Earl of Annandale and his mother the formidable Countess of Carrick. He lived through a turbulent time in Scottish history. For years he fought a guerrilla campaign against the English culminating in the defeat of the numerically superior English army at the Battle of Bannockburn in 1314. He is thought by many to be one of the greatest guerrilla fighters of all time. He died on 7th June 1329 and his body was buried at Dunfermline Abbey. His heart was taken at his request on a crusade headed for the Holy Land. It reached no further than Spain and was eventually returned and buried at Melrose Abbey.

Turnberry lighthouse stands on the site of the castle and close to the famous 9th tee of the Ailsa course. Thomas Stevenson examined the offshore rocks which claimed many ships, but decided they were not suitable to support a lighthouse. He, with his brother David, designed and built the present lighthouse on Turnberry Point. The light came into operation in 1873 and was fully automated in 1986.

A pleasant 4km walk is to start from the car park in Turnberry, walk north along the road, cross the golf courses to Turnberry Point and return along the beach or the footpath through the dunes just above the beach.

Troon Headland ♿ South Ayrshire

At Troon
Grid ref: NS 307316
Maps: OS Explorer 326 and 333, OS Landranger 70.

The town of Troon takes its name from the headland. Troon is Gaelic for 'nose' or 'headland'. (Compare the Welsh 'Trwyn") The town is almost completely surrounded by sea and golf courses. There are no fewer than six courses, several of championship standard. The rocky tip of the headland affords views of offshore rocks often covered with shags and other sea birds with the mountains of Arran in the background.

The banana-shaped headland points northwest with a natural harbour on the northeast side protected by breakwaters. Traditional occupations were fishing and salt-panning until the 4th Duke of Portland developed the port and installed quays, wet

The marina at Troon near the headland

and dry docks and launched the ship-building industry which brought prosperity to the town. Many of the ferries plying the Western Isles were built in these yards. Running along the south-west edge of the headland is a high bank, Ballast Bank, built from the ballast from ships calling at Troon to pick up cargoes of coal bound for Ireland. Troon was once a major coal port. In the late 19th century it was one of the top ten coal ports in Britain. The Duke of Portland built a railway to carry coal from Kilmarnock to Troon. Later carriages brought visitors to Troon opening the way to its popularity as a holiday resort. At first horses provided traction for the carriages until the Duke of Portland bought a steam engine from George Stephenson and named it 'The Duke'.

Nowadays the harbour is home to a large marina full of pleasure boats. There is no longer shipbuilding, but there is still an important fishing industry and fish market. Ferries sail from here to Larne and Belfast.

Farland Head   ♿   North Ayrshire

3 miles from Ardrossan
Grid ref: NS 179485
Maps: OS Explorer 341, OS Landranger 63.

Portencross Castle stands proudly on the shore at Farland Head and dominates the scene. A predecessor to the present building stood on Auld Hill above the village. The castle that stands today dates from the 14th century. It was inhabited till 1739 when a great storm blew away the roof. The impressive walls still stand to a height of four storeys. The castle played an important role in Scottish royal history. It was built during the reign of Robert II and several charters are known to have been signed within its walls.

A tiny harbour lies below the castle walls. It is believed that the bodies of Scottish kings from Cináed mac Ailpin (Kenneth

MacAlpine) (died 858) to Máel Coluim mac Donnachada (Malcolm MacDonald) (died 1093) were brought overland to Portencross then transferred by boat from the little harbour to Iona for burial.

Portencross Castle,
Farland Head

Just to the north are high cliffs, home to peregrine falcons, above a raised beach. Look out for pudding stone and a dolerite intrusion. Hunterston Nuclear Power Station stands on the coast just 3km to the north. Little Cumbrae Island is seen in the Firth of Clyde with a castle that, in the distance, looks very like the one at Portencross.

The village of Portencross lies just 3km west of West Kilbride. There are pleasant walks along the coast north towards the power station and in the opposite direction to West Kilbride.

Toward Point   ♿   Argyll and Bute

6 miles from Dunoon
Grid ref: NS 136672
Maps: OS Explorer 363, OS Landranger 63.

On the foreshore two distinct types of rock can easily be distinguished. To the northwest is Dalradian schist, a metamorphic rock about 500 million years old, while to the southeast is a sedimentary conglomerate rock laid down about

Toward Point

100 million years later in the Devonian Period. These two rock types are on either side of the Highland Boundary Fault that cuts obliquely across Scotland and demarcates the Highlands from the Midland Valley. The Highland Boundary Fault occurred when the Caledonian mountain range was formed as a result of the collision of two tectonic plates. Movement, both vertical and horizontal in the line of this fault was on a grand scale. The vertical movement has been estimated to be in the region of 4000 metres. On the east coast of Scotland the Highland Boundary Fault enters the sea again at Garron Point near Stonehaven.

Toward Point is the most southerly point of the Cowal Peninsula and lies 11km south of Dunoon. There are views west to Rothesay on the Isle of Bute, south to the island of Great Cumbrae and west to the Ayrshire coast. The lighthouse dates from 1812 and was designed by Robert Stevenson. It is operational and not open to the public.

Ardlamont Point   Argyll and Bute

27 miles from Lochgilphead
Grid ref: NR 982639
Maps: OS Explorer 362, OS Landranger 62.

Ardlamont Point is the southern tip of the tongue of land that separates Loch Fyne from the Kyles of Bute. An unclassified road runs from the village of Kames towards the point. It is possible to park near a telephone box where the road turns sharp right to Ardlamont House. A track leads 1.5km south to the point.

After passing Point Farm a large boulder with about a dozen cup marks stands in the pasture. The origin and purpose of these Neolithic or Bronze Age marks are unknown.

At the point are three rocky mounds. Two have vertical cliffs to seaward. All could have been fortified and one carries the name Dun nan Muileach indicating that it probably was.

Barmore Island   ♿   Argyll and Bute

2 miles from Tarbert
Grid ref: NR 870716
Maps: OS Explorer 357, OS Landranger 62.

Patronise the facilities of the Stonefield Castle Hotel 3 km north of Tarbert on the Kintyre Peninsula. Walk down through the hotel grounds and cross to Barmore Island along a causeway. Follow a defined track to the left round the north end of the 'island'. The path cuts back across the 'island' between two low hills and continues as a narrow path back to the causeway. Fish eagles, seals and the occasional otter may be seen. Wild flowers are abundant.

Stonefield Castle Hotel from Barmore Island

The hotel is mainly in the Scottish Baronial style with modern additions. When viewed from Barmore Island, thrusting its turrets through the trees, it forms a romantic picture loved of the Victorians. Only a little imagination conjures up a vision of a lone piper, a huge log fire, hunting trophies on the wall and a boar's head served to the laird and his lady sitting at either end of a long oak table.

Skipness Point   ♿   Argyll and Bute

13 miles from Tarbert
Grid ref: NR 913573
Maps: OS Explorer 357, OS Landranger 62.

The magnificent Skipness Castle dominates the area. Information boards give a clear picture of the castle's history. Construction started in the early 13th century and

183

Skipness Castle

some of this building is incorporated into the present castle. Most of what is seen today was built around 1300. The tower house at the northeast corner is 16th century. In succession the castle was in the hands of the MacSweens, MacDonalds, Forresters and Campbells. It was abandoned as a fortress in the 17th century. Today it is in a remarkably good state of preservation and is open to the public to enjoy.

Skipness Point is a low-lying spit of grass and rock at the end of a crescent pebble beach. The mountains of Arran form a fine backdrop.

Nearby stands the remains of Kilbrannan Chapel built in the 13th or 14th century. It was dedicated to St Brendan the Voyager (484 – 587) who also gave his name to Kilbrannan Sound, the sea that separates Kintyre from Arran. Legend has it that St Brendan undertook a seven-year voyage with a company of monks to the Land of Delights. The island of Madeira is one contender for this title. Legend apart; at the chapel are fine medieval grave slabs and several ancient gravestones with relief carvings depicting the trades of those buried there.

The B8001 becoming the B842 runs down the east side of the Kintyre Peninsula from Skipness to Campbeltown while the west side is served by the A83. From the car park at Skipness to the end of the point is an easy walk of a little over 1km.

Skipness is on the Kintyre Way, a long distance footpath that runs from Tarbert in the north right down to Dunaverty at the southern end of the Kintyre Peninsula. The whole distance is 141km as it sometimes follows the coast and also criss-crosses the peninsula several times. From Tarbert to Skipness is a 14km walk inland mainly through forest.

Carradale Point — Argyll and Bute

15 miles from Campbeltown
Grid ref: NR 815363
Maps: OS Explorer 356, OS Landranger 68 and 69.

At the end of the headland is Scotland's best preserved vitrified fort. The walls of this Iron Age fort were built of stone in a massive wooden framework. When the fort was burnt to the ground over 2000 years ago the heat was so great that the stones partially melted and fused together. There are many of these vitrified walls visible above ground.

There is a car park at the east end of the fine sandy beach of Carradale Bay. A footpath leads from the car park, running over rocks and across an isthmus that is covered by high spring tides, to the rocky tip of the headland 1km distant. On the way huge boulders of incredibly folded and faulted Dalradian schists litter the shore.

The little harbour of Carradale with its colourful fishing boats is chocolate box perfect. Carradale is on the long distance walking trail, the Kintyre Way. The section from Tayinloan on the west side of the Kintyre Peninsula across to Carradale is 26km and Carradale via Saddell to Campbeltown 32km for energetic hikers.

185

Carradale Harbour

Stones of the vitrified fort on Carradale Point

Island Davaar

Argyll and Bute

2 miles from Campbeltown
Grid ref: NR 762201
Maps: OS Explorer 356, OS Landranger 68.

Island Davaar stands high like a Rock of Gibraltar at the mouth of Campbeltown Loch. Instead of apes it supports a colony of wild goats. A 1km causeway of fine shingle, The Doirlinn, connects it to the southern shore about three hours either side of low water. Check with the Tourist Information Office in Campbeltown when it is safe to cross. The Gaelic name is Eilean Dà Bhàrr after Saint Barre.

Having crossed the causeway a wide grassy track reaches the lighthouse on the north side. It was designed by David and Thomas Stevenson, built in 1854 and automated in1983. In the opposite direction a tramp along the rocky shore leads to a cave.

Shingle Causeway to Island Davaar

187

In 1887 Archibald MacKinnon secretly painted a life-size depiction of the crucifixion of Christ on the wall of the cave. Some thought the painting had appeared miraculously, but the painter revealed his identity later the same year. Having venerated the painting when it was thought to be a miracle the local people now turned on the painter with anger and criticised the painting as worthless. MacKinnon left for England, but returned as an old man in 1934 to restore the painting. Such is the fickleness of public opinion that this time he was welcomed back by the civic authorities as a celebrity. In 2006 a vandal seriously defaced the painting, but it was quickly restored to its former condition.

Mull of Kintyre — Argyll and Bute

16 miles from Campbeltown
Grid ref: NR 587083
Maps: OS Explorer 356, OS Landranger 68.

The Mull of Kintyre at the southern end of the Kintyre Peninsula is one of Britain's major headlands. It is built on a grand scale and the views are huge, stretching from Islay, Fair Head on the Irish coast and right round to the coast of Ayrshire.

The lighthouse is on the western aspect of the smoothly rounded end of the peninsula. From a car park high above the lighthouse a road zigzags for a couple of kilometres and dropping about 250m down to the light which is itself about 80 metres above the sea. Thomas Smith, the founder of the engineering firm that subsequently employed members of the Stevenson lighthouse-building family, designed and built a lighthouse here. It became operational in November 1788. At that time there was no road down the length of the Kintyre Peninsula and material and supplies were brought by boat, landed six miles away and transported to the site on horseback. The lighthouse was rebuilt in

The lighthouse on the Mull of Kintyre

1821 and 1830, electrified in 1976 and fully automated in 1996. Lighthouse keepers cottages huddle round the base of the squat lighthouse and walls clearly demarcate the fields where the keepers would have grown vegetables and maybe kept a cow or a horse. The cottages are now holiday lets.

A memorial cairn beside the road down to the lighthouse remembers the four crew and twenty-five passengers of the Chinook helicopter that crashed here on 2nd June 1994. The passengers were senior members of the security forces flying from Belfast to Inverness. The cause of the disaster has never been established beyond doubt.

Memorial to those who died in the helicopter crash of 1994 on the Mull of Kintyre

A path leads south from the lighthouse along the cliff-top to a fog signal 1km away. Although overgrown it is easy to follow as it is equipped with a handrail for much of its length. The cliff scenery is majestic.

Dalradian rocks that form a great swathe across Scotland south of the Great Glen from Aberdeenshire to the Mull of Kintyre take their name from the ancient Kingdom of Dalreada. These are mainly schists that date from the late Precambrian to early Cambrian periods. (Adam Sedgwick (1785-1873) coined the term Cambrian for early fossil-bearing rocks in north Wales.) The Mull of Kintyre consists of late Dalradian schist of the early Cambrian period, about 560 million years old.

Only a fraction of those who have heard of the Mull of Kintyre from the song composed by Sir Paul McCartney will have visited the Mull in person. Here music is in the air and Campbeltown hosts a lively music festival each summer.

Rhunahaorine Point   ♿   Argyll and Bute

18 miles from Tarbert
Grid ref: NR 690493
Maps: OS Explorer 357, OS Landranger 62.

This low-lying spit of shingle and sand, rather like a miniature Dungeness, points across to the centre of Gigha Island. It is possible to park in the visitor's parking area of the caravan site and walk along an easy track past a pine plantation and a World War 2 lookout post to the end of the headland. Common and arctic terns nest here and small waders frequent the headland throughout the year.

The Covenanters gained a victory over Royalist forces in the Battle of Rhunahaorine Moss at this point in 1647.

Grace and speed at Rhunahaorine Point

Ardpatrick Point   Argyll and Bute

11 miles from Tarbert
Grid ref: NR 732578
Maps: OS Explorer 357, OS Landranger 62.

Near the west end of West Loch Tarbert an unclassified road leaves the B 8024 for Ardpatrick. Park beside the road near Ardpatrick and walk on past a pier and old Ferry House. The track becomes rough and later just a footpath. Go through a gap in the wall on the right and follow the high ground, there is no path, to the ruined cottage called Point House. The land then drops down steadily to the point where there is a small wooden shack. This is quite a strenuous hike of about 3km to the point.

This is a low rocky headland composed of Dalradian quartzite. There are views of the Kintyre coast to the east and the hills of Jura to the west. It is purported to be where St Patrick landed on his way from Ireland to Iona.

View from Ardpatrick Point

Point of Knap　　　　Argyll and Bute

19 miles from Lochgilphead
Grid ref: NR 700721
Maps: OS Explorer 358, OS Landranger 62.

There is interest here for the energetic and the more sedentary, for the lovers of nature and of art. The tramp to the point just 2km away can be heavy going, but rewarding. From a small car park at Balimore an ill-defined path crosses a swampy area to a track which soon peters out. Continue in the same direction keeping to high ground and passing a cairn and trig point on the right. The final descent to the point is rough going with a scramble down between two cliffs. The views of Islay and Jura make the effort worthwhile. The grain of the land along the coast all the way from the Great Glen to Knapdale is northeast to southwest. The headlands point southwest and along the coast are numerous thin linear islands like splinters. The Point of Knap is composed of epidiorite, a metamorphic rock of the Dalradian series of late Precambrian age.

Kilmory Chapel stands 1.5km back along the road from the car park. This 13th century chapel contains a fine collection of medieval carved grave slabs and crosses, many of which were brought in from the sur-rounding graveyard for pre-servation. One of the finest is the MacMillan Cross that was carved around 1500.

Depicted on the cross

MacMillan Cross in Kilmory Chapel. Point of Knap

are the crucifixion of Christ, his Mother and St John. On the shaft beneath the crucifixion is a finely carved sword. On the reverse side are elaborate interlaced patterns and a hunting scene. This is one of the best-preserved and most beautiful medieval crosses in all Scotland. Crosses were erected to the glory of God and were never grave markers. Several medieval grave slabs at Kilmory Chapel show knights in armour and the tools of the trade of the deceased.

Stone carvers came from Ireland to Iona in the first millen-nium. Scottish stone carvers learnt the art and brought it to the mainland where it took root, particularly in Argyll where five separate styles of carving can be distinguished. Notable sites in the vicinity are Keills Chapel on the adjacent headland of Rubha na Cille, Kilberry Castle on the Kintyre Peninsula at NR708642 and Keil Church at Lochaline on the Morvern Peninsula.

Tip of the Point of Knap looking across to Jura

Further back along the road is Castle Sween, the oldest stone castle still standing in Scotland dating from the 12th century. It was held successively by the Sweens (Suibhne or MacSween), Earls of Menteith, MacDonalds Lords of the Isles, Campbells Earls of Argyll and was finally seized in 1645 by Alexander MacDonald a Royalist in the Civil War. It has not been occupied since.

The Crinan Canal cuts across from Crinan to Lochgilphead. Turn off the B 8025 about 2km south of the Crinan Canal along a road signed to Achnamara, Castle Sween and Kilmory Chapel. Drive along this road as far as possible, about 20km, to the small car park at Balimore.

Rubha na Cille
(Keills Point)　　Argyll and Bute

17 miles from Lochgilphead
Grid ref: NR 682791
Maps: OS Explorer 358, OS Landranger 55/62.

The Gaelic name Rubha na Cille means 'The Headland of the Church or Burial Ground'. The chapel here must be visited. (See the headland 'Island of Danna' how to get here by road.)

Meanwhile the route to the end of the headland is along a narrow, often indistinct path that starts at a stile near the chapel where a sign directs to Keills Point. There is no danger of getting lost as the path simply follows the crest of a very narrow finger of land just over 1km long. Erupting along this ridge are columns

Looking along the length of Rubha na Cille

195

8th Century cross at Rubha na Cille

and slabs of jagged rock like dragon's teeth. One day there may be a car ferry between Keills and Lagg on Jura, but the end of this headland will remain remote.

In the chapel is a fine collection of medieval carved crosses and grave slabs. The chapel may date from the 12th or early 13th century. Of particular note is a superb cross probably carved as early as the 8th century. It is carved just on one face. At the crossing is a boss surrounded by four beasts representing the evangelists. Above stands St Michael and beneath is the seated figure of Christ. The shaft is richly decorated with animal, foliated and abstract designs.

Just to the east lies the Island of Danna. Here is complete solitude. Once an island it is now joined to the mainland by a short causeway. It is possible to park beside the road on the 'island' just over the causeway. Walk along a track past New Danna Farm. Just past a gate across the track take the gate through a fence to the right. Follow a trod, often indistinct, along high ground. At the end of the headland are three thin finger-like projections with shallow bays between. To the end and back is about 5km. To the west are the entire length of Rubha na Cille and the island of Jura beyond.

Craignish Point　　　Argyll and Bute

27 miles from Oban
Grid ref: NR 760989
Maps: OS Explorer 358, OS Landranger 55.

The Craignish Point ends in the three prongs of Rubha na Traighe, Rubh a Chrainn and Rubh' an Lionaidh. The Craignish Peninsula is a Mecca for artists and craftsmen, a St Ives of Argyll. Ardfern is the largest community where there are shops selling artwork and locally produced crafts. The town sports a bustling marina.

The B 8002 turns of the A 816 about 31km south of Oban and passes through the village of Ardfern. At the end of the road a well-defined path leads from a car park to the tip of Rubha na Traighe just over 1km distant. Along the shore several basalt

Stac na-h-Iolaire to the left, mountaineering sheep to the right.

197

dykes cut through the bedrock. The most prominent is named Stac na h-Iolaire. The north end of Jura is a few kilometres across the Sound of Jura to the east. Between Jura and the Island of Scarba to the north is Corryvrechan, the third largest whirlpool in the world. George Orwell knew its power when his boat capsized. He, and the others with him, managed to scramble onto a small rocky island where they stayed until they were rescued. At certain states of the tide this channel is virtually un-navigable

A couple of kilometres back along the road near Craignish Castle is Kirkton Chapel. This 12th or 13th century chapel houses a fine collection of carved grave slabs and tomb chests. It was common practice to reuse these slabs. There is a good example here of the new name and date crudely carved across the original decoration. It must have made the original owner turn in his grave.

Rudh' Arduaine   Argyll and Bute

19 miles from Oban
Grid ref: NM 791105
Maps: OS Explorer 359, OS Landranger 55.

Arduaine Gardens, open to the public and owned by the National Trust for Scotland, occupy most of the headland except for its tip. J. Arthur Campbell having made his fortune from tea estates in Ceylon, returned to his native land and bought the promontory and built his large house in the 1880s. He began work on the gardens in 1895. Rhododendrons were his great love and by the time he died in 1929 the garden contained 220 species. Arduaine Gardens are a delight at any time of year, but to see the rhododendrons at their best come in the last week in April or the first two weeks in May.

The name Arduaine means Green Promontory. The end of the headland can be reached by entering a field adjacent to the hotel, making for the bottom right-hand corner, through another gate

The garden headland of Rudh' Arduaine

and following a path along the shoreline. The going is moderately difficult. At the end is a cairn of stones acting as a daymark for boats. Nearby is an up-ended blue plastic fish-box, not so elegant, but probably more visible than the cairn. The highest point of the promontory is An Cnap, an outcrop of granite.

Rudh' Arduaine is 30km (19miles) south of Oban on the A816.

Degnish Point — Argyll and Bute

18 miles from Oban
Grid ref: NM 773121
Maps: OS Explorer 359, OS Landranger 55.

Off the A816 about 22km south of Oban a narrow road runs it's, switchback course along the north shore of Loch Melfort. The views are spectacular. There is room

199

Degnish Point

to park at the end, just before the derelict Degnish farm where a track leads off signed to Ardmaddy Castle. Walk the track on the south (left) side of Degnish farm through a wood and into a pasture field. In the diagonally opposite corner a gate opens onto rough ground. From here the going is quite heavy. As the end of the headland is approached there seems to be a building with a doorway and a turf roof. It turns out to be a natural arch. The effort of reaching the end is rewarded with superb views along Loch Melfort and up Seil Sound. There is no sight of the open sea, no horizon to be seen, the whole area appears to be landlocked.

Dunstaffnage Castle
(Rubha Garbh)   ♿   Argyll and Bute

4 miles from Oban
Grid ref: NM 883345
Maps: OS Explorer 359 and 376, OS Landranger 49.

The popular attraction of Dunstaffnage Castle, in the care of Historic Scotland, is open to the public throughout the year. It stands on a rocky promontory, Rubha Garbh, meaning Rough Headland, just 5km north of Oban. at a strategically important site. It guards the entrance to Loch Etive. Loch Etive in turn leads up to the Pass of Brander and central Scotland.

Dunstaffnage Castle

201

The Stone of Destiny came to Dunstaffnage from Ireland via Iona. It was moved to Scone in the mid 9th century because of the threat from the Viking raiders.

Duncan MacDougall, Lord of Lorn, the grandson of Somerled, King of the Hebrides, built the present castle in the early 13th century. He, together with the MacDonalds of Kintyre to the south and the MacRuaris to the north were semi-independent rulers. Other major players in the power game at the time were Scotland and Norway who both claimed the Isles of Hebrides as their own. The castle was wrested from the MacDougalls by Robert Bruce in 1308/9 following which it remained in the hands of the Kings of Scotland. The loyal Campbells were appointed keepers and the castle was used as a launching pad against the MacDonalds, Lords of the Isles. The Campbells, Dukes of Argyll, remained owners of the castle until it was passed into state ownership in 1958.

Research laboratories of the Scottish Association for Marine Science occupy part of the base of the headland and the adjacent Dunstaffnage Bay.

If travelling north by road to Fort William it is worth taking a minor road at Duror to Cuil Bay. From there a walk of about 2km leads to three small headlands, Rubha Beag (Little Headland), Rubha Meadhonach (Middling Headland) and Rubha Mòr (Big Headland) that define two small bays. When I visited a pair of black-throated divers was fishing in one of them.

Auliston Point   Highland

52 miles from Fort William
Grid ref: NM 547580
Maps: OS Explorer 383, OS Landranger 47.

From the small jetty at Bonnavoulin towards the west end of the Morvern Peninsula walk through the broadleaved woodland of the Drimnin Estate. Continue behind the

Abandoned croft at Auliston Point

house following the sign to Doirlinn. After a little less than 3km at a sharp hairpin bend go through a gate and down an old track to the deserted village of Auliston. A steep scramble almost down to sea level reveals the remnants of a few more crofts and an inlet of the sea where boats may once have been dragged ashore. The tip of the headland is about 330m further on. The whole walk is a fairly strenuous 10km.

The Morvern Peninsula bears the remains of many villages that thrived before the time of the notorious Highland Clearances. Many of the ruined cottages at Auliston have rounded corners which are typical of buildings in this area. Thirteen families comprising a total of 58 souls lived in Auliston in 1779. By 1841 there were 107 people living in 21 houses and their ages ranged from 1 month to 90 years. The great potato famine hit the Highlands from 1846 to 1857. A combination of famine and the policy of land clearance to make way for sheep farming tolled the death-knell for many crofting communities. Thousands of the more able-bodied emigrated to the New World, especially to the Maritime Provinces of Canada, leaving the old and infirm behind to mourn.

The Morvern Peninsula is composed of basaltic lava from the huge volcano of Mull which spewed out layer upon layer of lava about 60 million years ago in the Paleogene Period (Tertiary) (66 — 23 million years ago). These layers can be made out on Morvern and across the Sound of Mull on Mull itself.

Ardnamurchan   ♿   Highland

57 miles from Fort William
Grid ref: NM 415675
Maps: OS Explorer 390, OS Landranger 47.

Ardnamurchan means 'The High Headland of the Flowing Seas' and is the most westerly point of the British mainland. What a magnificent headland it is! It is reached along a narrow, twisty road through oak woodlands, with their resident pine martens, and then open moorland. Despite its remoteness there is much to see and do and many visitors make the long journey to reach the end of the peninsula.

At the point are a lighthouse, accommodation for previous lighthouse keepers, fields where they grew crops, a stable block housing a welcome cafe and an excellent permanent exhibition.

Tradition has it that if a mariner successfully passes Ardnamurchan Point he can hoist a sprig of white heather up his mast as a gesture of gratitude. A lighthouse was needed to mark this dangerous headland. Alan Stevenson built the lighthouse and surrounding houses in the Egyptian style, as he did at Chanonry Point. The Egyptian features are seen most clearly just below the light. Each stone block of the tower is dovetailed into its neighbours to each side and also above and below. The lowest course is cemented and bolted into the rock. The stone of the tower and the keepers' houses is granite from the Isle of Mull. The tower stands 36m high and first shone out over the Minch on October 5th 1849. A great storm raged in January 1852 when the tower was struck by

Ardnamurchan Point

lightning and a length of boundary wall and road was washed away. The tower appears as secure today as the day it was completed. The light was automated in 1988. The keepers cottages, built of granite in the same style, are available to rent.

People have lived in the vicinity from at least the Bronze Age. A small offshore island bears the name Eilean Chaluim Cille meaning the Island of Saint Columba. It is possible that he visited Ardnamurchan, but the facts are lost in the mists of time. More recently the Jacobite rising of 1745 began near here. The boat carrying Bonnie Prince Charlie lay at anchor on the north side of the Ardnamurchan Peninsula before his standard was raised at Glenfinnan at the head of Loch Shiel. Lachlan Campell, a local minister and Protestant supporter, saw the boat and alerted the Sherrif-Depute of Argyll, thus starting the resistance to the Jacobite rebellion.

There are many places of interest nearby. I will mention two. Camas nan Geall is a small bay and one of the finest natural views in Scotland. Just behind the beach is a collapsed chambered cairn and nearby a superb ancient cross slab adjacent to a small walled cemetery, overgrown and rather difficult to find, but worth the effort. Within are two fine headstones, one bearing the Campbell coat of arms, the other a depiction of the crucifixion. Around the bay are traces of the deserted settlement of Camas nan Geall. The name has several meanings: Bay of Strangers, or Bay of Promise, or even Bay of Love.

The road to Sanna crosses an area of great geological interest. The underlying rock of the Ardnamurchan Peninsular is around 100 million years old. These are the Moine sediments which, on Ardnamurchan, are less deformed than elsewhere. Sedimentary rocks deposited on the Moine in subsequent periods have largely been eroded away, but not entirely. When the north Atlantic formed and America split away from Europe there was intense volcanic activity on Ardnamurchan. At first this was to the east, later moved southwest and was finally centred near the hamlet of Achnaha. From here, on the road to Sanna the circular configuration of the hills with a diameter of about 3km is apparent. These encircling hills are known as the Great Eucrite. They were formed when molten rock in a ring formation was forced up through overlying layers and solidified as it cooled. These ring formations on Ardnamurchan are of international geological significance.

Rubh' Arisaig   Highland

38 miles from Fort William
Grid ref: NM 611847
Maps: OS Explorer 398, OS Landranger 40.

The scenery is breathtaking. There are fine views across to Eigg, Rum and Skye. Across the mouth of Loch nan Ceall are numerous low rocky islands, known as a skerry-guard,

Rubh' Arisaig with Eigg, Rum and Skye beyond the skerry-guard.

joined at low tide by white sand or shingle. Highland cattle roam free. Take a picnic and linger to soak up this scene.

From Arisaig a minor road runs for 5km along the south shore of Loch nan Ceall. A track leads on. Where it turns sharp left just continue across rough country to the end of the headland, total walk of 4km. Or why not walk from Arisaig, you may not meet a single motor vehicle.

Knoydart (Dun Ban)   Highland

43 miles from Fort William. Reached by ferry.
Grid ref: NG 701036
Maps: OS Explorer 413, OS Landranger 33.

Knoydart is one of the most romantic and atmospheric of all Scottish headlands. For a start it is so remote that it must be reached by ferry. It is one of three mainland

Leaving Inveree, Knoydart

peninsulas with a road system that does not link with the rest of Britain. The others are Scorraig and Cape Wrath. Access to Knoydart is by ferry from Mallaig to Inveree or by private boat charter. From Inveree the single road runs east to the Kilchoan Estate a couple of kilometres away and west 10km to Airor. Inveree consists of a row of whitewashed low buildings facing the sea, some further houses along the coast, a post office/shop, a restaurant, the offices of the Knoydart Foundation and The Old Forge, the most remote pub in Britain.

The most prominent point on the coast of this peninsula is Dun Ban at the hamlet of Doune. Walk from Inveree along the mountain road toward Airor for about 7km. A sign saying 'Doune here' points down a track that zigzags 1km down to the sea. A handful of houses and a small bay with a couple of boats are sheltered from the west side by a small rocky headland. This was the site of an Iron Age promontory fort, Dun Ban. Some remains of vitrified walls of the fort can be seen. There are fine views of Skye, Rum, Eigg and the mainland at Mallaig.

Knoydart suffered as much as anywhere from the Highland Clearances and potato famine of the mid 19th century. Before its decline it supported a population of about 2000. In 1853 the final 322 tenants were cleared from their crofts and put on board the *Sillary* bound for Canada. Those who refused to leave had their crofts burnt to the ground. There was then a succession of landlords, the most notorious being Lord Brocket, a Nazi sympathiser. During his tenure in 1948 the famous Knoydart Seven conducted a land raid to reclaim their ancestral property. Lord Brocket challenged them in the courts and, regrettably, won. Even though they could not take up their rightful inheritance their spirit lives on. A cairn to their memory stands in Inveree with the inscription in Gaelic and English that reads *"Justice! In 1948, near this cairn, the Seven Men of Knoydart staked claims to secure a place to live and work. For over a century Highlanders had been forced to use land raids to gain a foothold where their forebears lived. Their struggles should inspire each new generation of Scots to gain such rights by just laws. History will judge harshly the oppressive laws that have led to the virtual extinction of a unique culture from this beautiful place."*

In the latter half of the 20th century Knoydart has been divided into a number of smaller estates. The Knoydart Foundation was formed in 1997 to manage 17,000 acres at the western end of the peninsula in a sustainable way in accord with the wishes of the resident population.

Plock of Kyle — Highland

At Kyle of Lochalsh
Grid ref: NG 756273
Maps: OS Explorer 413 and 428, OS Landranger 33.

'Plock of Kyle' is Gaelic for 'Lump of the Narrows' — an appropriate name. A short walk or drive up the hill from Kyle of Lochalsh reaches an extensive picnic area and

The Skye Bridge, Plock of Kyle

viewpoint. The scene of mountain, sea and sky is superb. This is the springboard for the bridge across to the Isle of Skye. The whole elegant sweep of the Skye Bridge is spread out below. A bronze plaque points out and names the peaks of the Culin range of mountains on Skye that can be seen from this viewpoint. Below the summit a track, which later becomes a rather indistinct footpath, leads across what was once a golf course to the sea.

The bridge leapfrogs over the island of Eilean Bàn to Kyleakin on Skye. Eilean Bàn (meaning White Island) was the last home of Gavin Maxwell. It is now a nature reserve where otters, the descendents of those that gave Gavin Maxwell so much pleasure, may be seen. On the island is a lighthouse and holiday cottages available to rent. The lighthouse was built by David Stevenson and his brother Thomas in 1857 and is reached by one of only two iron walkways in Scotland.

Rubha na h-Uamha Highland

45 miles from Kyle of Lochalsh
Grid ref: NG 722348
Maps: OS Explorer 428, OS Landranger 24.

'Rubha na h-Uamha' means 'Headland of Caves'. At the tip of the headland there is a beautiful, entirely natural, sandstone rock garden. The coastal views make the tramp to the end supremely worthwhile.

This headland is the southern tip of the Applecross Peninsula. To reach the end a 1:25,000 map, compass and walking boots are virtually essential. Start from the snug south-facing little harbour of Toscaig and allow three hours there and back. There is a path, but it is often indistinct. Walk over a footbridge and follow a path signed to Na h-Uamhagan/Uags. This path runs over fairly rough terrain that can be very wet. Just before Uags it runs through a little wood of oak and silver birch. Uags is a small collection of crofts. They were all in ruin, but are being renovated. No doubt the easiest way to reach Uags is by boat. The end of the headland is just a few metres beyond Uags.

Natural rock garden at
Rubha na h-Uamha

211

Red Point

18 miles from Gairloch
Grid ref: NG 725672 and NG 725687
Maps: OS Explorer 433, OS Landranger 19 and 24.

The Queen was particularly fond of Red Point. The Royal Yacht would anchor offshore and the royal party would come to the beach at Red Point for barbeques. At that time Red Point was even more secluded than it is today.

About 5km south of Gairloch along the A832 turn right along the B8056 and follow the road 14km to a small car park just before Red Point Farm. Walk south through the farm, currently deserted, to a sandy beach just 1km away. The winch and slipway marked on the OS map can be seen, but the winch is now a rusting wreck. Walk on to the southern point. From there it is quite a strenuous hike north across numerous peat cuttings up to the

Red Point with view across to Skye

northern point. Here there is another fine sandy beach backed by dunes. From there it is a short step back to the car park. The round walk is about 5km.

Rubha Rèidh   ♿   Highland

12 miles from Gairloch
Grid ref: NG 740918
Maps: OS Explorer 434, OS Landranger 19.

The lighthouse stands defiant against the wildest westerly gales. It is planted securely on gently dipping beds of Torridonian sandstone that slide down into the sea. The scenery is magnificent. Numerous geos cut into the rocky shore. These are a feature of sandstone coasts. A small jetty sits in one of these where boats used to moor loaded with supplies for the lighthouse before the road was built. David Stevenson first

Rubha Reidh on a stormy day

suggested a light here in 1853, but it was not until 1908 that the go-ahead was given and his son, David Alan Stevenson, built it. The light first shone out over the sea on 15th January 1912. Three lighthouse keepers manned the light and lived with their families in accommodation around its base. A three-mile walk along a rough track brought them to the nearest habitation. The road was built in 1962. In the same year it was re-designated as a rock station and keepers manned it for a month at a time while their wives lived elsewhere. The last keeper left in 1986 when the light was automated. The original light, clockwork mechanism and foghorn are now in the Gairloch Heritage Museum. The lighthouse keeper's premises are now open as holiday lets specialising in walking tours with guides who have expert knowledge of the area and its wildlife. A café here is open to the public one day a week.

A 15-minute walk along the cliffs to the east brings the beautiful sandy bay of Camas Mor into view, although another 45 minutes are needed to reach it. Here there is a large natural arch.

North from Gairloch the B 8021, later to become an unclassified road, leads through stunning coast and mountain scenery all the way to the lighthouse at Rubha Reidh.

Rubha nan Sasan   ♿   Highland

9 miles from Poolewe
Grid ref: NG 816920
Maps: OS Explorer 434, OS Landranger 19.

The two words 'Arctic Convoy' speak loudly of hardship, loss, heroism and raw courage in the war at sea. Loch Ewe is where these convoys assembled. Rubha nan Sasan is a high rocky headland guarding the entrance to Loch Ewe. This loch, unique among west-coast lochs, runs north/south and is, therefore, sheltered from the predominantly westerly gales. This fact, together with its deep water and distance from German air bases in Norway made it the clear choice for a naval base in World War 2.

When Hitler invaded Russia this made Russia an ally, albeit a reluctant one. From September 1941 to May 1945 convoys of merchant ships with naval escort left Loch Ewe bound for the northern Russian ports of Murmansk and Archangel. The cargoes included military materiel such as Hurricane aircraft and tanks and on the return journey pit-props destined for Britain's coal mines. A

Memorial to those lost in the Arctic Convoys

total of 78 convoys sailed to or from the Russian ports with a loss of 85 ships. These bald numbers give no indication of the horrors and hardships endured by merchant seamen and naval personnel alike. There was the bitter cold. Ice 6 inches thick would form from condensation on the un-insulated steel roof above the bunks. The ship's superstructure would be caked in frozen spray. Storm force winds were a regular occurrence. Added to dangers posed by nature almost the whole route was within range of German aircraft, the north Atlantic was patrolled by U-boats and surface ships, including the *Tirpitz* lurking in nearby Norwegian fjords. The most ill-fated convoy was PQ17 that sailed on 27th June 1942. Thirty-six merchant ships with an Anglo-American naval escort set off, two returned, and enemy aircraft sank a further three. The Admiralty then called off the escort vessels to face what turned out to be a false threat from the German surface fleet and gave the order for the convoy to scatter. Of the remaining virtually unprotected 31 merchant ships only 11 reached their destinations.

A memorial stone set up near the headland by the Russian Convoy Club honours those who died on these missions. It reads *In memory of our shipmates who sailed from Loch Ewe during World War II. They lost their lives in the bitter Arctic sea battles to north Russia and never returned to this tranquil anchorage. We will always remember them.*

The headland is still crisscrossed with concrete roads and dotted with the remains of gun emplacements and command posts.

Another tragic episode of the same war was the wreck of the Liberty Ship *SS William Welch* just off the headland on 26th February 1944 with the loss of 62 of a crew of 74 men. An information board gives a graphic account of the incident. Local crofters struggled to rescue the crew and a Mrs Mackenzie trudged three miles through the snow with a large jug of tea to revive the frozen seamen who had made it to the shore. One wonders if it was covered with ice by the time she reached them.

Liberty Ships were mass-produced in USA as general freighters in World War 2. At peak production 140 ships were being launched each month. The fastest construction was the *Robert G. Peary* which was launched just four days and fifteen-and-a-half hours after the keel was laid and was fitted out in a further three days!

From Poolewe drive the 14km along the west shore of Loch Ewe to the car park at the headland.

Greenstone Point   Highland

13 miles from Poolewe
Grid ref: NG 860985
Maps: OS Explorer 434, OS Landranger 19.

The Gaelic name for the headland is *Rubha na Lice Uaine* meaning the 'Point of Green Slabs'. The rock is Torridonian Sandstone. To detect the green requires the eye of an artist.

At Laide on the A832 about 13km (8 miles) north of Poolewe a minor road runs north past the beautiful beach at Mellon Udrigle to Opinan. It is possible to park at either place. From Opinan there is rough walking across open land where peat has been cut. Occasionally there is an indistinct path near the sea. The walk from Opinan is only 3km, but seems longer. The point itself is low and marked by a small cairn with two ugly uprights of rusty iron. The scenery is improved by a number of attractive lochans

Greenstone Point with Summer Isles in the distance

and wild flowers: devil's bit scabious *(Succisa pratensis)*, orchids, bog asphodel *(Narthecium ossifragrum)* and in the wetter areas the carnivorous sundew *(Drosera rotundifolia)*.

Stattic Point Highland

22 miles from Poolewe
Grid ref: NG 973962
Maps: OS Explorer 435, OS Landranger 19.

Gruinard Island stands off Stattic Point to the west. During World War II it was feared that Germany would conduct biological warfare with anthrax and the Allies also considered using it. An experiment was conducted in 1942 when Gruinard Island (520 acres) was bombed with anthrax spores. Sheep that were tethered nearby began dying of anthrax within three days. So dangerous are anthrax spores when inhaled that the island was put in quarantine for years. Scientists from Porton Down made periodic visits to assess the level of continuing contamination. In 1986 decontamination of the island began. The whole area was sprayed with 280 tonnes of formaldehyde diluted in seawater. The island was declared free of anthrax in 1990, 48 years after the spores were introduced.

About half way between Ullapool and Gairloch at Badcaul on the southern shore of Little Loch Broom a minor road runs above the loch to Badluarach with its jetty. From there it is a rough walk of 2km with no path to the point. Below on Little Loch Broom is a pattern of circular fish cages. The view up the loch is superb, backed by the distinctive twin peaks of Beinn Ghobhlach. The Summer Isles are spread out to the northeast.

Cailleach Head · Highland

22 miles from Poolewe. Reached by ferry.
Grid ref: NG 985985
Maps: OS Explorer 435, OS Landranger 19.

Few headlands in Britain are as remote as this. Here is one that is reached by boat, the others being Dun Ban on Knoydart and Cape Wrath. By prior arrangement Bill, the postman (Tel: 01854 633333), will take passengers across Little Loch Broom from Badluarach to Scoraig in a small open boat. The only other way is to walk along a 9km (5 mile) path from Badrallach along the north shore of Little Loch Broom.

In modern Gaelic Cailleach means an Old Woman. In mythology a Cailleach can be a female divine creator or a deified ancestor.

A footpath from Scoraig leads out to Cailleach Head 3km away where there is a modern, Tardis-like, lighthouse. (The old lighthouse has been moved to Carnach, a community to the east of Scoraig, and rebuilt to house a small museum.) The view east from Cailleach Head is to the wild and rocky part of the headland — Carn Dearg.

The community on this peninsula numbers about 90 souls. There can be few

Rather strange lighthouse on
Cailleach Head

219

places of similar size in Britain that contain such a variety of people and talents. Every house is powered by a wind turbine or small hydroelectric generator designed and built by one of the residents. Although this area is remote, and that is a major attraction for anyone wishing to live here, the locals are anything but cut off from the rest of the world. A wide range of skills and enterprises is found at Scoraig. These include alternative medicine, archaeology, authorship, ceramics, commercial herb growing, computer technology, guesthouse accommodation, live music and violin making. Further details are on the Scoraig website.

A small jetty at Scoraig serves the whole population. Scoraig merges with Carnach along the shore of Little Loch Broom. A school is here that takes children to the age of 14. A track runs over to the north side of the peninsula to Annat and Achmore. The word Annat implies the existence of an ancient church and there are indeed the remains of an Anchorite monastery that might even predate Iona.

Rubha Cadail   ♿   Highland

3 miles from Ullapool
Grid ref: NH 092974
Maps: OS Explorer 435 and 439, OS Landranger 19.

Rubha Cadail stands at the entrance to Loch Broom and the approach to Ullapool. In 1773, just 27 years after the Battle of Culloden, the *Hector* sailed from Loch Broom laden with Highlanders and their families, picked up more passengers from Greenock and headed for Pictou, Nova Scotia. Eighteen died at sea of smallpox and dysentery. The exact number that survived the journey is not known, somewhat less than 190. By the time they reached their destination they were near starvation. They were the vanguard of many thousands of Highlanders who, partly as a consequence of the 'Highland Clearances', emigrated to that part of Canada where they preserved the Gaelic language and customs.

Thomas Telford designed Ullapool which is today a bustling community. The ferry to Stornoway sails from Ullapool's busy harbour.

There is a car park at Rhue 5km northwest of Ullapool. The end of the headland and the lighthouse are less than 1km further along a footpath. The lighthouse at Rubha Cadail was built in 1952 and is solar-powered and is in the hands of Ullapool Harbour Trust. It is known locally as 'Dr Who', though it is less like a tardis than the light at Cailleach Head just down the coast.

'Dr Who' at Rubha Cadail

Rubha na Còigich   Highland

27 miles from Ullapool
Grid ref: NB 981181
Maps: OS Explorer 439, OS Landranger 15.

Here is the Scottish coast at its most wild and desolate, and the views are second to none. Overhanging cliffs and deep-cut inlets (geos) give the coastline an appearance of being smashed to smithereens by the waves. Roseroot *(Sedum*

The wild end of Rubha na Còigich

rosea), an attractive member of the Stonecrop family, thrives on ledges on the sandstone cliffs. In every little trickle running down from boggy areas the carnivorous sundew *(Drosera rotundifolia)* flourishes. This is the haunt of divers and arctic skuas with their unmistakeable tail feathers. The lighthouse on the Point of Stoer is seen to the north. There are superb views of the Sutherland Mountains, Suilven, Quinag and others.

Take the A835 north from Ullapool for 15km and turn left at Drumrunie. This minor road runs 25km to Reiff. First it skirts the north shore of Loch Lugainn, Loch Bad a' Ghaill and Loch Osgaig. At a junction turn right, not left to Achiltibuie. At one more junction turn right again to Reiff. From the A835 to Reiff is 25km. If you turn left at the last junction you reach Polbain where the view of the Summer Isles is thought by many to be one of the finest views in the whole of in Scotland. Park off-road at Reiff. A track leads on along the east shore of Loch of Reiff. A boulder bar cuts the loch off from the sea at the little bay of Camas Eilean Ghlais. Follow a rather indistinct path past a small stone house then all the way to the headland following the coast. Further inland the ground is very boggy. This walk is 4km one way. I lost a pair of binoculars somewhere along this way in 2005, so if you find them.......

An Fharaid Bheag Highland

40 miles from Ullapool
Grid ref: NC 050249
Maps: OS Explorer 442, OS Landranger 15.

A more idyllic spot would be hard to imagine. An Fharaid Bheag is a small headland beside a beach. Achmelvich beach, campsite and car park are 6km northwest of Lochinver along a narrow road. Walk up onto the headland from the car park.

The rock here is one of the oldest found in the British Isles called Lewisian Gneiss. It takes its name from the Island of Lewis

An Fharaid Bheag

in the Outer Hebrides. A Gneiss is a metamorphic rock that has been subjected to intense pressure and high temperature giving it a characteristic foliated appearance with alternating dark and light crystals. Lewissian Gneiss dates from the Precambrian Period about 3,000,000,000 years ago. At that time the seas only contained soft-bodied creatures and there was no oxygen in the atmosphere. It is found down the coast of northwest Scotland from Cape Wrath to the Isle of Skye and gives the scenery an unmistakable character. The landscape is part rock and part grass, sometimes one predominates and sometimes the other. The rock has been worn down and smoothed over millions of years. The headlands composed of Lewissian Gneiss are mainly low. Cape Wrath with its high cliffs is an exception. In many places the gneiss is overlain with a sedimentary rock that has not been metamorphosed, the Torridonian Sandstone. (See Point of Stoer.)

On the headland is a small, but intricate, Wendy-house-type structure built of concrete. It is all irregular angles, has square holes for windows, a concrete bed and shelves and a chimney. It is said that David Scott, an architect from Yorkshire, lived in a hut nearby for two years and built his 'castle' in the 1950s. He spent one night in it and nearly choked to death on the fumes from his fire.

Point of Stoer   Highland

46 miles from Ullapool
Grid ref: NC 021355
Maps: OS Explorer 442, OS Landranger 15.

A car park at the Stoer Head lighthouse is the starting-point for a 7km walk to the Point of Stoer and back. The rather indistinct path runs up the west side of the headland. There are fine vertical cliffs on both sides. The going can be strenuous and very wet underfoot. Just before the tip of the

Point of Stoer lighthouse

headland stands the Old Man of Stoer. This is the best of the mainland offshore stacks of Scotland and at 60m (200ft) high is a challenge to rock-climbers. The views along the coast are dramatic. To the northeast Eddrachillis Bay is studded with islands. This is a good area for spotting whales and dolphins. No fewer than 21 species of cetaceans have been seen within 60km of the coast and 11 are present all the year or are regular visitors.

The whole headland is composed of Torridonian Sandstone which overlies the older Lewisian Gneiss. The sandstone is itself old dating from the late Precambrian period about 1,000 million years ago. It, therefore, contains no fossils of hard-shelled organisms as are seen in sedimentary rocks of the Cambrian Period. The distinctive high mountains of Sutherland are made of Torridonian Sandstone. Near the lighthouse there is a deep cleft where the cliff has begun to fall away providing a microclimate where a profusion of ferns flourishes.

David and Thomas Stevenson, who were brothers, designed the lighthouse. They were brothers to Alan and sons of Robert

Stevenson who was the first of the family to build lighthouses. Thomas was the father of the novelist Robert Louis Stevenson. The light was built in 1870 and was automated in 1978. It now provides holiday accommodation although it is still a functioning light.

The residents of the North Assynt Estate, which includes the Stoer peninsula, purchased 21,500 acres from its previous owner for a sum of £300,000 in 1993. The local population now manage the estate for the first time since the infamous Highland Clearances by the Duke of Sutherland more than two centuries ago, but which are remembered clearly today.

The narrow road to the lighthouse leaves the B869 2km north of the village of Stoer.

Rubha Ruadh   Highland

6 miles from Scourie
Grid ref: NC 162513
Maps: OS Explorer 445, OS Landranger 9.

Rubha Ruadh is a remote, desolate, beautiful spot. Go armed with a compass and 1:25,000 scale map. Five km north of Scourie take a minor road for another 5 km through Tarbet to Fanagmore. Walk north onto rough pasture. The lower ground to the right down by the sea is lush with hazel, rowan and goat willow. There is no way through there. Keep to high ground and walk northwest, through a gate in a wall. Continue in the same direction (there is no path), crossing a number of ridges and small inland cliffs. The ground can be very boggy and there are several small lochans. Bog myrtle is everywhere. Small inlets chop up the end of the headland. The total walk is only 4km but the terrain makes it seem longer. The view back along Loch Laxford with its islands is magnificent.

Tarbet is the place to take a small boat over to the bird sanctuary of Handa Island. There is a little restaurant at Tarbet,

The Shorehouse, renowned for its fish dishes made from fish caught locally. Freshness is guaranteed. Rick Stein commends it and so do I.

Cape Wrath   Highland

13 miles from Durness. Reached by ferry.
Grid ref: NC 259747
Maps: OS Explorer 446, OS Landranger 9.

The name Cape Wrath summons up a picture which is appropriate for this most north-westerly headland in Britain with its high cliffs, crashing seas and exploding 1000lb bombs. It is mildly disappointing to learn that the word 'wrath' (rhyme with 'hath') comes from Old Norse meaning 'a turning'. An important turning it is though, where Viking explorers after sailing west from Norway turned south along the west coast of Scotland. To the east within sight of the tip of the cape are the sandstone cliffs of Clo Mòr which at 281m (921ft) are the highest sheer cliffs on the British mainland. The cliffs at

Eagle's eye view of Cape Wrath

Cape Wrath (121m, 397ft) are of Lewisian Gneiss. It is very unusual to have such high cliffs made of this type of rock. Numerous ledges provide nesting sites for gulls and auks.

Cathedral Stack at Kearvaig, Cape Wrath

It is not possible to drive to Cape Wrath as the single road to the headland does not link up with any other and there is no car ferry. The usual and easiest way is to catch a small open ferry across the Kyle of Durness. A minibus that runs from May to September then takes passengers the 11 miles to Cape Wrath lighthouse. Red deer are often seen from the road. Keep an eye open for a hen harrier gliding low over the ground. At the lighthouse it feels like the very end of the country. Due north there is no land between here and the North Pole. Energetic folk can walk up the west coast from a little north of Oldshoremore via the beautiful sands of Sandwood Bay. This is a rough hike of about 20km.

Robert Stevenson designed the lighthouse which was built and became operational in 1828. It was automated in 1998. Like all foghorns around the coast the one here is now silent. The light, however, still warns ships and acts as a navigation reference point. In the days when the lighthouse was manned supplies were landed at a small jetty nearby at Clais Charnach. The beautiful small sandy beach at Kearvaig is visible from the road. Here Cathedral Stack with its twin towers stands just offshore.

Cape Wrath is the only site in Europe where 1000lb bombs are dropped live in exercises. The target is the small island of An Garbh-eilean (Garvie Island). Combined exercises involving land, sea and air elements of European and NATO forces conspire to demolish the island, but still it stands. Beneath the surface and well out of sight to the west of Cape Wrath a Vanguard submarine armed with trident missiles may well be patrolling.

Faraid Head   Highland

1 mile from Durness
Grid ref: NC 391719
Maps: OS Explorer 446, OS Landranger 9.

Along the Kyle the mists of evening stole
To huddle in the hollows on the hill.
The August moon just waning climbed the sky
And redness from the settled sun glowed still.
From out that eerie scene two sounds I heard,
A piper's lone lament
And the breaking of the surf at Balnakeil.

Autumnal Atmosphere Alan Herman

A minor road from Durness passes a collection of interesting craft workshops in converted army buildings. It runs on to reach the village of Balnakeil that lies at the end of a fine sandy beach that leads north to Faraid Head. The road from Durness crosses limestone country. This Durness Limestone was laid down in shallow seas over 50 million years in the late Cambrian and Ordovician periods. Similar rock is found in Greenland and Newfoundland, the reason being that Scotland was once part of the same ancient continent of Laurentia and was split away by the development of the Atlantic Ocean.

229

Walk along the beach to a tarmac track through high dunes. The distance is about 6km there and back. The road serves a Ministry of Defence establishment that occupies the tip of the headland. It is associated with the gunnery ranges on the other side of the Kyle of Durness. The headland to east and west of the M.o.D. land is open access. Two fine sea stacks stand to the east. There is a solitary circular sheepfold similar to those seen in Northumbria. There is an annual fun-run from Balnakeil to Faraid Head and back. The winner is the person who completes the run closest to the time that he/she predicted. The slowest runner may win!

Ruined church and graveyard at Balnakiel. Faraid Head in the background

St. Maelrubha is said to have founded a monastery at Balnakeil in AD 722, the year of his martyrdom at the hands of Danish Vikings in Strathnaver. Certainly he travelled widely in northwest Scotland and founded many churches during his journeys. The present ruined chapel surrounded by a graveyard dates from the 17th century. Set in a deep alcove, as if trying to be half in and half outside the church, is the grave of Donald

MacMurdo, Domhnull MacMhurchiadh, Donald "macMurdo macEan Mor" Mackay, a notorious highwayman with the blood of eighteen victims on his hands. However, he donated a large sum for the rebuilding of the church in 1619 on condition he was buried within it so that nobody would interfere with his bones. The inscription may be read as

> *Donald Makmurchou here lies low.*
> *Was ill to his friend, and worse to his foe.*
> *True to his master in prosperity and woe.*
>
> *DMMC 1623.*

The poet Rob Donn Mackay, described as the Robert Burns of the Gaelic language, is buried at Balnakeil and the granite obelisk in the churchyard is his memorial. Another memorial is to the crew and passengers, mainly emigrants, of the *Canton* that was wrecked off Faraid head with the loss of all lives in 1849. Balnakeil House, the most prominent building in the area, was one of the seats of the Chief of the Clan Mackay.

Farr Point   Highland

3 miles from Bettyhill
Grid ref: NC 720648
Maps: OS Explorer 448, OS Landranger 10.

Borve Castle has been so comprehensively destroyed that hardly a trace remains, yet the site it once occupied is impressive. It was built on a small promontory with sheer cliffs, pierced by a natural arch and connected to the mainland by a narrow saddle. It is on the east side of the headland terminating at Farr Point. For many years this stronghold of the Mackays remained impregnable. For centuries the Mackays and the Sutherlands were archenemies and were continually skirmishing or engaged in major battles. In 1554 while the Earl of Sutherland was away in France the Mackays attacked his territory. The Queen Regent, mother of Mary Queen of Scots summoned the Chief of the Clan Mackay to her presence, an order he ignored. She then gave leave to the Earl of Sutherland to wreak his revenge. He invaded Strathnaver in 1555 and the Mackays took refuge in Borve Castle where they thought they would be safe. Meanwhile the Sutherlands hauled a cannon overland all the way from Edinburgh, 427 km by road today, and positioned it on a higher promontory overlooking Borve Castle. From there they were able to reduce the castle to rubble, the defenders surrendered and their Chief, Rory Mhor Mackay was hanged there and then. The remnants of the castle were systematically demolished. The footings of a few walls and the site of a well are all that can be seen today.

Site of Borve Castle, Farr Point

From the A836 2.5km east of Bettyhill take a narrow road to Farr. Near the telephone box walk along a tarmac road serving a few houses. This then becomes a track. At the end of the track turn left and over a stile and you are at Borve Castle.

The short walk north from Borve Castle to Farr Point along the rugged cliffs affords spectacular, wild coastal views. It is just 2km from Farr to Farr Point. The rocks here are Moine Schists. (See Rubha Bhra)

Ardmore Point   Highland

8 miles from Bettyhill
Grid ref: NC 770665
Maps: OS Explorer 448, OS Landranger 10.

The deserted village of Poulouriscaig is a vivid illustration of the rigours suffered by those displaced from their livelihoods at the time of the Highland Clearances. From Armadale walk 3km along a track signed to Poulouriscaig A green hollow opens up surrounded by higher rocky ground. A small stream runs down to the sea. In this silent spot are the ruins of several buildings and tumbledown field walls. Each building comprised a living area and adjoining byre for animals. They were constructed carefully with stones of varying size. The windows were chamfered to let in maximum daylight. The best preserved of the houses has dressed stone for the door-jambs and chimney. A small inlet of the sea provided minimal safety for small fishing boats.

Close by are the rocky headlands of Rubha nam Meallan and Ardmore Point. The latter is a narrow, tapering strip of rock sliding gently into the sea and looking for all the world like the snout of a crocodile. In the position of the eye is a large round boulder below which are vertical columns of rock like 'crocodile tears'.

The valley of Strathnaver running inland from Bettyhill saw some of the most brutal displacements of crofters from their land in the early 19th century. The Duke of Sutherland owned 1.5 million acres in the Highlands. Patrick Sellar, his Factor, was responsible for evicting 15,000 people from their homes to make

Poulouriscaig, near Ardmore Point, where crofters were settled during the clearances.

way for sheep farming on a grand scale. He was not averse to burning their houses so that they could not return. In 1814, two years after the evictions in Strathnaver, Sellar stood trial on the charge of homicide and fire-raising. The establishment closed ranks and he was acquitted. Those who were evicted were given inferior land, barely enough to support them, usually on the coast where they were expected to supplement their diet with fish. They were crofters and not fishermen and had to learn this dangerous occupation from scratch. Some families from Strathnaver settled at Poulouriscaig. This was a relatively successful venture and the last inhabitants did not leave until the 1930s.

Strathy Point

Highland

12 miles from Bettyhill
Grid ref: NC 828698
Maps: OS Explorer 449, OS Landranger 10.

Strathy Point is a clenched hand with index finger pointing due north. A car park sits at the base of the finger, Lochan nam Faoileag towards the tip and the lighthouse at the tip itself. On a clear day Cape Wrath, Dunnet Head and the Orkneys are within sight. From the car park to the lighthouse and back is just 2.5km.

The lighthouse is one of Scotland's most recent. It was the first that was built to be powered by electricity from the outset, was operational in 1958 and automated in 1997. The tower and surrounding buildings are white. The traditional round tower has been abandoned for a square one. The buildings round the tower are also arranged in a square giving a pleasing uniform appearance to the whole complex. P H Hyslop, Engineer to the Northern Lighthouse Board, designed the buildings.

Looking west from Strathy Point

235

The small settlements on Strathy point received evicted tenants from the hinterland, including Strathnaver, at the time of the Highland Clearances in the early 19th century. Today the crofting life attracts people who want to escape the pressures of the city. One hardy lady keeps sheep which follow her around, rather than having to be driven or rounded up with sheepdogs. Her secret is to bribe them with digestive biscuits from the supermarket in Thurso. Twenty-five packets a week make for expensive lamb.

Rubha Bhrà — Highland

13 miles from Bettyhill
Grid ref: NC 865668
Maps: OS Explorer 449, OS Landranger 10.

The west side of Melvich Bay is guarded by the small headland of Rubha Bhrà. The rocks here are Moine Schists while to the east all the way to Duncansby Head they are Old Red Sandstone. Moine Schists are ancient Precambrian metamorphic rocks. A short way to the west extending from Loch Eriboll as far south as the Isle of Skye these older metamorphic rocks can be seen to lie above younger sedimentary rocks such as Durness limestone and Torridonian sandstone. How could metamorphic rock that has been subjected to high pressure and temperature lie above

Rubha Bhra Image kindly provided by the British Geological Survey

sedimentary rock that has not undergone such treatment? The answer is that two tectonic plates collided about 430 million years ago, throwing up the Caledonian Mountains and forcing the older rocks to slide over the younger. This is the famous Moine Thrust.

The village of Portskerra at the base of the headland has an almost landlocked natural harbour. Nearby is a memorial to three disasters that befell the local community. In 1848 eight fishermen were lost at sea, in 1890 eleven were drowned and in 1918 seven more fishermen were lost, all from the tiny local community.

Sandside Head   Highland

12 miles from Thurso
Grid ref: NC 953665
Maps: OS Explorer 449, OS Landranger 11.

The typical field boundaries of Caithness are flat stones like large roofing slates placed upright to form a low wall. These stones are Thurso Flags. Sandside Head is composed of this rock. The bedding planes are very apparent and it is easy to appreciate how the rock splits readily into flat plates. Deep geos cut into the headland, the largest being Geodh Sheumais on the western side. A natural arch pierces a huge cube of rock that

Sea mist at Sandside Head

is an island at high tide. The Scottish primrose *(Primula scotica)* and mayweed *(Tripleurospermum maritimum)* with its large daisy-like flowers grow in profusion.

237

Dounreay is a ruined castle on the coast and also the name of two small settlements of Upper and Lower Dounreay, but is now better known as Dounreay Nuclear Establishment. It can be seen along the coast 3km to the east. Three reactors at Dounreay fed electricity into the national Grid from 1959 to 1994. The Vulcan Naval Reactor Test Establishment is part of the complex, but under the Ministry of Defence. It develops and tests nuclear propulsion systems for submarines. In 2005 the Nuclear Decommissioning Authority took over the UK Atomic Energy Authority site and is undertaking one of the most extensive and complex decommissioning tasks in the world. The clean-up may take until 2033, but it could be over 300 years before the area reverts to a brown field site. Children and animals are advised not to venture onto the firm sands of Sandside Bay and nobody is allowed to dig or remove material from the beach because of the small risk of contamination with radioactive particles. No fresh radioactive material is escaping now.

There is a car park beside the trim little harbour of Sandside about 1.5km north of the hamlet of New Reay on the A836. The end of the headland is less than 1km from the car park.

Holborn Head   Highland

2 miles from Thurso
Grid ref: ND 109716
Maps: OS Explorer 451, OS Landranger 12.

A short walk from Scrabster, past the ferry terminal where boats leave for Stromness, leads to Holborn Head lighthouse. David and Thomas Stevenson built this light in 1862. It is unusual in that it is integral with the lighthouse keeper's house. It was decommissioned in 2003 and the buildings are now divided into apartments. Holborn means *Stream in the Hollow*.

A path continues past the lighthouse for 1km over several stiles to the end of the headland. A couple of deep geos come in from the east terminating in impressive blowholes. The whole head is riddled with large sea-caves. One with a huge square entrance is seen just to the west of the tip of the headland. The rocks here are Thurso Flags, a variety of Old Red Sandstone, which are finely foliated into thin sheets. In places they are crushed and twisted and in others are flat and uniform.

An Iron Age ditch and wall cut the headland from the mainland to provide a safe enclosure for people and stock.

Thurso flags at Holborn Head

Dunnet Head   ♿   Highland

12 miles from Thurso
Grid ref: ND 202768
Maps: OS Explorer 451, OS Landranger 12.

D unnet Head is the most northerly point on the British mainland. A short walk up from the car park near the lighthouse leads to the top of a small hill. From here there are 360 degrees panoramic views. The Orkneys and even the Old

Huge cliffs at Dunnet Head

Man of Hoy are seen clearly to the north. On a very clear day Cape Wrath can be made out way to the west. Don't ignore the view inland to the mountains of Morven and Maiden Pap. Energetic folk can walk from Castletown the length of the fine sandy beach of Dunnet Bay and then along the road to the lighthouse, a distance of 22km there and back.

The 300ft (91m) high vertical cliffs of Old Red Sandstone at the end of the headland support Dunnet Head lighthouse. The ferocity of the sea has been such as to throw up stones and shatter windows in the lighthouse. Robert Stevenson designed the lighthouse which was operational in 1831 and automated in 1989. At one time three keepers with their families would have occupied the surrounding buildings. Much of the headland is an extensive area of peat bog dotted with lochans.

Scattered over the high land are the remains of buildings dating from World War II. The master station of the Northern Gee chain was here with slave stations near Cape Wrath, Fraserburgh and the Shetlands. The Gee chain system was a navigation aid to allied aircraft, based on very short radio signals transmitted from a master station and from up to three slave stations a matter of milliseconds later. A receiver in the aircraft would measure the delay in receiving the signal from the slave stations relative to the master station. If signals were received from the master and one slave then charts in the cockpit would show a position line and if from two slaves then two position lines and where they intersected would give the accurate position of the aircraft. The system was used throughout much of World War 2 and only became obsolete in 1970.

The little village of Brough at the base of the headland houses an interesting information centre and the Dunnet Head Tea Rooms which is another mine of local information.

My wife and I had parked our car beside the road to Dunnet Head and were enjoying a picnic when a police car drew up. A very polite policeman asked us if we would mind moving on and have our picnic somewhere else. The reason? There were red-throated divers nesting nearby. What a nice reason for being moved on by the police!

Duncansby Head   ♿   Highland

21 miles from Thurso
Grid ref: ND 405734
Maps: OS Explorer 451, OS Landranger 12.

Britain's northeast corner is a noble headland of high sandstone cliffs cut by deep geos. Those who visit John o' Groats without venturing just 2.5km east to this headland miss a real treat. A car park by the lighthouse means it is accessible to non-walkers.

Duncansby Head is known as Seabird City. The cliffs are made of nearly horizontal beds of Old Red Sandstone providing numerous ledges which make very desirable tower-block residences for guillemots, razorbills, shags, kittiwakes, fulmars and others. In places the sandstone strata look like piles of coins. The ledges

241

are white with guano. The guillemots inhabit the lower storeys. With all that guano above them who in their right minds would select one of the lower ledges? Nesting birds are to be seen everywhere in season, but the best sight is the cliffs of the Geo of Sclaites about 300m south of the lighthouse. A further 1km south stand the famous natural arch of Thirle Door and the pinnacles of Duncansby Stacks with tips as sharp as needles just off-shore. The coastal views are magnificent. The view north from the lighthouse takes in the Island of Stroma, the Pentland Skerries and beyond them the Orkneys across the Pentland Firth.

Duncansby Stacks

The lighthouse is a castellated square tower surmounted by the lantern. It was built in 1924 by David Stevenson and automated in 1997. The tide flows through the Pentland Firth from the Atlantic to the North Sea then ebbs in the opposite direction. In places it can flow at 10 knots. So treacherous are these tide-races that sailors have given them names such as The Duncansby Bore and The Merry Men of Mey. Even today when ships have powerful engines and sophisticated navigation equipment these waters must be treated with the utmost respect.

Noss Head   Highland

3 miles from Wick
Grid ref: ND 388551
Maps: OS Explorer 450, OS Landranger 12.

The Sinclairs have been prominent in Scottish affairs for a thousand years. Here at Girnigoe Castle was one of their most important seats. The Laird, Ian Sinclair currently lives in the lighthouse complex at Noss Head and is active in researching the history of the Sinclair clan and preserving what remains of their castle. The buildings contain a study centre and extensive library holding some rare books of historical interest. The end of the headland is private property and permission to walk on the estate must be obtained in advance from Ian Sinclair who will then ensure that the bull is kept safely out of the way! A previous laird, John Sinclair, was the model for Long John Silver in Treasure Island by Robert Louis Stevenson. He took objection to this and as a consequence the Stevenson firm of engineers lost the contract to build the harbour at Wick.

The lighthouse is functional. Alan Stevenson designed the light and Robert Arnot of Inverness built the tower. It was completed in 1849 and automated in 1987. This was the first lantern to have diagonal rather than vertical framing. The stronger diagonal frame became the standard design.

The ruins of Girnigoe Castle, which are open to the public, stand on the northern aspect of the headland. Although many of the buildings have crumbled away this is still one of the most extraordinary and impressive coastal castles in Britain. It is built on a thin finger of land running parallel with the coast and almost completely separated from the mainland by a deep geo. Walls rise up from the top of cliffs and it is difficult to see where natural rock ends and masonry begins. Construction of the oldest part of the castle including the keep began in 1470 on orders of William St

243

Sinclair Castle, Noss Head

Clair, the first Sinclair Earl of Caithness. A great vaulted way right through the castle allowed a horseman to enter without having to dismount. A passageway with steps leads down to a cave allowing escape by boat if necessary. The fireplace in the kitchen was large enough to roast a whole ox. George, the 4th Earl Sinclair of Caithness, was renowned for his cruel ruthlessness. It was he who extended the castle around 1600 and named the extension Sinclair Castle, but it was never separate from the older Girnigoe Castle. The 6th Earl bequeathed his estate to John Campbell of Glenorchy. As the new owner marched north to take possession of the castle the Campbells marched to the pipes playing the tune they had just composed, "The Campbells are Coming." Later the Sinclairs attacked the castle with cannon and recaptured it, but in the process reduced it to a ruin such that it was never subsequently inhabited. The Clan Sinclair moved its seat to the Castle of Mey. In the Castle of Mey is an old Dutch map that refers to Groëngho Castle. Could this mean Green Geo?

There is a car park about 5km north of Wick beyond the airport from which it is just a short step of about 500m to Girnigoe/Sinclair Castle.

Tarbat Ness   Highland

12 miles from Tain
Grid ref: NH 948878
Maps: OS Explorer 438, OS Landranger 21.

Between Dornoch Firth and Moray Firth is a strip of land, off the beaten track, but well worth a visit, which ends at Tarbat Ness. On the way to the headland is the pretty little village of Portmahomack. Back to that in a moment.

At the tip of the headland beyond the lighthouse the Upper Old Red Sandstone rocks slide gently into the sea. The sea has eroded the rocks into fantastic shapes with pot-holes and sharp ridges. On the west side are numerous small geos and rock pools. Further back along the east coast there are low cliffs showing marked cross-bedding. Jurassic outliers are found along the foreshore. The peninsula forms the north-western side of an extension of the Great Glen. The whole area is farmland with a gentle atmosphere, just the sort of place a migrating bird from Norway would appreciate. Indeed this is the first landfall for many such migrants like wheatears, redwings and field-fares. The headland has SSSI status for maritime heath and salt spray flora.

A Pictish Queen at the Tarbat Discovery Centre Museum, Portmahomack.

245

The lighthouse with its alternating red and white bands is at 47m the highest on the Scottish mainland and one of Robert Stevenson's finest. A great storm in 1826 wrecked sixteen ships in the Moray Firth. In response to that disaster the lighthouse was built and was operational in 1830. It was automated in1985. The lighthouse is not open to the public, but the surrounding buildings are let as holiday cottages.

An old church at Portmahomack is now the site of the Tarbat Discovery Centre Museum. A church has stood here since the 8th century. In fact here was the only Pictish monastery discovered in Scotland so far. The museum houses many examples of Pictish art found locally. Active archaeology is still going on and yielding more information. Outside the museum is a fine modern statue of a Pictish queen. A raiding party of Sutherland Mackays led by one Angus Mackay in the 15th century took refuge in the crypt. The Rosses set fire to the church and Angus and some or all of his men perished in the flames. Signs of burning are evident in the crypt today.

There is a car park near the lighthouse. Alternatively walk the 5km from Portmahomack along the road.

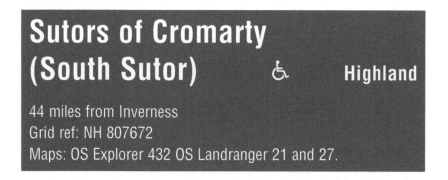

Sutors of Cromarty (South Sutor)   ♿   Highland

44 miles from Inverness
Grid ref: NH 807672
Maps: OS Explorer 432 OS Landranger 21 and 27.

In times long ago when giants roamed the land the baker made off with the blacksmith's wife. The enraged blacksmith threw a hammer at the baker, but missed. The hammer struck the ground with such force that the earth divided to form the two headlands, the Sutors of Cromarty, and allowed the sea to flood into the Cromarty Firth. Two other giants who were cobblers took up residence on the two headlands and when one needed a tool the other would throw it to him across the water. The word 'sutor' means a cobbler or shoemaker.

North Sutor from South Sutor across the entrance
to Cromarty Firth

The two high headlands guard the entrance to Cromarty Firth where huge oilrigs stand like aliens. They are built and serviced at Nigg and Invergordon. Rowan and beech cover South Sutor. If allowed to grow unchecked the views of the coast will be lost.

The town of Cromarty, largely dating from the 18th century, is beautiful and unspoilt. George Ross bought the estate, built the harbour, introduced hemp weaving, nail and spade manufacturing, brewing and agricultural innovations which transformed the fortunes of the town. At one time the hemp factory was turning out 1000 yards of cloth per day.

There are several buildings of architectural and historical interest. Hugh Miller was born and worked here. His birthplace, the only thatched building in Cromarty, and the house where he lived later are open to the public. Coming from a poor family he earned his living as a stonemason. His acute powers of observation allowed him to see the variety of fossil fish in the local Old Red Sandstone with which he worked. He wrote scientific articles and was acknowledged by the leading palaeontologists of his day. He was influential in church affairs, moved to Edinburgh and edited a widely read and respected newspaper, the 'Witness'. Throughout his life he never forgot his humble origins, fought for the rights of the common man and felt most comfortable when wearing the working clothes of a stonemason.

A 2km footpath from Cromarty leads up to South Sutor. There is also a road terminating in a small car park at the headland.

Chanonry Point   ♿   Highland

14 miles from Inverness
Grid ref: NH 750557
Maps: OS Explorer 432, OS Landranger 27.

Chanonry Point is possibly the most rewarding place to watch dolphins anywhere round the coast of Britain. The narrowest part of the Moray Firth is the 1 km of water that separates Chanonry Point from Fort George. Crowds gather on the tip of the headland to watch dolphins as they pass close to the shore following salmon or shoals of herring. They often play in the disturbed water where tidal currents sweep round the headland.

The bottlenose dolphin is the species most likely to be seen, but you may be lucky and spot a whale. The common dolphin occurs more on the west coast of Britain than the east. The harbour porpoise, the only porpoise to frequent these waters, is rather secretive. It is more likely to be heard than seen when it blows through its blowhole on surfacing. Dolphins and porpoises are mammals that belong to the order *Cetacea* and suborder *Odontoceti*. Porpoises, of which there are six species are in the family *Phocoenidae*, whereas there are 26 species of oceanic dolphins belonging to the family *Delphinidae*. Porpoises can be distinguished

248

from dolphins by a number of features: they have no beaks and their heads are small and round, their dorsal fins are triangular rather than curved, their flippers are small and tail flukes notched. Dolphins have prominent bulging foreheads called 'melons' which porpoises lack. Dolphins live in larger groups (schools) than porpoises and are more acrobatic. Bottlenose dolphins vary in colour, but usually are grey above fading to a paler shade down the flanks. Common dolphins have an hourglass or figure-of-eight colour pattern on their flanks. Although apparently moving in a leisurely and effortless manner through the water it is amazing how quickly they cover a long distance and have disappeared from sight. Dolphins are most numerous in the Firth during summer when salmon are returning to rivers to spawn. Dolphin behaviour is described by various terms. 'Breaching' means jumping out of the water and often coming down with a great splash. 'Tail-breaching' is slapping the tail onto the water surface. 'Logging' is lying still on or near the surface of the water. 'Porpoising' refers to jumping clean out of the water while moving fast forward. Despite the term if you see a cetacean porpoising it is more likely to be a bottlenose dolphin than a porpoise.

Chanonry Point seen from Fort George

The lighthouse on Chanonry Point was designed by Alan Stevenson and built in 1846 in his Egyptian style. It was fully automated in 1984.

On the point is a memorial stone to Brahan Seer who was also known as Kenneth Mackenzie or Coinneach Odhar (Kenneth the dun-coloured). In the mid 17th century he gained a reputation as a soothsayer, a Highland Nostradamus. Legend states that Isabella, 3rd Countess of Seaforth enquired of him why her husband was late returning home from Paris. His eventual reply indicated that he was enjoying the female company of Paris too much to return to his wife. She took her revenge on the seer rather than her husband and his reward was to be convicted of witchcraft and tipped into a barrel of boiling oil on Chanonry Point.

Fort George   ♿   Highland

14 miles from Inverness
Grid ref: NH 760566
Maps: OS Explorer 160, OS Landranger 27.

The battle of Culloden on 16th April 1746 was the last land battle to be fought on British soil. The Hanoverian army of George II won a decisive victory over the Jacobites. Charles Edward Stewart (Bonnie Prince Charlie) escaped to the Continent and died in Rome in 1788. King George was determined that there should be no armed rebellion from the Highlanders in the future. Fort George was an important element in maintaining peace in the Highlands by the threat of overwhelming force. A chain of forts across the Highlands linked by 1,100 miles of military road built by General Wade would be supplied and garrisoned from the largest fort of all, Fort George on the Moray Firth near Inverness.

From its inception it was to be the largest and most advanced coastal artillery fort in Europe. The site chosen was the promontory

Fort George

of Ardersier controlling the sea approach to Inverness. Colonel William Skinner provided the design based on the latest military thinking and the contract to build it went to the architect William Adam. He died in 1748 leaving the work to his sons John, Robert and James. The fort is huge, covering 42 acres and able to house a garrison of over 2,000 men. Around the perimeter is a truly massive rampart with strategically placed bastions and demi-bastions where heavy guns could be mounted to give 360 degrees of fire-cover. The landward eastern approach is further protected by a wide moat and ravelin. Beyond this a glacis was formed and many acres of land were flattened so that any advancing army would be deprived of cover. Within the fort were barracks, magazine, ordnance stores,

provision stores, bakery, brewery, workshops, garrison chapel, governor's house, barrack square, parade ground etc. Beneath one of the bastions was a jetty for bringing equipment, stores and men by sea.

Cannon guarding the Moray Firth at Fort George

Part of a barrack block has been converted into a museum giving a clear indication of life in the fort in the 18th century. The Grand Magazine houses the Seafield Collection of arms and equipment mainly dating from the Napoleonic wars. In the Fort Major's House is the Regimental Museum of the Queen's Own Highlanders with an extensive display of gallantry medals, regimental silver, uniforms and weapons.

Fort George is 24km east of Inverness. The B9006 off the Inverness to Nairn road (A96) leads directly to the fort. Although open to the public, who are allowed access to most of the fort, it is still a military establishment with a resident garrison. The overall impression is of military neatness, short clipped grass and spit and polish.

Burghead   ♿   Moray

8 miles from Elgin
Grid ref: NJ 108692
Maps: OS Explorer 423, OS Landranger 28.

Burghead is the largest known Pictish coastal fort and was probably the seat of the ruler of the Northern Pictish Kingdom. It thrived from the 4th to 9th centuries AD. It must have been as impressive in the 4th century as Fort George, just a short way along the coast to the west, was in the 18th. The fort covered an area in excess of 7 acres and was protected to landward by three large ramparts and ditches. Unfortunately the town has swallowed up these defences. On the promontory

Storm signal building at Burghead

side of these banks and ditches there are upper and lower levels separated by a high rampart running along the centre of the headland like a spine. This and its extension along the north shore give an indication of the layout of the fort. The upper level may have contained the royal quarters. Excavation has revealed that the outer walls were truly massive, 8m thick and 6m high on a

253

foundation of large boulders, faced with dressed stone on the outer aspect and oak planks on the inner, tied from inner to outer surfaces with oak logs and in-filled with rubble.

The Picts were maritime people and the beaches near the fort could have been places where boats drew up and trade conducted. Archaeological evidence points to destruction of the fort by burning in the 9th or 10th centuries, possibly in a Viking raid.

Nearby is Burghead Well. Twenty rock-hewn steps lead down to a rock cistern filled with fresh water fed by an underground spring. Its origin and use are open to conjecture. It could have been the water supply to the Pictish fort. It might have had pagan ritual significance or be a place of execution, as the Picts executed criminals by drowning. Later it could well have been a Christian baptistry.

While in this area go to see the Sueno's Stone at Forres close to the A96. This huge stone nearly 7 metres tall is the largest Pictish carving in existence. On one side is carved a cross and on the other a battle scene of more than 100 figures.

At the most prominent point on the headland is a round white building with an external staircase leading onto the roof. This is a storm signal dating from the mid 19th century. Originally a mast rose from the roof and when a storm was imminent a large cone would be hoisted to warn shipping. In World War 2 it was a lookout guarding the entrance to the Moray Firth.

Portknockie   ♿   Moray

21 miles from Elgin
Grid ref: NJ 483688
Maps: OS Explorer 423, OS Landranger 28 and 29.

Portknockie is built on a grid plan on a cliff-top high above the small harbour. The houses are neat with large ashlared quoins. The cliff, known as the Green Castle was the site of

254

a Pictish fort similar to that at Burghead. Archaeologists claim that it was fortified for the best part of 2000 years, from about 1000 BC till the Vikings burnt it to the ground. Below the cliffs are three small shingle inlets in the rocky shore. Here over 50 wooden fishing boats, mainly of the Zulu Drifter design developed at Lossiemouth, were built between 1883 and 1905 when the herring fishing industry was in its heyday. At one time the little harbour was the home port for 100 fishing boats. It is still an active fishing port.

Bow Fiddle Rock, Portknockie

At the tip of the headland is a fine oblique natural arch of Cullen Quartzite. One side is remarkably thin giving it the name of Bow Fiddle Rock. The base fans out like the fluke of a whale. The arch is home to colonies of raucous seabirds.

The public bar of the Victoria Hotel displays a fine collection of old photographs of the fishing fleet, fish market and local wrecks.

Castle Point, Cullykhan

Aberdeenshire

11 miles from Fraserburgh
Grid ref: NJ 839662
Maps: OS Explorer 426, OS Landranger 29 and 30.

The small headland at Cullykhan Bay has a long history, much of it unrecorded. This is Castle Point. An information board describes how this site served for defence for the last 3000 years. The headland was successively a fort for Bronze Age, Iron Age and Pictish people. Later a medieval castle was built here whose remains can still be made out. Finally Fort Fiddes protected these shores in the 18th century.

There is a fine view east to the village of Pennan built along the shoreline. There is just room for a single row of houses between cliff and sea. Scenes in the film *Local Hero* were shot

The picturesque village of Pennan from Castle Point

256

here. The red telephone box that featured in the film still stands and is even a listed structure.

There is a small car park close to Castle Point. Access to Troup Head to the northwest is hazardous and not to be recommended. There is no cliff-top path from either east or west.

Kinnaird Head   ♿   Aberdeenshire

At Fraserburgh
Grid ref: NJ 998677
Maps: OS Explorer 427, OS Landranger 30.

Kinnaird Head is within a few minutes' walk of the centre of Fraserburgh. The Gaelic An Ceann Àrd means a High Headland. This rocky headland is the site of the Museum of Scottish Lighthouses. The history of Scottish lighthouse building and the dominance of the Stevenson dynasty are graphically portrayed. There is a superb collection of lighthouse lenses and outside the buildings, a large number of buoys stranded on dry land. The older ones are iron and the newer ones fibreglass. A visit to the museum includes a climb up

Kinnaird Head and the port of Fraserburgh

Kinnaird Head lighthouse. This unique lighthouse was built by Thomas Smith in 1787 and was the first to be commissioned by the Northern Lighthouse Board. Thomas Smith was the father-in-law of Robert Stevenson, the first of the famous Scottish lighthouse engineers bearing that name. Thomas Smith built his lighthouse up through the unoccupied castle on Kinnaird Head. This is the only instance of such a mode of construction. The original light was a series of whale-oil lamp set at the focal points of parabolic mirrors composed of many small reflecting silvered glass. Although sounding primitive these were highly effective. Robert Stevenson's son Alan made improvements to the light and Alan's nephew David completed the cluster of keepers' cottages. The light was decommissioned in 1991 and a new automatic light set up beside the old light tower.

It is likely that as early as the second century AD the Alexandrian geographer Ptolemy knew of Kinnaird Head and its importance at the entry to the Moray Firth. The port of Fraserburgh gets its name from one Alexander Fraser, a member of a long line of Frasers who came originally from East Lothian. They acquired lands in this area through marriage and built Cairnbulg Castle to the southeast of the little fishing village of Faithlee. In 1546 Faithlee became a Burgh of Barony giving it the right to trade widely. Later the name was changed to Fraserburgh. In the meantime the Frasers improved the harbour and completed Kinnaird Castle on Kinnaird Head around 1570.

Near to the Lighthouse Museum is the so-called Wine Tower, a misleading name. This three-storey building with a turf-covered roof is of unknown purpose and is not open to the public. It may have been a chapel for Catholic worship at the time of the Reformation.

Next to the Lighthouse Museum is the award winning Fraserburgh Heritage Centre that vividly portrays the history of Fraserburgh through the ages. A restaurant with large windows gives views out to sea where passing pods of dolphins can often be seen.

Fraserburgh has a fine sandy beach bounded at its eastern end by Cairnbulg Point, an exposed and rather bleak headland with a small harbour and two breakwaters.

Rattray Head

Aberdeenshire

10 miles from Peterhead
Grid ref: NK 105580
Maps: OS Explorer 427, OS Landranger 30.

Sand is the theme at Rattray Head. The sand dunes are huge, up to 23m (75 feet) high and back a beach 18km (11 miles) long. The sheer scale of dunes, beach and sea makes mere humans seem very small. It is remote, lying 40km (25 miles) south-east of Fraserburgh and reached along a rather rough track. A small cluster of old lighthouse keepers' cottages provides holiday lets and an unexpected, but welcome, café.

Lighthouse at Rattray Head

On climbing over the dunes the lighthouse comes into view. It stands on a wave-washed rock (The Ron) that can be reached by a causeway at low tide. The remnants of old shipwrecks in the sand show how necessary this light is. The lighthouse was designed

259

by David Alan Stevenson and was operational in 1895 and automated in 1982. In World War 2 the Luftwaffe attempted to bomb the light and strafed the lantern with machine gun fire, but inflicted little damage. It is said that when lighthouses were lit with whale oil they had a range of 12 miles and the lighthouse keeper could be smelt at 6 miles.

Keith Inch (Peterhead)   ♿   Aberdeenshire

At Peterhead
Grid ref: NK 140458
Maps: OS Explorer 427, OS Landranger 30.

Keith Inch is now part of the port area of Peterhead forming the northeast limit of Peterhead harbour. It carried a fishing village before Peterhead existed. It was once an island until the channel between it and the mainland was filled in with stones in 1739. John Smeaton (1724-1792) built the South Harbour in 1773. The Eddystone Lighthouse, built on rocks on the approach to Plymouth, was perhaps, Smeaton's most famous construction. Thomas Telford built the North Harbour fifty years later. Keith Inch protected it from the northeast. The area of Keith Inch shows signs of its ancient origin in the pattern of its streets — Ship Street, Pool Lane, Castle Street, Greenhill Road etc. It is now given over to the fishing and oil industries.

The Peterhead Lifeboat Station is seen across the harbour from Keith Inch. It was the first station in Scotland to receive a state-of-the-art Tamar class lifeboat.

By 1840 Peterhead was Britain's major whaling port and over half of Britain's whaling fleet sailed from here. As whaling subsided the emphasis turned to herring. Herring in its turn declined and attention swung to white fish. In the late 20th century

Harbour at Keith Inch, Peterhead

it was Europe's leading white fish port with Europe's largest fish market. Large boats dock here with holds full of fish held in seawater. The contents are pumped out of the holds, under a road and on to the next stage to get the fish to the table. As limits have been placed on fish catches by the quota system Peterhead has become a major supply port for the North Sea oil and gas industry. Here is an example of a community surviving by adapting to new circumstances.

Buchan Ness Aberdeenshire

3 miles from Peterhead
Grid ref: NK 138422
Maps: OS Explorer 427, OS Landranger 30.

Just off the town of Boddam is a large slab of granite connected by a bridge to the mainland, but accessible across the rocks dry-shod at most states of the tide. Before the island of Keith Inch was connected to the mainland at Peterhead this was the most easterly point on the Scottish mainland. Robert Stevenson built a 35m high lighthouse on this rock in 1827. It came close to destruction during the Second World War when a mine drifted onshore and exploded about 50m from the tower. Amazingly it caused only minor damage. The light was electrified in 1978 and automated a decade later.

Robert Stevenson's lighthouse at Buchan Ness

Slains Castle, Port Erroll ♿ Aberdeenshire

7 miles from Peterhead
Grid ref: NK 097356
Maps: OS Explorer 427, OS Landranger 30.

Port Erroll, built on its headland with its small harbour, is the oldest part of the town of Cruden. Paths lead out onto the headland. Very unusually the coast on either side of the headland holds more interest than the headland itself. To the southwest is the sweep of the sands of Cruden Bay and to the northeast is a steep valley with a small stream and beyond are seen the ruins of Slains Castle.

Slains Castle

Along a rather rough track 1km from Port Erroll stand the romantic ruins of Slains Castle. (A car park on the A975 serves the castle. There is still a 1km walk, but an easy one from there.)

There was an Old Slains Castle 10km down the coast that was blown up in 1594. Francis Hay 9th Earl of Erroll built this New Slains Castle in 1597 on the site of another older castle, Bowness Castle. The ruins are massive. It is not possible to walk round the castle as the seaward wall is built right on the edge of the cliff. In 1836 it was largely rebuilt, faced with granite and became a private house. Having fallen into a dangerous state of dilapidation the roof was removed in 1925 as it was in danger of collapse. Bram Stoker stayed in Cruden Bay in 1895 and it is said that Slains Castle was the inspiration for Count Dracula's Castle.

Girdle Ness   ♿   Aberdeen

3 miles from Aberdeen
Grid ref: NJ 972053
Maps: OS Explorer 406, OS Landranger 38.

Girdle Ness projects into the North Sea and guards the approach to Aberdeen docks. The entrance to the docks lies between the South breakwater that springs from Girdle Ness and the North Pier on the opposite side of the River Dee. Pilot boats constantly ply in and out to escort larger vessels. There is a dramatic view of the docks from the north side of the headland.

The lighthouse on Girdle Ness is a building of architectural and historic interest. As was so often the case it needed a maritime disaster to ensure that a lighthouse was built. The trigger in this instance was the wreck of the whaling ship *Oscar* in 1813 with the loss of 43 lives from a crew of 45. Robert Stevenson designed the lighthouse which did not shine until 1833. At first there were two fixed lights, one at the top of the 37m high tower and the other about one third of the way up. The lower light was discontinued in 1890. Originally fuelled by paraffin, it was later electrified and

Girdle Ness at the approach to Aberdeen harbour

converted to a revolving light on a bed of mercury. It was automated in 1991.

Torry Battery stands on the north side of the headland. A medieval blockhouse was built during the 1490s to protect Aberdeen from the English, but has long gone. The present fortifications date from 1860 to counter a French threat. The battery was armed during both World Wars. After each war homeless families were housed here where at least they had water, drainage and a roof over their heads. When the families were finally re-housed in the 1950s the battery fell into decay. During these years migrating birds, including several rare species, frequented the site. Eventually it was smartened up, debris cleared away and some structures strengthened or rebuilt to make the area safe. It is now a scheduled ancient monument and the birds have not been frightened off.

A road winds round this headland and several car parks give the opportunity to leave the car and walk.

Garron Point Aberdeenshire

1 mile from Stonehaven
Grid ref: NO 893877
Maps: OS Explorer 396, OS Landranger 45.

Garron Point just north of Stonehaven is where the Highland Boundary Fault runs into the sea. It crosses Scotland to the southwest to reach the sea again at Toward Point. Rocks to the northwest of this fault are known as Dalradian, after the ancient Kingdom of Dalreada. They are, for the most part, schists 850 to 540 million years old. Southeast of the fault the rocks are much younger, for instance Old Red Sandstone of the Devonian Period about 380 million years old. Both vertical and horizontal movement occurred along this fault line. To the north are the Highlands and to the south the Central Lowlands. The Lowlands dropped relative to the Highlands by as much as 4000m. The geological process then was similar to what is occurring in the Rift Valley in East Africa today.

At a car park in the northern part of Stonehaven signs point the walker to the Highland Fault just a couple of kilometres away. The path runs beside a golf course to the point.

Stonehaven has an attractive harbour. It was home to R W Thomson, the inventor of the pneumatic tyre.

Dunnottar Castle ♿ Aberdeenshire

There is hardly a site for a coastal castle in Britain more dramatic than Dunnottar. A large rock with a flat top more than three acres in area stands in the sea surrounded by vertical cliffs 50m high and only attached to the mainland by a narrow spine of rock. To make the site even more impregnable much of the connecting spine was removed. The rock of Dunnottar is a particularly hard conglomerate or 'pudding stone'. It consists of pebbles and small boulders of varying size set in a red matrix. The matrix is so hard that when a fissure occurs the rock splits through the pebbles and not round them.

Dunnottar Castle

267

Dunnottar was a place of defence in Pictish times. It is thought that St. Ninian visited Dunnottar and built a chapel here in the late 5th century. These early buildings would have been of wood and nothing of them remains. The present chapel is 13th century and may be built on the site of the chapel of St. Ninian. The imposing stone keep, standing towards the landward end of the site, dates from the late 14th century. At the other end of the site is a courtyard surrounded by elegant 17th century buildings giving a degree of comfort not known before. In addition there are extensive stables, storehouses and other buildings that give a vivid impression of life at Dunnottar over the centuries.

Dunnottar Castle has played a prominent part in the history of Scotland. It is particularly remembered for two episodes, one heroic and the other shameful all in the space of half a century.

On 1st January 1651 Charles 2nd was crowned at Scone the year after his father had been beheaded. Cromwell was incensed and invaded Scotland. One objective was to capture the 'Honours of Scotland' the name given to the royal regalia: a crown, sceptre and sword. These were taken to Dunnottar which was defended by just 69 men and 42 guns. Cromwell laid siege to the castle which held out for eight months. The most widely accepted account is that before the castle fell the Honours of Scotland were lowered down a cliff in a basket to a waiting peasant woman who was collecting seaweed. They were then hidden beneath the floor of the nearby church at Kinneff.

Covenanters were a group that rejected the interference of the king in the affairs of the Presbyterian Church of Scotland. In 1685 from 24th May till the end of July 122 men and 45 women who were Covenanters were imprisoned under appalling conditions at Dunnottar. They had no sanitation and had to buy food and water from their jailors. Thirty-seven recanted and signed an oath of allegiance, 5 died in custody, 25 managed to escape, 2 fell to their deaths in the attempt and 15 were recaptured and tortured. Eventually the remainder were deported to the West Indies, but about 70 died on the journey or soon afterwards.

A tour of the castle includes the buildings where these events took place.

There is a car park at Dunnottar Castle. Alternatively it can be approached along a 2km coastal path from Stonehaven. Along this path first Downie Point is reached, but this is inaccessible. A war memorial stands at its base. Next is the small headland of Bowden Head which can be explored with care. The third headland is Dunnottar.

Scurdie Ness   ♿   Angus

3 miles from Montrose
Grid ref: NO 733567
Maps: OS Explorer 382, OS Landranger 54.

The lighthouse, designed by David and Thomas Stevenson, is a building of architectural and historic interest. It is beautiful in its simplicity. The smooth tower rising to 39m is painted white but for yellow ochre down to a gallery just below the lantern and a thin yellow ochre line a short way below that. During World War 2 it was painted black so that it could not be used as a daymark to guide German bombers. However, it was marked on Luftwaffe maps as The Black Pencil! The light first shone in 1870 and was automated in 1987.

The River South Esk runs into a large basin of mud and

Scurdie Ness lighthouse

269

sand before escaping to the sea at Montrose. This salt marsh is a haven for birds. The town of Montrose lies on the northern bank of the river and the much smaller village of Ferryden on the southern. What Ferryden lacks in size it makes up for in history and the attractiveness of its buildings. Ferryden had the first Nursery School in Scotland opened in 1835 by the daughter of the local laird. There are picturesque fishermen's cottages with doors at ground and first floor levels. The hard rock of Scurdie Ness is lava of Devonian age.

Walk from Ferryden to the Scurdie Ness lighthouse 1.5km. On the way are the remains of World War 2 pill-boxes and two conical daymarks to guide boats into Montrose harbour.

Red Head   Angus

6 miles from Arbroath
Grid ref: NO 701474
Maps: OS Explorer 382, OS Landranger 54.

A massive headland stands at the south end of the beautiful sandy beach of Lunan Bay. The northern point is Lang Craig and the southern is Red Head. Both are rather difficult to reach, but well worth the effort. Why is there no lighthouse on this headland? Here are magnificent cliffs 81m high dropping to the sea in two great leaps. Gulls, fulmars and guillemots are in profusion.

The rock of Red Head is Old Red Sandstone. Over an immense period of time two ancient tectonic plates collided. One carried what would become North America and Scotland and another the future England and part of Europe. The force of this collision thrust up a great mountain chain of Himalayan proportions, the Caledonian Mountains, remnants of which persist in Norway, Scotland and Greenland. Erosion of these mountains yielded sediments deposited in huge fresh-water lakes.

High cliffs at Red Head

Compression of these sediments produced the rock known as Old Red Sandstone. Many headlands in northeast Scotland are composed of this rock.

From Inverkeilor on the A92 take the road via Anniston Farm, Raesmill and Ethie Barns then turn left to Red Head. The path from the car park to Red Head is narrow and right on the edge of the cliff. Do not attempt it in a high wind or mist and be very careful with children or dogs.

Banks and ditches of an Iron Age fort are nearby. The path continues northward to a small geo and the remains of St. Murdoch's Chapel. Of this medieval chapel only one gable end remains. (But who was St. Murdoch?) It stands close to a small reservoir. At Lang Craig the rock has changed from Old Red Sandstone to basalt and the superb view north along Lunan Bay opens up. There is no access up onto the headland from Lunan Bay. Beneath the cliffs lies the tiny settlement of Ethie Haven, once home to fishermen, now holiday lets.

Tentsmuir Point
Fife

11 miles from St Andrews
Grid ref: NO 496282
Maps: OS Explorer 371, OS Landranger 54 and 59.

Scottish Natural Heritage owns and manages the internationally important nature reserve and SSSI of Tentsmuir Point. The dunes are grazed by highland cattle to prevent them being colonised by scrub. Outside the reserve to the north this is exactly what has happened. The habitats contained within the reserve include sand bar, sand dunes, wet heath, fen, salt marsh, grassland and woodland. In winter 8000 pink footed geese roost on the inter-tidal mudflats together with 15% of the British population of eider duck. In the summer 2000 grey seals and 750 common seals haul out onto the sand. An information board at the point lists important and rare species of plants and insects found in the reserve such as coralroot orchid *(Corallorhiza trifida)*, grass-of-Parnassus *(Parnassia palustris)*, seaside centaury *(Centaurium littorale)*, green hairstreak butterfly, burnet moth and over 450 species of beetle.

From the town of Tayport a combined cycle track and footpath runs eastward about 3km through Tentsmuir Forest (a conifer plantation) to Tentsmuir Point. To make a round trip go one way along this track and back along a footpath that skirts the edge of the plantation and follows the shoreline. Tree roots and rocks strew the path making it fairly hard going. Concrete blocks to slow down an invasion with tanks and the occasional pillbox remain of World War 2 defences of the Tay estuary. The sound of gunfire from artillery ranges across the water is a reminder of present day military activity.

Out Head   ♿   Fife

2 miles from St Andrews
Grid ref: NO 494197
Maps: OS Explorer 371, OS Landranger 59.

S t Andrews is the Home of Golf. The dunes on the southern side of the estuary of the River Eden that terminate at Out Head hold no fewer than seven 18 hole golf courses. The Royal and Ancient Golf Club traces its origins back to 1754, but the game of golf goes back much further to the 15th or even the 11th century. Scots, Dutch and Chinese all lay claim to inventing the game. Wherever it originated there is no doubt that its heart is in St Andrews.

Extensive sands at Out Head

In addition to golf the town of St Andrews boasts fine architecture, a university, a cathedral, a ruined castle and fine sandy beaches. A great bonus is that it is small and can be explored on foot.

A road (West Sands Road) runs from the town along the east side of the headland to its tip where there is ample parking. To the right is a sandy beach and the Jubilee Golf Course to the left. The sandy beach at the tip of the headland is patterned by swirls of shells deposited by retreating waves. Peace is shattered from time to time by the roar of jets taking off from RAF Leuchars on the other side of the estuary.

Fife Ness   ♿   Fife

10 miles from St Andrews
Grid ref: NO 638098
Maps: OS Explorer 371, OS Landranger 59.

Fife Ness is given over to two golf courses. For a small fee it is possible to park at the Balcomie clubhouse at the end of the headland. Alternatively walk 3km along the coast path from the attractive fishing village of Crail. The footpath is part of the extensive Fife Coastal Path.

Of major interest are two man-made features to be seen on the shore. Facts about both are given on an information board. One is the site of a medieval tide mill. A reservoir in the flat rocks of the foreshore filled with seawater at each tide and while it discharged turned an undershot waterwheel which powered an adjacent corn mill. Various features of this ingenious structure can still be made out although nothing remains of the mill itself.

Nearby is a flat area of rock on which are carved perfect concentric circles and various straight lines. These were templates for cutting stones to construct an offshore lighthouse on the nearby North Carr Rocks. Stones were cut accurately to shape here then taken out to the rocks to construct the lighthouse. Each stone would lock into adjacent stones to right, left, above and below. Robert

Stevenson was the designer. After 5 years work in the early 19th century the light tower was almost complete when a storm brought it crashing down. Later it was replaced with an iron beacon.

Fife Ness

Template on the foreshore of Fife Ness for cutting stone for a lighthouse

The modern lighthouse on Fife Ness is a low structure established in 1975. It does not have the beauty of the Stevenson lighthouses, but no doubt functions as well as any. Previously the entrance to the Firth of Forth was guarded by the light on the Isle of May erected as early as 1636.

Two wildlife reserves, Fife Ness Muir and Kilminning Coast Reserve give ample bird-watching opportunities, particularly for observing the great migrations year on year.

Danes Dyke is a low embankment that nearly cuts across the headland. There is a legend that it was built by the Danes in one night in 874. They had been defeated at the Water of Leven and were awaiting rescue by their fleet.

Headlands at Elie and Earlsferry   ♿   Fife

13 miles from St Andrews
Maps: OS Explorer 371, OS Landranger 59.

The headlands at Elie

Lighthouse at Elie Ness

Elie Ness Grid ref: NT 496993

This small headland with its dainty lighthouse built in 1908 affords a fine view of Earlsferry across the bay. A walk of about 300m leads to Lady's Tower, a summerhouse built in the late 18th century for Lady Janet Anstruther. When she bathed she would send a bell-ringer round the town warning folk to stay away. She would change in the tower and bathe in the pool below. She was not popular when she removed the village of Balclevie in 1771 to improve the view from Elie House. A spey-wifie laid a curse upon her that only six generations of Anstruthers would live in the house. This came true, but six generations was not bad going. There is a car park on the east side of Elie just 500m from this headland and the next.

Headland by Elie Harbour Grid ref: NT 492995

There is a good view of Elie waterfront and harbour. A view indicator on the high ground of the headland pinpoints places on both sides of the Firth of Forth and as far away as Bass Rock and St Abb's Head (33 miles).

Chapel Ness Grid ref: NT 481993

This marks the western end of the bay on which Earlsferry and Elie are built. From here a ferry used to cross the Firth of Forth. A small ruined chapel stands here. According to legend it marks the site of a chapel built by MacDuff in gratitude to local fishermen who ferried him across the Firth while he was escaping from King MacBeth in the 11th century. The present ruins are of a chapel and a hostel provided by the nuns of North Berwick for travellers crossing by ferry.

Kincraig Point Grid ref: NT 465997

This is by far the highest of this series of headlands. The east side is composed of dramatic columns of basalt. Some remains of World War 2 defensive structures and gun emplacements are evident. The intrepid can round the base of the headland, except at high tide, along the Chain Walk. Only the sure-footed and those with a head for heights should attempt this. Do not try it when the tide is coming in as there is a real danger of being caught by the rising water.

Ruddon Point Grid ref: NT 453003

This is a contrast to high, rocky Kincraig Point. Ruddon Point is a range of low sand dunes terminating in rocks.

Gullane Point   East Lothian

5 miles from North Berwick
Grid ref: NT 462830
Maps: OS Explorer 351, OS Landranger 66.

Here is another headland of golfing fame. Gullane Golf Club has three courses. Championship matches are played regularly at Gullane, the first was the British Ladies Championship in 1897. The links here boast some of the finest views from any courses in Britain.

An information board stresses the fragile nature of sand dunes and how they can be seriously damaged by erosion. This happened in the 17th century when so much marram grass had been cut for thatching that blown sand threatened to swamp the village of Gullane. In the early 20th century further erosion was caused by holiday makers and vehicles. During World War 2 it was a training area for the D-Day landings and this caused more damage. Antitank defences can still be seen. The dunes were stabilised by marram grass planted by prisoners of war. The headlands here are composed of hard intrusive igneous rock resistant to erosion by the sea.

A coastal path runs right round Gullane Point and, for the energetic, on to the village of Aberlady and then round Aberlady Point and Craigelaw Point. A high path from Gullane Bents avoids a steep scramble up from the beach. The high path passes through thickets of sea-buckthorn *(Hippophae rhamnoides)* with its enormous thorns.

Park in the car park at Gullane Bents. The name refers to the area of dunes behind the magnificent Gullane Beach.

Tantallon Castle   ♿   East Lothian

3 miles from North Berwick
Grid ref: NT 596851
Maps: OS Explorer 351, OS Landranger 67.

A great curtain wall nearly 4m thick stretches across this small headland from one side to the other. In front of it a deep ditch was dug. Intruders would need to scale the cliffs round the headland or the curtain wall itself to gain access to the castle. The only weak point was the central gate through the wall. William, the first Earl of Douglas built the castle and its curtain wall in the mid 14th century. The gatehouse was extended and strengthened several times. As cannon technology advanced it became necessary to build defensive earthworks and a ravelin. Although previously impregnable it fell to Cromwell in 1650. A

279

fine 17th century lectern style dovecote stands on flat ground in front of the castle. The castle is now in the hands of Historic Scotland and is open to the public.

Tantallon Castle with Bass Rock in the distance

The Bass Rock stands in solitary splendour beyond the castle in the Firth of Forth. During the nesting season the rock is white with gannets that swoop and wheel around it like bees round a hive.

Tantallon Castle is just off the A198 4km east of North Berwick.

St Baldred's Cradle   East Lothian

7 miles from Dunbar
Grid ref: NT 637813
Maps: OS Explorer351, OS Landranger 67.

The cradle is a small sea inlet towards the end of this headland. An information board informs that it is called a cradle because of the gentle lapping of waves on the shore.

Strangely there is a long depression in the ground nearby with rib-like rocks running across it reminiscent of a cradle or the skeleton of a wooden sailing vessel fossilised in stone. The stone of the headland is the remains of a volcano from the Ordovician period.

Woods near St Baldred's Cradle

St Baldred was born in the mid 6th century and was commissioned as a missionary by St Kentigern, more commonly known as St Mungo. St Baldred is commemorated at several sites along the coast. He founded a monastery at Tyninghame and it is stated that he lived as a hermit on Bass Rock and died there.

Tyninghame was the seat of the Earls of Haddington. Thomas Hamilton, the 6th Earl, together with his wife Lady Helen Hope, planted extensive acres of woodland on the estate. They were among the first to establish woodland plantations. An information board at the car park at Tyninghame gives details of their achievements.

Park in the car park at Tyninghame, bear right along a path in a south-easterly direction, turn left along a track through woodland to the coast then right to the headland, a little over 1km level walk from the car park.

Dunbar   ♿   East Lothian

At Dunbar
Grid ref: NT 662793 to NT 682794
Maps: OS Explorer 351, OS Landranger 67.

Much of Dunbar is built on a wide headland with the golf course to the west and harbour to the east.

Dunbar Castle stands as a ruin on a high rock overlooking the entrance to Victoria Harbour. This was one of the earliest and most powerful castles in the whole of Scotland. There is evidence that it was a stronghold of the Votanidi, an ancient British tribe of the Iron Age. In the 7th century AD it was held by the Kingdom of Northumbria and later became a Pictish fortress. The first stone castle dates back to the late 11th century. A famous incident in its history was in 1338 when 'Black Agnes', Agnes Randolph, Countess of Dunbar, led a successful defence of the castle throughout a siege by the English that lasted five long months. The castle was not impregnable and it subsequently changed hands on several occasions. Mary Queen of Scots came here following her abduction by the Earl of Bothwell and again after their marriage. The castle suffered extensive damage when part of the rock on which it was built was removed by explosive charges to form an entrance to the newly constructed Victoria harbour in the 1840s. The technique of firing explosives by electricity was invented and first used on this occasion.

Dunbar is, or certainly should be, famous for another important invention. Beside the quay of Victoria harbour is a screw propeller and an information board describing its significance. Robert Wilson (1803-1882) as a young boy heard that the paddle wheel lost its efficiency in rough weather. By the time he was a mere nine years old he had conceived the idea of the screw propeller. He constructed many different models to discover the most efficient design. Despite the screw propeller being installed and its efficiency over the paddle demonstrated this failed

282

to satisfy the noble lords of the Admiralty and Wilson became increasingly frustrated. He did, however, continue to invent and innovate and headed the Manchester engineering firm of Nasmyth, Wilson and Co. The superiority of the screw over the paddle was finally demonstrated in 1845. Two sloops, H.M.S. Rattler with a screw and H.M.S. Alecto with paddles ran two races in calm and rough conditions. Rattler won on both occasions. Finally they were roped stern to stern and while steaming under full power Rattler towed Alecto at a speed of 2.5 knots. Belatedly in 1880 at the age of 77 Wilson was awarded a prize of £500 by the War Office for his invention of the screw propeller.

Dunbar harbour where the idea of the screw propeller was born.

Dunbar was the birthplace of John Muir (1838-1914), the father of modern conservation. When he was 11 years old he and his family emigrated to Wisconsin and farmed there. He had the intelligence, enthusiasm and powers of observations to become a largely self-taught authority on Natural History, particularly Geology and Botany, with little in the way of formal education in these subjects. He was a passionate advocate of the preservation of nature and was instrumental in persuading President Roosevelt in 1903 to protect the pristine nature of the Yosemite Valley by federal law. On 6th December 2006 the California Museum for History, Women and the Arts inaugurated a Hall of Fame. Thirteen prominent individuals and families were honoured by admission to the Hall of Fame and one of them was John Muir.

Barn's Ness   ♿   East Lothian

4 miles from Dunbar
Grid ref: NT 723773
Maps: OS Explorer 351, OS Landranger 67.

From a car park and campsite a track leads to the lighthouse. David Stevenson designed the 37m high tower and it was operational by 1901. It was automated in 1986. Following a review of all navigation aids by the Joint Lighthouse Authorities of UK and Ireland it was declared that Barn's Ness was redundant and the light was finally extinguished in October 2005 after over a century of uninterrupted service.

Information boards describe the geology of the area. The rock here dates from the Carboniferous Period (354 to 290 million years ago). It consists of beds of limestone, sandstone, mudstone and thin coal seams. Fossil corals are prominent. The Carboniferous Period is so called because all coal deposits date from this time. Land destined to be Britain lay close to the equator. The predominant plants were tree ferns. There were no flowering plants or grasses. Insects were the major members of the animal kingdom and some were huge compared with their modern counterparts. The seas teemed with fish and amphibians were colonising dry land while still needing an aquatic environment for part of their life cycle. Scotland is an ancient country in geological terms and these rocks are some of the youngest to be found in Scotland. The rocky foreshore is backed by thin dunes behind which flat land is crossed by the John Muir Way. This long-distance coastal

Barns Ness lighthouse

footpath extends from Edinburgh along the coast of East Lothian. The path is still under construction and there are plans to continue it to the border at Berwick. It forms part of Nortrail, an ambitious project of coastal paths in countries that form a ring around the North Sea.

Torness nuclear power station is seen across the water to the east.

Torness Point   ♿   East Lothian

6 miles from Dunbar
Grid ref: NT 748755
Maps: OS Explorer 351, OS Landranger 67.

You either like them or you hate them, but you can't ignore them. Nuclear power stations by their sheer size dominate the area for miles around them. Torness is an Advanced

Gas-cooled Reactor built between 1980 and 1988 and due to be decommissioned around 2023. Currently it supplies about a quarter of Scotland's electricity.

Torness Power Station from Barns Ness

A public footpath on two levels rounds the point which has been completely taken over by the power station. It is advised to take the higher path in stormy weather. Various information boards describe the workings of the power station. The sea defences are designed to withstand the fiercest storm likely to be encountered in 10,000 years. The power of the waves is dissipated by a barrier of 17,500 huge concrete blocks called 'dolos' shaped like two hammer-heads attached at right-angles. Each weighs 5.4 tons and those in the breakwater 13 tons apiece. They absorb energy five times as efficiently as the same weight of rock. They do not form a friendly environment for seabirds and very few can be seen around the point.

Torness Point is 9km southeast of Dunbar. There are public car parks just over 1km from the point at Thorntonloch and Skateraw and also at the nuclear power station itself, although the visitor centre at the power station no longer exists.

Siccar Point   Scottish Borders

11 miles from Dunbar
Grid ref: NT 812709
Maps: OS Explorer 346, OS Landranger 67.

For a geologist this is one of the most famous headlands in Britain. If geology were a cult then Siccar Point would carry a temple and be a place of pilgrimage. James Hutton (1726 – 1797) is rightly considered to be the father of modern geology. His ideas, based on his own acute observations, were to lay the foundations of this new science. He, it was, who concluded that

Hutton's unconformity at Siccar Point

the earth is subject to the dual processes of erosion and new land formation and that these processes which had been operating over vast aeons of time are active in the present. These ideas completely shattered the concept, widely held at the time, that the earth was only about 6,000 years old based on a crude reckoning from individual biblical verses. At Siccar Point he defined what he termed an 'unconformity'. By this word he described a buried land surface on which a sedimentary rock had been deposited at a later period. At Siccar Point nearly vertical beds of greywackes and shales of Silurian age are overlain by nearly horizontal beds of Old Red Sandstone of the Devonian Period.

From the A1107 take a minor road signed to Pease Bay. After about 200m bear right to a complex of buildings that is a vegetable distribution centre. Park here and walk through the complex keeping to the road to the left and be wary of lorries and forklift trucks. Beyond the complex climb up to the left and through a number of field gates until the point is reached. The slope down to the point is steep and can be slippery.

Fast Castle Head   Scottish Borders

10 miles from Eyemouth
Grid ref: NT 86710
Maps: OS Explorer 346, OS Landranger 67.

A path runs through the heather high above the ruins of Fast Castle seen far below. From this elevation there are superb views along the coast. The ruins of the castle are reached across an isthmus just a metre or two wide with iron chain railings for support. This is not for the vertiginous. Take particular care of children. All that remain today are fragments of standing and

Fast Castle

fallen masonry. This is a strange site for a castle. It stands 30m or so above the sea. Yet much higher ground above the castle gives an advantage to any attacker. The stone castle dates from before 1333. As would be expected of a castle so close to the Scottish/ English border it was captured on a number of occasions: by the English 1346, Scottish 1410, English 1547. It passed through the hands of several Scottish landowners until it finally fell into its present ruinous condition.

288

A minor road branching off the A1107 about 8km west of Coldingham leads to a car park at Downlaw Farm where the path is signed to Fast Castle just 0.5km away.

St Abb's Head & Scottish Borders

4 miles from Eyemouth
Grid ref: NT 912692
Maps: OS Explorer 346, OS Landranger 67.

This magnificent headland stands high above the sea and is made of lava from an ancient volcano. Between this great block of rock and the 'mainland' lies a valley with a man-made lake terminating to the northwest in the little cove of Pettico Wick. From here there is a superb view along the wild coast. The coastline round the headland is extremely rugged and cut by numerous small inlets. The ledges on the cliffs and offshore stacks are ideal nesting sites for an estimated 60,000 sea birds. Kittiwakes and guillemots are the most numerous.

Wild coast of St Abb's Head

St Abb's Head is a nature reserve and offshore is the first of Scotland's marine nature reserves established in 1984. Many more such marine parks are needed. It has been shown that if a total ban on all fishing, including sea floor fishing for shellfish, that areas that had been denuded of most life could regenerate within

289

a very few years. These waters, with their numerous wrecks, are popular with divers.

Peace of the lochan at St Abb's Head

The lighthouse was designed by David and Thomas Stevenson and was established in 1862. The light is part way down the cliff and reached by a staircase. A lighthouse built on top of the cliff would often be swathed in mist. (See Beachy Head.) The first light was oil fired. Electricity was introduced over a century later in 1966 and it was automated in 1993. St Abb's had the first siren fog signal in Scotland operational in 1876. The light still shines, but the foghorn is silent.

The name St Abb's Head is derived from St Ebba or Æbbe, a sister of a 7th century King of Northumbria. She founded a monastery on or near the headland. Shortly after her death it burnt down and was never rebuilt. Its exact location is unknown. Kirk Hill is a high point of the headland where monks from Coldingham Priory built a small oratory in the 12th century dedicating it to Our Lord and St Ebba. Some authorities state that St Ebba in the 7th century built a religious house on Kirk Hill. Much remains clouded in mystery, but it is certain that she was a powerful influence in bringing Christianity to the pagan Angles of Northumbria.

Above the picturesque village of St Abbs is a visitor centre and National Trust for Scotland car park. Disabled people can drive to the lighthouse. The able-bodied must walk the 3km along the road to the headland. From the lighthouse it is possible to climb to the highest point of the headland for magnificent views. Another footpath follows the shore of the lake.

Fort Point, Eymouth   ♿   Scottish Borders

At Eyemouth
Grid ref: NT 944649
Maps: OS Explorer 346, OS Landranger 67.

Little remains of the important, yet short-lived, forts that once occupied this headland. In the 16th century advances in cannon technology made the old forts with vertical stone walls obsolete. They had been designed to repel armies equipped with little more than bows and arrows and battering rams. New forts were designed in Italy to withstand artillery fire from modern cannon. They had low walls fronted with sloping earth embankments to deflect the cannon ball and absorb its energy. Bastions were placed at the corners. The design was called Trace Italienne. In 1547

Cannon at Fort Point, Eyemouth

291

the English on the orders of the Duke of Somerset, who was the protector of the boy king Edward VI, built the first Trace Italienne fort in the British Isles at Eyemouth. A mere three years later it was abandoned and the structure dismantled. The French, at the request of the Scots, built another Trace Italienne fort of stronger design in 1557. This only lasted for two years until it was demolished in 1559 when peace was established between England and France. The earthworks outlining the French fort can still be made out.

Just to the west of Fort Point is the promontory of Hairy Ness, the site of an Iron Age fort called Corn Fort.

In a great storm in October 1881 no fewer than 129 fishermen from Eyemouth were drowned. One hundred years later the womenfolk of Eyemouth embroidered a beautiful tapestry in memory of the disaster. It can be seen in Eyemouth museum.

A notice board gives the grizzly information that in the 17th century Eyemouth was a principal centre of witch mania. No fewer than two dozen women and several men were convicted of witchcraft and burnt at the stake along this shore.

Castle Point, Lindisfarne   &♿;   Northumberland

14 miles from Berwick-upon-Tweed
Grid ref: NU 140416
Maps: OS Explorer 340, OS Landranger 75.

The Holy Island of Lindisfarne is one of the most important sites in the history of Christianity in the whole of Britain and has played a crucial role in the development of these islands. Northumbria became the dominant power in the region under the Christian king Oswald in 634 AD. He sent to Iona for a missionary to preach to the pagan Northumbrian people. Corman was sent, but found the people too obstinate and

Lindisfarne Castle

barbarous. St Aidan succeeded him in 635AD and founded a monastery on Lindisfarne within sight of the king's stronghold of Bamburgh Castle. Aidan, followed later by St Cuthbert established Lindisfarne as the most important Christian influence in the northeast. It was here that the beautiful Lindisfarne Gospels, displayed now in the British Museum, were written in 698AD and illuminated in memory of St Cuthbert.

The Vikings raided Lindisfarne in June 793AD, one of the first places in Britain to suffer under the Norseman's axe. The Anglo-Saxon Chronicle and Alcuin, a Northumbrian in the court of Charlemagne, give lurid accounts of this raid that certainly sent shivers down the back of western Christendom. There is no doubt that monks were killed, buildings destroyed and booty removed, but the community survived, albeit in a weakened state and its church rebuilt. Today the extensive ruins of the medieval church and other monastic buildings are a powerful reminder of its former glory. Statues of Aidan and Cuthbert stand among these remains.

The Lindisfarne Centre in the village provides the visitor with a clear and detailed account of the history of Lindisfarne. The rich beauty of the Lindisfarne Gospels can be seen in facsimile and on screen by touch-screen 'turning pages' technology.

Saint Aidan

Lindisfarne Castle stands proudly on top of its hill of dolerite, part of the Great Whin Sill and the highest point on the island. The Tudor Fortress was built to control the unruly border with Scotland. The castle lost its strategic importance with the unification of the Kingdom, but it remained a minor military garrison into the 17th century. Sir Edwin Lutyens extended and converted it into a stylish Edwardian private house in the early years of the 20th century. Today it is in the hands of the National Trust and is open to the public. Gertrude Jrkyll designed the nearby walled garden.

The Heugh is another block of dolerite beside the harbour. On it stand a simple war memorial cross, a solar powered light, the remains of a 17th century artillery fort and an 18th century watchtower.

Access to Lindisfarne is along a causeway during the lower half of the tidal range. Do not attempt to walk or drive to Lindisfarne without first consulting a tide timetable and making sure that it is safe to cross. Lives have been lost here. The sand and mud flats and much of the island itself are a nature reserve and haven for waders, geese, ducks, swans, divers, grebes and seabirds. A white, pyramidal daymark stands at Emmanuel Head at the most north-easterly point of the island. There are distant views of Bamburgh Castle and the Farne Islands from the castle and the Heugh.

Lindisfarne is a fine place to explore on foot. Climb the Heugh and walk round the small harbour with its overturned boats converted into sheds. The castle is just over 1km from the village. Beyond the castle a walk to the north along the coast brings you to Emmanuel Head.

Budle Point, Bamburgh Northumberland

19 miles from Berwick-upon-Tweed
Grid ref: NU 162361
Maps: OS Explorer 340, OS Landranger 75.

Bamburgh Castle stands foursquare on a dolerite mound. Its massive walls look as capable of withstanding the onslaught from wind, wave and cannon as the rock itself. Excavation has shown that the site has been occupied for more than two millennia. There is so much of architectural interest beneath the present ground surface which is 5 metres above the bedrock. It was successively a citadel of Ancient Britons, Romans, Britons again, Anglo-Saxons and Normans. The Normans built the massive keep that stands today. When it became obsolete as a fortress it gradually fell into ruin until it was bequeathed to a Dr John Sharp for charitable use in the 18th century. He restored the keep. The first Lord Armstrong purchased the castle in 1894. He performed extensive repairs and extensions. Today it is partly the private dwelling of the current owner, partly divided into flats, but much of it is open to the public. This part is a museum of the life of Lord Armstrong and displays the treasures of a great Victorian industrial magnate.

At one time two cannon were mounted on top of the keep and were fired to alert the local population when a ship was in distress. There was also a speaking horn to hail the stricken vessel.

A wide sandy beach backed by dunes sweeps round Budle Point 2km northwest of Bamburgh. A road leads from

Bamburgh to a golf club house from where a path through the golf course continues to the point. Bamburgh Lighthouse stands by the clubhouse. It is a squat tower attached to a low building looking for all the world like a face. The door is an open mouth and two round windows form the eyes. The light was established in 1910.

Bamburgh Castle near Budle Point

The Farne Islands can be seen out to sea. These are renowned for bird and sea life and for the heroic action of the lighthouse keeper's daughter Grace Darling on 5th September 1838. Her courage in rowing a small boat in heavy seas to reach shipwrecked survivors stranded on a rock is one of the most inspiring of all sea rescues. Her action did much to stimulate others to establish lifeboats around the coast.

The village of Bamburgh hosts the Grace Darling Museum and the fine, historic Church of Saint Aidan.

Dunstanburgh Castle Point

Northumberland

28 miles from Berwick-upon-Tweed
Grid ref: NU 258221
Maps: OS Explorer 332, OS Landranger 75.

Whatever the weather this most evocative of Britain's coastal castles makes a profound impact on the visitor with a spark of romance in his soul. Don't miss the experience on account of a thick sea mist. Even then the headland with the silhouette of its majestic castle ruins looms out of the haar and it only takes a little imagination to hear the sound of galloping hooves and the clash of steel. The castle stands on a dolerite headland, part of the Great Whin Sill, with precipitous cliffs providing nesting sites for thousands of kittiwakes and other

Ghostly Dunstanburgh Castle in the haar

297

seabirds. The cliffs also give the castle natural protection and on the remaining aspect a deep ditch was cut through the hard dolerite rock.

Thomas of Lancaster started to build the first recorded fortifications on this headland in 1312. His gatehouse is still the most impressive feature of this largely ruined castle. It served as a stronghold against the raiding Scots. Later he rebelled against the king, was defeated at the Battle of Boroughbridge and executed for treason in 1322. John of Gaunt, through his first marriage, became Duke of Lancaster and inherited Dunstanburgh. He added to the castle and made Thomas of Lancaster's gatehouse his keep. It played a part in the War of the Roses and fell to Yorkist forces after a long siege in 1462. At no time in its history was Dunstanburgh Castle armed with cannon. It is a throwback to the era of bows and arrows and boiling tar. From the mid 15th century it served no defensive purpose and fell into decay. Today the castle is owned by the National Trust, managed by English Heritage and is open to the public.

There is no vehicular access to the castle. To reach it entails a walk of about 2km from a car park near Embleton, or a little further away from Craster. The path follows the coast. On the boulder-strewn shore towards the castle lies Greymare Rock. This is an unusual saddle-shaped outcrop of folded limestone.

Newbiggin Point Northumberland

7 miles from Blyth
Grid ref: NZ 318880
Maps: OS Explorer 325, OS Landranger 81.

Newbiggin Point shelters Newbiggin Bay from the north and forms the limit of the town of Newbiggin-by-the-Sea. The headland is a grassy area with steps leading down to a gently sloping wave-cut platform. Dominating the scene is the 14th century church of St Bartholomew whose spire has been a guide to sailors for centuries. Beneath a large stone lies a time capsule with mementos of the 20th century chosen by children to mark the new millennium.

St Bartholomew's Church, Newbiggin-by-the-Sea

The historic town of Newbiggin-by-the-Sea was once a major port for shipping grain and coal. A lifeboat was established here in 1851 following a disaster when ten local fishermen lost their lives. Walking from the town to the headland you pass Newbiggin Lifeboat Station. This is a Discover station whose doors are open to the public in summer months. The lifeboat station is the oldest in continuous operation in the country. It is equipped with an Atlantic 85 lifeboat for inshore rescues.

Standing resolutely out in the bay are huge figures sculpted by Sean Henry of a young man and woman gazing out to sea.

St Mary's or Bait Island   ♿   North Tyneside

4 miles from Tynemouth
Grid ref: NZ 352755
Maps: OS Explorer 316, OS Landranger 88.

St Mary's Island 6km north of Tynemouth is joined to the mainland by a causeway, but cut off at high tide. The corresponding part of the mainland is called Curry's Point. On the 4th September 1739 Michael Curry was hanged for the murder of Robert Shevil, the landlord of the Three Horseshoes Inn at Hartley. His body was hanged in chains from a gibbet at the site known since then as Curry's Point. Why do we commemorate the criminal rather than the victim, but that's the usual way it is. Who can remember those who Al Capone rubbed out?

The lighthouse has been operational since 1898 and replaced a previous one at Tynemouth Priory. It is open to the public. Also on St Mary's Island are attractive low buildings round the lighthouse including a shop and conference room. A small garden is maintained by the Friends of St Mary's Island. A bird-watching hide looks out to sea.

Lighthouse at St Mary's Island

300

Along this stretch of coast from Seaton Sluice to Tynemouth Upper Carboniferous coal measure rocks are seen as clearly as anywhere in Britain. A geological fault runs close to the lighthouse. Rock to the north of the fault has moved down relative to rock to the south. The fault is seen as a gully to the seaward side of the lighthouse.

Tynemouth, Pen Bal Crag   ♿   North Tyneside

At Tynemouth
Grid ref: NZ 374695
Maps: OS Explorer 316, OS Landranger 88.

The extensive ruins of Tynemouth Priory dominate the rocky headland on the north side of the mouth of the River Tyne. They give clear evidence of the importance of this ecclesiastical house. The structure that remains dates mainly from the 11th and 12th centuries and demonstrates Norman and Early English styles. The only part with a surviving vaulted roof is the small Percy Chantry from the 15th century. There was an earlier Christian community on the site. It was attacked by the Danes in 800 and finally destroyed in 875. Three kings are reputed to be buried here: Oswin, King of Deira, Osred, King of Northumberland and Malcolm III King of Scotland. North Tyneside coat of arms carries three crowns.

From the headland springs a 1km long breakwater that balances one on the south bank of the river. The headland is notched by a tiny bay and beach called Prior's Haven. The northern part of the headland is known as Pen Bal Crag meaning 'The Headland of the Rampart on the Rock'. Indeed across its neck runs a ditch and bank. This area has been of strategic importance throughout history. In addition to the Priory the

Pen Bal Crag, Tynemouth. The ruins of Tynemouth
Priory are seen in the centre of the headland.

headland carries the remains of a medieval castle and gun emplacements of a World War 2 battery. Access to the headland is through the 14th century gatehouse of the medieval castle. This is a substantial three-storey building with outer and inner barbicans, hall and other rooms. Walls would have run round the whole defended part of the headland. Some remain, but much has been lost by natural erosion. Artillery pieces from different periods are displayed around the headland.

On the southern part of the headland beyond Prior's Haven is a vast statue of

Admiral Lord Collingwood. He was born in Newcastle-upon-Tyne. He it was who on his ship 'Royal Sovereign' was first to engage the enemy at the Battle of Trafalgar. For a whole hour his was the only British ship within range of French or Spanish vessels.

Lizard Point   ♿   South Tyneside

3 miles from South Shields
Grid ref: NZ 410643
Maps: OS Explorer 316, OS Landranger 88.

L izard Point, just 2km south of South Shields, is in a beautiful stretch of coast with limestone cliffs, offshore stacks and a natural arch at the point itself. As the ports of Sunderland on the Wear to the south and Newcastle and South Shields on the Tyne to the north developed there was a great increase in the amount of shipping along this coast. In the single year of 1869 twenty ships were wrecked between South Shields and Sunderland. A considerable tonnage was lost on an underwater reef just offshore.

Plans were laid for a lighthouse at Souter Point over 1km south of Lizard Point. James Douglass was given the responsibility

Souter Lighthouse at Lizard Point

to design and build the light, but he chose Lizard Point over Souter Point as there the cliffs were higher. That is why Souter lighthouse is at Lizard Point. The name was left unchanged to avoid confusion with the lighthouse at the Lizard in Cornwall. The lighthouse was operational in 1871 and was the first in the world to be powered by electricity. The light was discontinued in 1988. The lighthouse is in the hands of the National Trust and is open to the public.

Coastal paths extend most of the way from the Tyne at South Shields to the Wear at Sunderland, a distance of 11km and well worth the walk.

The Heugh, Hartlepool   ♿   Hartlepool

At Hartlepool
Grid ref: NZ 532338
Maps: OS Explorer 306, OS Landranger 93.

On the 16th December 1914 three German cruisers, SMS Blücher, SMS Seydlitz and SMS Moltke fired 1150 shells into unsuspecting Hartlepool killing 112 including 8 British soldiers, the first military casualties on British soil of World War 1. The shore battery on The Heugh retaliated with 120 shells that killed 80 German sailors. Two other German cruisers, SMS Derfflinger and SMS Von der Tann, completed the flotilla that shelled English east coast towns. (See Castle Headland, Scarborough.)

The defensive importance of the headland at Hartlepool, The Heugh, had been recognised since the 16th century. Today the Heugh Battery is a scheduled Gun Battery Museum with a display of artillery from World War 2 back to Napoleonic times. Near the battery is a winged statue "Triumphant Youth" a memorial to those killed in the Hartlepool bombardment, together with memorials to those who died in subsequent conflicts.

The Heugh, Old Hartlepool

The Heugh, or The Headland, was once an island. Long-shore drift brought in material that eventually linked it with the mainland. Old Hartlepool was built on this headland and West Hartlepool on the mainland proper. The headland curls round the old harbour providing shelter from the north and east. Look on the headland for the little statue of Andy Capp, the comic strip character created by Reg Smythe who hailed from Hartlepool.

The first lighthouse was built on The Heugh in 1846 and was probably the first in the world to be lit reliably by gas. This lighthouse was dismantled during World War 1 as it obstructed the lines of sight of the coastal battery. A temporary light served the purpose until the present lighthouse on the headland was built in 1927. The lighthouse that can be seen today is made of cast iron painted white.

Prominent on the headland stands the Church of St Hilda. Hilda was the abbess of the monastery at Hartlepool from 649 to

657 when she founded the monastery at Whitby. Nothing remains of her monastery at Hartlepool which was destroyed by Danish Vikings in the 9th century.

Andy Capp in his home town of Hartlepool

The Historic Quay in Hartlepool must be one of the finest maritime museums in Britain. The prize exhibit is HMS Trincomalee, the oldest British ship afloat, built in Mumbai (then Bombay) in 1817.

The story did the rounds that a French warship during the Napoleonic Wars was wrecked and the sole survivor was a monkey. Local fisherman hanged the unfortunate creature thinking it to be a French spy. This was all an invention of the Victorian music hall with the popular song *Fishermen hung the Monkey-O*. A monument to the fictitious monkey stands on the headland and his image pops up all over the place.

Saltwick Nab   ♿   North Yorkshire

1 mile from Whitby
Grid ref: NZ 914113
Maps: OS Explorer OL27, OS Landranger 94.

The headland of Saltwick Nab is 1.5km along the coast path, part of the Cleveland Way, from Whitby Abbey. The coast here is National Trust property. Look down from the path onto a moonscape. The headland has been nearly completely removed on account of its alum rich shales. (See Old Peak,

Quarrying erosion at Saltwick Nab

Ravenscar). Only a thin strip of still un-vegetated quarried land remains.

A seam of jet runs along this coast around low-water line. It has largely been worked out, but occasionally pieces of jet can be found on the shore. Jet is the black (hence 'jet black') fossil of the Monkey Puzzle tree *(Araucaria araucana)*. Jewellery made of jet was a fashion 'must have' in Victorian times.

Spend more time at the ruins of the Benedictine Abbey of Whitby. Oswy, King of Northumbria founded the abbey in 657 and appointed Hilda as the first Abbess. It was a monastery for both Nuns and Monks. Cædmon, the medieval poet, was a monk here. He is the earliest English poet whose name we know who composed verses in his native tongue. The Synod of Whitby in 664 within the walls of the abbey determined that the English Church would follow the direction of Rome rather than the Celtic tradition. The abbey was destroyed by Vikings in 867, rebuilt about 200 years later and was finally dissolved by Henry VIII in 1540. The gaunt ruins that served as a landmark for shipping are still impressive.

Just 10km north along the coast is the rather similar headland of Kettle Ness. The Jurassic rocks of the Yorkshire coast from Redcar in the north to the Cretaceous chalk of Flamborough Head in the south are rich in fossils. The largest dinosaur fossil found along this coast was dug out of the shale at Kettle Ness in the mid 19th century. It was a Plesiosaur. These aquatic dinosaurs sometimes grew to 15metres in length. The fossil is now in the National Museum of Ireland and a cast resides in the Natural History Museum in London.

Old Peak (or South Cheek), Ravenscar North Yorkshire

12 miles from Scarborough
Grid ref: NZ 980023
Maps: OS Explorer OL27, OS Landranger 94.

Although this is now a peaceful scene it was once an industrial site of one of Britain's earliest chemical industries. Alum is a white crystalline compound (Hydrated Aluminium Potassium Sulphate) that had many applications, most importantly as a mordant in the dyeing of cloth and in the leather industry to make leather supple. In the early 17th century it had to be imported from Italy and was very expensive. It was then discovered that shales along the coast of Yorkshire could yield this important commodity. The Peak Alum Works at Ravenscar operated for more than two centuries from about 1650 to 1862. Layers of alternating shale and brushwood were burnt for no less than 9 months and up to a year. The resultant 'calcined shale' was washed and the liquor subjected to a series of boilings to remove impurities. The concentrated liquor was alkalinised with stale human urine and pure alum crystallised out. Parallel ruts on the flat rocks of the foreshore show where carts plied between the alum works and flat-bottomed ships. There's also a small rectangular 'harbour' cut into the rocks and several postholes. The carts could follow these rutways even when the rocks were under water. Coal would be brought ashore and alum sent to the ships. The rutways are difficult to find and are immediately below the old alum works. The Peak Alum Works was one of thirty along the north Yorkshire coast. Well-marked footpaths run through the old workings and information boards bring them to life.

A path from Ravenscar passes a hotel and crosses a golf course on its way to the base of the headland of Old Peak. The distance is only about 700m, but down to the head-land the path is very steep and a bit of a scramble. This heather-clad head-land runs down to a flat wave-washed rock platform. The ledge on the right (east) side of the headland marks a major geological fault. The land to

Rock patterns in Robin Hood's Bay
seen from Old Peak

the southeast has dropped 150 meters and moved seaward by 400 meters. The rocks to the south are younger than those to the north, but still within the Jurassic Period. The reef extending from the tip of the headland is known as Peak Steel and is made of a hard sandstone. Look for fossil ferns.

The view across Robin Hood's Bay at low tide to the headland of Ness Point or North Cheek shows dramatic swirls of alternating Limestone and Shale rock called 'scours'. The land that once filled this bay was pushed up to form a low dome. As this dome was eroded it left these concentric patterns. The rocks at the centre are the oldest and those round the outside the youngest, though all are Jurassic.

Near the hotel stands a reinstalled rocket post. If a ship were stranded on the rocks rockets carrying a line would be fired from such a rocket post across the stricken ship. A heavier line would be attached and hopefully the crew rescued by Breeches Buoy.

The National Trust Visitor Centre at Ravenscar gives information about local items of interest including the Whitby to Scarborough Railway and the history of the Alum Works. Ravenscar was planned as a seaside resort to rival Whitby and Scarborough, but these grandiose Victorian plans were never realised.

The trig point above Ravenscar is one end of the Lyke Wake Walk that crosses the North York Moors from Osmotherley. There are many shorter walks around Ravenscar. A pleasant one of about 5km is to follow the Cleveland Way north-west along the cliff top to a road just before Stoupe Bank Farm. Turn left up the road to the old railway line and walk along it back to Ravenscar. There are steps down to the shore at Stoupe Bank Farm.

The headland of Ness Point (North Cheek) on the north side of Robin Hood's Bay provides fine views of the town and the bay itself.

Castle Headland, Scarborough   ♿   North Yorkshire

At Scarborough
Grid ref: TA 051892
Maps: OS Explorer 301, OS Landranger 101.

Scarborough claims to be Britain's oldest seaside resort. It boasts two magnificent sandy beaches separated by Castle Headland that juts out into the North Sea from the centre of the town. The Old Harbour clings to the southern part of the headland. Scarborough Castle stands in a dominant position on the highest part of the headland about 100m above the sea. Elegant terraced houses overlook the two bays and the harbour. Marine Drive runs right round the headland just above sea level. The cliffs are rich in fossil ammonites, starfish and bivalves.

Castle Headland, Scarborough

The defensive capability of the headland was exploited during the Iron Age. In their turn the Romans built a signal station on the headland to give warning of Anglo-Saxon raiders. This was one of a chain of signal stations around the eastern and southern coasts of England. The castle dates from the mid 12th century. Although it is largely ruined it is still an impressive structure today. During the Civil War it changed hands on several occasions and was partially dismantled on the order of Parliament. Further damage was inflicted on the morning of 16th December 1914 when two German battle cruisers, SMS Derfflinger and SMS Von der Tann, shelled the town before steaming north to inflict damage on Whitby (See The Heugh, Hartlepool). The fatalities and injuries suffered by the civilian population by the bombardment produced a wave of public anger. "Remember Scarborough" became a rallying cry and appeared on recruiting posters.

St Mary's church, on the neck of the headland, dates back to the 12th century, though much of it was constructed at later dates. Anne Brontë's grave can be found in the churchyard.

William Smith (1769-1839), honoured as the Father of English Geology, lived in Scarborough from 1824 to 1826 when he built the Rotunda as a geological museum. It has been modernised and opened in 2007 as the William Smith Museum of Geology. William Smith produced the first geological map of Britain. By his meticulous observation and encyclopaedic knowledge of fossils he was able to place strata of sedimentary rocks anywhere in the country in their correct chronological sequence. For most of his life he did not receive the recognition he was due, but his immense contribution to the science of Geology is now acknowledged.

Filey Brigg   North Yorkshire

At Filey
Grid ref: TA 138813
Maps: OS Explorer 301, OS Landranger 101.

No other headland in Britain even remotely resembles Filey Brigg. The headland projects 1.6km out to sea. The landward half is high and goes by the name of Carr Naze. Filey Brigg refers to the low narrow rocky extension to seaward that is covered at high tide. The north side of Carr Naze is composed of high cliffs affording challenging rock climbs. The contrast with the south side is stark. Here cliffs of boulder clay have been eroded by rainwater into vertical gullies and ridges. This is the best example in Britain of Badlands scenery, but not on quite the scale of the Badlands of Nebraska and Wyoming! Straddling the Naze are the foundations of a Roman signal station much of which has been eroded away into the sea. The Naze is narrow and one day the sea will cut it in two. The name Filey possibly means 'Promontory shaped like a sea monster'.

Filey Brigg itself is composed of a hard sandstone called Birdsall Calcareous Grit lying on limestone. The beds slope gently

Rough sea breaking over Filey Brigg from Carr Naze

to the south. Bivalve fossils are found in the rocks of the Brigg. Also the fossilised tunnels of burrowing creatures are abundant in limestone boulders scattered along the Brigg.

An erected stone on Carr Naze marks the end of the Wolds Way and the Cleveland Way.

An enigmatic line of rocks extends southwards from Filey Brigg. There is still an ongoing debate as to whether this is a natural feature or part of a harbour wall dating from Medieval or even Roman times.

Cobles are small fishing boats characteristic of the northeast coast of England and may be seen at Filey and other fishing villages. Originally of a Norse design their basic shape has not changed for hundreds of years, but there are many minor variations. The most striking feature of the Coble is the high prow, essential for launching it from a beach through heavy surf.

The headland stands just 1km north of the town of Filey and can be reached along a footpath or via the beach.

Flamborough Head ♿

East Riding of Yorkshire

6 miles from Bridlington
Grid ref: TA 257706
Maps: OS Explorer 301, OS Landranger 101.

This is one of Britain's major headlands. Here the great band of chalk that crosses England from SW to NE reaches the North Sea. The highest cliffs are on the northern aspect. The coast is made more dramatic by stacks, arches, caves and wave-cut chalk platforms. The chalk here is harder than along the English Channel coast and more resistant to erosion.

Flamborough Head

314

Bempton Cliffs on the northern side rise sheer out of the sea to 122m (400 feet). This is an RSPB nature reserve. It is an important breeding site for puffins, guillemots, kittiwakes and the only place on the British mainland where gannets nest.

Danes Dyke has nothing to do with Denmark. It is a massive 4km long Iron Age earthwork that crosses the headland to defend 13 square kilometres (5 square miles) of territory. Nature trails run along the dyke.

Flamborough village contains several houses built of chalk. To north and south are two small bays called, appropriately, North Landing and South Landing.

The Oldest surviving lighthouse in England built 1674

Near the tip of the headland is a tall octagonal chalk tower. Sir John Clayton built the tower in 1674 and it is the oldest surviving light tower in England. It was designed to carry a beacon fired by coal and brushwood, but it is not known if this was ever lit. Samuel Wyatt designed and John Matson of Bridlington built the present lighthouse in 1806. Prior to that date over 170 ships were wrecked off Flamborough Head in 36 years, about one every 12 weeks. The light was converted from oil to electricity in 1974 and automated in 1996.

The American War of Independence was not only fought on American soil. One September evening in 1779 a fierce naval battle raged just off Flamborough Head. John Paul Jones (1747-1792) was born in Scotland and is now revered as the founder of the US Navy (see Southerness Point). He was commanding a squadron of five ships when he encountered a large fleet of merchantmen from the Baltic protected by two British warships under the command of Captain Richard Pearson. The ensuing battle could be seen clearly from the mainland. Although Jones's ship, *Bonhomme Richard*, was severely damaged and sank in Bridlington Bay his fleet won the encounter. The merchantmen found shelter in Scarborough and other ports along the coast. Captain Richard Pearson had to face a court martial, but was acquitted and later knighted by King George III.

There is plenty here for the walker. There are several car parks, for instance at South Landing and North Landing, adjacent to the stunning cliff-top path that runs round the whole headland. Many paths cross the headland so you can construct a circular walk of a length to suit your time and energy. South Landing is the site of Flamborough Lifeboat Station. This is classed as a Discover Station and is open to visitors in summer months.

Spurn Head ♿ East Riding of Yorkshire

25 miles from Hull
Grid ref: TA 397105
Maps: OS Explorer 292, OS Landranger 107 and 113.

December 5th 2013 saw the worst storm surge on the east coast of England for many years. The sea smashed over the central part of this land spit tearing up the road and cutting off essential services to the community at the far end of the headland. Repair work is underway but whether the community can return to its previous condition is uncertain. The following description dates from before the damage was inflicted. It is hoped that it is also a true description of how things will be again one day.

Spurn Head is a 5km long hook-shaped shingle and sand spit curling back into the mouth of the Humber. At the 'entrance' to Spurn Head a visitor centre provides a wealth of local information and literature. Nearby there is a bird observatory. On payment of a toll it is possible to drive the 6km almost to the tip of the headland. It is, of course, possible to walk along this narrow spit and enjoy the contrasting views on each side. Much of the spit is extremely narrow being just 50m wide and looks to be vulnerable to breaching by the sea. To seaward on the eastern side waves break on the sandy shore. On the other side in the shelter of the spit are extensive salt marshes that provide habitat for thousands of waders. Along the way are fragments of rail track dating from World War 1. The spit widens out at its tip where there is a collection of houses, a jetty, a lifeboat station, a pilot station and two lighthouses.

The Holderness Coast north of Spurn Head is the fastest eroding coast in Europe. Material from here is carried south by 'longshore drift' (see Blakeney Point) to build Spurn Head. It was here in 1066 that the defeated Viking Norwegian forces took refuge after the battle of Stamford Bridge before returning home. The spit is constantly changing and over the last few hundred years has altered considerably. Many villages have been lost to the sea. Among the most remarkable were Ravenser and Ravenser Odd. In the early 13th century an island appeared off the tip of Spurn Head and as it seemed to be stable a village was established on it

Spurn Head

called (appropriately) Ravenser Odd. In the mid 13th century it was even taking trade from Hull and Grimsby and had its own mayor. A century later, though, the island and the town it carried had disappeared beneath the waves.

Spurn is still continuously changing shape. Marram grass helps to prevent erosion and sea-buckthorn (Hippophae rhamnoides) with its long thorns and bright orange berries forms a dense covering. The dunes, salt marsh and grassland provide habitats for many wild flowers, invertebrate life and birds.

There have been many lighthouses on Spurn Head and the sea has washed away at least eight of them. The earliest records go back to 1427. Lighthouses were built in pairs; a high light and a low light. The present high light tower was completed in 1895, but ceased to shine in 1985. The low light was redundant as the high tower carried lights at two levels. The low light tower was used as a water tower and now stands derelict. Currently a small metal structure near the tip of the headland is the only functioning light.

Pilot boats are moored at the jetty. They are constantly taking pilots to and from the large freighters bound for Immingham and the Humber ports. The lifeboat is the only one in the country with a full-time crew resident at the station.

Between the car park and the tip of the point are numerous reminders of the fortifications installed here during World War 2 to guard the mouth of the Humber.

Blakeney Point   Norfolk

14 miles from Cromer
Grid ref: TF 987456
Maps: OS Explorer 251, OS Landranger 133.

There is no better way to view seals around the whole of the British coastline than from a small boat off Blakeney Point. Both Grey and Common Seals bask on the shingle while young seals play in the whirlpools and eddies that form round the tip of the spit. Common Seal pups are born from June to August and the Grey from October to December. The resident population is around 500. Regular boat trips run from Morston Quay and the boats draw in close to the seals. It is dramatic to watch an incoming tide remorselessly filling the muddy channels and creeks of the salt marshes.

For while the tired waves, vainly breaking,
Seem here no painful inch to gain,
Far back, through creeks and inlets making,
Comes silent, flooding in, the main.

Arthur Hugh Clough 1819—1861

Seals at Blakeney Point

Blakeney Point, now owned by the National Trust, was the first nature reserve in Norfolk. As well as being a breeding ground for seals this shingle spit is an important site for ground-nesting birds. Four species of Tern nest here: Common, Arctic, Little and Sandwich. In addition to shingle the habitats comprise sand dunes, brackish and salt marsh. Several bird-watching hides are free for the public to use.

The 5km long spit with Blakeny Point at its tip is formed by 'longshore drift'. Waves hitting the coast at an angle push material such as shingle along the shore to form a spit. Spits formed in this way, such as Spurn Head have a typical hooked shape due to wave refraction. The River Glaven used to enter the sea at Cley next the Sea, but has been diverted westward by the spit. A prominent

319

building on the point is the Old Lifeboat Station. This is now a botanical field research station owned by University College London.

Visit the picturesque village of Blakeney that seems to be half on land and half in the sea.

Orford Ness   Suffolk

25 miles from Felixstowe
Grid ref: TM 449489
Maps: OS Explorer 212, OS Landranger 169.

Like Blakeney Point and Spurn Head this is a shingle spit constructed by 'longshore drift'. The spit starts at Aldeburgh and runs southward for 18km along the coast. About half way along, opposite the village of Orford, the spit is widest and projects into the North Sea as Orford Ness. Access to Orford Ness is by open ferry across the River Ore from Orford Quay. Once ashore it is advised to obtain the National Trust Orford Ness booklet and follow the well-marked trails that lead to places of historical and wild life importance. They vary from 7 to 11km. There are restrictions of access during the bird-nesting season. Information boards are placed at strategic points.

The National Trust owns this stretch of coast. There is a wide range of natural habitats making this an internationally important site for flora and fauna. Habitats comprise strand line shingle, poorly vegetated or disturbed shingle, shingle heath, salt marsh, freshwater marsh, brackish marsh, brackish lagoons, estuarine mud and reed beds. If it were not for continuous maintenance of sea defences and ditches the rich diversity of habitats would soon disappear. After Dungeness Orford Ness has the largest area of vegetated shingle in Europe. Storms throw up the shingle in a series of ridges. These are seen clearly from the roof of the Bomb Balistics Building or the Black Beacon. Shingle provides the habitat for many ground-nesting birds such as several species of terns, gulls and plovers.

Horned Poppy at Orford Ness

Scattered over Orford Ness are buildings dating from the time when this was a key military research establishment. Some of the buildings are open to the public and house information panels. Before and during World War 1 Orford Ness was home to the Central Flying School's Experimental Flying Section. Between the two World Wars important experimental early work on radar was conducted here. Also ballistic experiments continued throughout World War 2 and subsequently on the trajectory of bombs. In the huge concrete buildings known as 'pagodas' research was conducted into trigger mechanisms for nuclear bombs. For many decades Orford Ness kept its developmental work a tightly guarded secret.

Now the BBC World Service is transmitted from Orford Ness.

On a single night in 1627 no fewer than 32 ships were wrecked on the shingle spit of Orford Ness with hardly a survivor. The first light was raised in 1634. The present tower was designed by William Wilkins, the son of a Norfolk plasterer and built by Lord Braybroke in 1792. It underwent several modifications as technology advanced and was fully automated as early as 1964.

'Orford Ness' from 'Suffolk Suite' by Mary Alwyn, born Doreen Carwithen, (1922-1985) conjures up the spirit of the place.

Landguard Point   ♿   Suffolk

2 miles from Felixstowe
Grid ref: TM 282312
Maps: OS Explorer 197, OS Landranger 169.

Defence is the dominant feature of Landguard Point. Henry VIII commanded the first Landguard Fort (1545-1588) to be built. It was garrisoned till 1588 to protect the Orwell Estuary from the Spanish. Nothing of this fort remains. A huge fort (Fort 2) was built in 1628. This was square with a bastion at each corner. This was the fort that was attacked by the Dutch in 1667, the only occasion that Landguard was fired on from the sea. Fort 3 was erected in 1717 during the reign of George I. It housed 20 guns in the form of a closed lunette. Fort 4 (1744-1871) was a red brick five-sided fort with a bastion at each corner. It incorporated part of the walls of Fort 3. The building we see today is Fort 5 built in the reign of Queen Victoria around 1875. The internal buildings were removed and casemated batteries built. Very little has changed since 1875. The fort is open to the public.

Adjacent to the fort is Felixstowe Museum in the Ravelin Block. Here are exhibits varying from local Roman and Medieval history, models of pleasure steamers, military history of Landguard Point to a grocer's shop from the early 20th century. Something for everyone.

There is a car park at a point for viewing Felixstowe container docks built on the north bank of the Orwell Estuary looking across to Harwich. A walk of less than 1km along the shingle reaches the tip of the point and a small wooden pier. The seaward side of the headland is a nature reserve. A small fenced area protects the very rare and charmingly named 'stinking goosefoot' *(Chenopodium*

Shipping passing the tip of Landguard Point

vulvaria) that smells of rotting fish. Little terns breed on the shingle. All around is the detritus of previous military installations in the form of concrete bases of gun emplacements, housings for searchlights to pick out enemy ships and concrete tank barriers.

The Naze, Walton-on-the-Naze   Essex

At Walton-on-the-Naze
Grid ref: TM 266246
Maps: OS Explorer 184, OS Landranger 169.

Just north of Walton-on-the-Naze is the Naze proper, meaning 'nose', an open area of grass, farmland, scrub, woodland, fresh water and salt marsh protected from the North Sea by a sea-wall and low cliffs that are rich in fossils.

323

There is a car park close to the Naze Tower. The Naze Tower rising to 21m dates from 1720. It was built as a daymark to guide shipping. It is open to the public and shows exhibitions of art on eight floors. The view from the top is superb. Paths run through and round The Naze. A walk round The Naze is just 5km.

Down on the beach are two concrete blockhouses of World War 2 vintage that had been built on the cliff-top. They are a vivid demonstration of the erosion of this coast estimated to be 2m each year. How long will the Naze last? Recent landslips are evident. Sand martins nest in these cliffs where ancient shark's teeth are found.

During the Paleogene geological period (Tertiary) (66 — 23 million years ago) two very different processes were going on at opposite ends of the British Isles. In the northwest a line of volcanoes was erupting and spreading thick sheets of lava over the land (see Auliston Point), whereas here in the southeast great rivers were depositing London Clay up to 155m deep. The Naze is composed of London Clay.

Kite flying at Naze Tower

The Stevenson Dynasty of lighthouse builders

Robert Stevenson's father died when Robert was an infant. His mother, Jean, then married Thomas Smith, the founder of the engineering firm that became famous for the building of lighthouses. Robert married Thomas Smith's daughter by a previous marriage. All those in upper case were lighthouse engineers. Robert Louis Stevenson left engineering for a life of literature. This is a greatly simplified family tree.

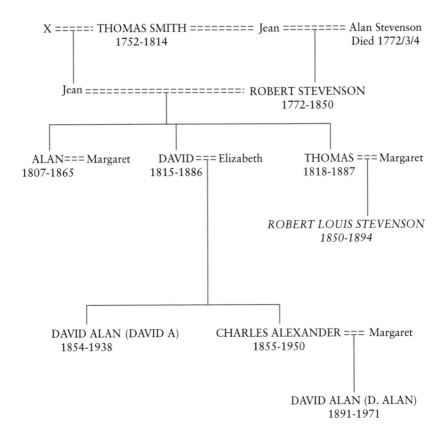

Headlands with access for wheelchairs (Many other headlands have partial access)

Ardnamurchan, Barmore Island, Barns Ness, Beachy Head, Berry Head, Braich y Pwll, Burghead, Cape Cornwall, Castle Headland Scarborough, Castle Hill Tenby, Castle Point Lindisfarne, Castle Point St Mawes, Chanonry Point, Corsewall Point, Criccieth Castle, Dodman Point, Dunbar, Duncansby Head, Dungeness, Dunnet Head, Dunnottar Castle, Dunstaffnage Castle, Durlston Head, Farland Head, Fife Ness, Flamborough Head, Foreland Point, Formby Point, Fort George, Fort Point Eyemouth, Girdle Ness, Godrevy Point, Great Orme, Hartland Point, Headlands at Barry, Headlands at Elie, Hengistbury Head, Heysham Head, Hurst Castle, Isle of Whithorn, Keith Inch, Kinnaird Head, Landguard Point, Lands End. Lizard Point, Mull of Galloway, Mumbles Head, Nare Head, North Foreland, Out Head, Pendennis Point, Pentire Point East, Perch Rock, Peveril Pont, Point of Ayr, Portknockie, Portland Bill, Rhunahaorine Point, Rubha Cadail, Rubha nan Sasan, Rubha Reidh, Saltwick Nab, Scurdie Ness, Selsey Bill, Skipness Point, Slains Castle, Port Errol, Southerness Point, Southsea Castle, Spurn Head, St Abb's Head, St Agnes Head, St Mary's or Bait Island, St Michael's Mount, Start Point, Strumble Head, Sutors of Cromarty, Tantallon Castle, The Heugh, Old Hartlepool, The Island St Ives, The Lizard, Tonfanau Headland, Torness Point, Towan Head, Toward Point, Troon Headland, Trwyn y Witch, Turnberry Point, Tynemouth Pen Bal Crag, Walney Island, Zone Point and St Anthony's Head.

Index of Headlands

General Index

Items in bold type are towns with headlands that are nearby.

L

Ravenser Odd 317
Ray xv
Razorbills xv, 106, 241
Rebecca 41
Reculver 4
Red Point Farm 212
Red Squirrels 149
Redcar 23, 308
Redruth 67
Redstart, common 34
Redwings 245
Reed beds 103, 320
Rees, Robert 139
Regulbium 4
Reiff 222
Rest Bay 98
Rhinns 156, 174, 175
Rhiw 135
Rhiwledyn 144
Rhododendrons 198
Rhossili Bay 105, 106, 107
Rhue 221
Rhygyfarch 119
Rhyolite 129
Rias xi, 46
Richard, Duke of York 28
Richborough 3
Richmond, Earl of 56
Ridge and Furrow 168
Rift Valley 266
Rigg Bay 167
Rutupiae 4
River Carnon 46
River Dart 34
River Eden 273
River Fal 46
River Glaven 319
River Helford 50
River Lune 150
River Percuil 46

River South Esk 269
River Thames 3
River Tyne 301, 302, 303, 304
Rob Donn Mackay 231
Robert 2nd 179
Robert the Bruce xxiv,177, 202
Robin Hood's Bay 309, 310
Rock (village) 77
Rock climbing xxiv, 57, 91, 111,
    113, 144, 225
Rock of Gibraltar 187
Rockcliffe 162
Rocket Post 76, 310
Rock-rose, Common Yellow 102,
    144
Rock-rose, Spotted 136
Rock-rose, White 90
Rodin, Auguste 109
Roman/Romans xvii, xxi, xxii, 3,
    4, 6, 13, 19, 25, 30, 54, 72,
    73, 94, 98, 136, 140, 173, 295,
    311, 312, 313, 322
Romano-Celtic Temple 90
Rome xxii, 13, 169, 250, 307
Roosevelt, President 283
Roseland 46
Roseroot 221
Rosudgeon 53
Ross, George 247
Ross, The Clan 246
Rothesay 181
Rough Firth 163
Round Hole 75
Roundheads see Civil War
Royal and Ancient Golf Club 273
Royal Anne 51
Royal Flying Corps 177
Royal Marines 24
Royal Naval Dockyards 39

351

Some useful websites

Tide Times — http://www.tidetimes.org.uk/#axzz2ygV8SQ7O
National Trust coast — http://www.nationaltrust.org.uk/visit/places/
coast-and-countryside/
English Heritage — http://www.english-heritage.org.uk
Historic Scotland — http://www.historic-scotland.gov.uk/heritage.htm
Scottish Natural Heritage — http://www.snh.gov.uk
Northern Lighthouse Board — https://www.nlb.org.uk
Trinity House Lighthouses — http://www.trinityhouse.co.uk/
lighthouses/lighthouse_list/
National Coastwatch Institution — http://www.nci.org.uk
Royal National Lifeboat Institution — http://rnli.org/Pages/default.aspx
Heritage Coasts of England and Wales — http://www.naturalengland.
org.uk/ourwork/conservation/designations/heritagecoasts/
Jurassic Coast — http://jurassiccoast.org
Cetacean sightings — http://www.seawatchfoundation.org.uk
Flowers of the coast — http://www.aphotomarine.com/marine_plants.html
Coastal Erosion — http://apps.environment-agency.gov.uk/
wiyby/134808.aspx
Photographs of headlands and Geology — http://geoscenic.bgs.ac.uk/
asset-bank/action/viewHome
Castles and Forts of England and Wales — http://www.ecastles.co.uk
Castles and Forts of Scotland — http://www.scotland.com/castles/
Visit Wales (Castles) — http://www.visitwales.com/things-to-do/
attractions/castles-heritage

Putting the name of a headland into a search engine can often yield
interesting facts. A degree of scepticism is important as some websites
give false information or are not kept up to date.

Lightning Source UK Ltd.
Milton Keynes UK
UKOW07f1433161116
287812UK00013B/112/P